Sizing Up Measurement

Sizing Up Measurement

Activities for Grades 3–5 Classrooms

Chris Confer

Math Solutions Publications
Sausalito, CA

Math Solutions Publications
A division of
Marilyn Burns Education Associates
150 Gate 5 Road, Suite 101
Sausalito, CA 94965
www.mathsolutions.com

The publisher would like to thank those who gave permission to reprint borrowed material: pages 202–203: *The Fewest Weights* is based on an idea from *Good Questions for Math Teaching: Why Ask Them and What to Ask, Grades 5–8* by Lainie Schuster and Nancy Canavan Anderson. © 2005 by Math Solutions Publications.

Library of Congress Cataloging-in-Publication Data

Confer, Chris.
  Sizing up measurement. Activities for grades 3–5 classrooms / Chris Confer.
    p. cm.
  Includes bibliographical references and index.
  ISBN-13: 978-0-941355-80-3
  ISBN-10: 0-941355-80-2
  1. Mensuration. 2. Mathematics—Study and teaching (Elementary)—Activity programs. [1. Measurement.] I. Title.
  QA465.C688 2007
  372.35′044—dc22
                                            2007018884

Editor: Toby Gordon
Production: Melissa L. Inglis
Cover design: Isaac Tobin
Interior design: Jenny Jensen Greenleaf
Composition: ICC Macmillan Inc.

Printed in the United States of America on acid-free paper
11 10 09 08   ML   2 3 4 5

A Message from Marilyn Burns

We at Math Solutions Professional Development believe that teaching math well calls for increasing our understanding of the math we teach, seeking deeper insights into how children learn mathematics, and refining our lessons to best promote students' learning.

Math Solutions Publications shares classroom-tested lessons and teaching expertise from our faculty of Math Solutions Inservice instructors as well as from other respected math educators. Our publications are part of the nationwide effort we've made since 1984 that now includes

- more than five hundred face-to-face inservice programs each year for teachers and administrators in districts across the country;
- annually publishing professional development books, now totaling more than sixty titles and spanning the teaching of all math topics in kindergarten through grade 8;
- four series of videotapes for teachers, plus a videotape for parents, that show math lessons taught in actual classrooms;
- on-site visits to schools to help refine teaching strategies and assess student learning; and
- free online support, including grade-level lessons, book reviews, inservice information, and district feedback, all in our quarterly *Math Solutions Online Newsletter*.

For information about all of the products and services we have available, please visit our website at *www.mathsolutions.com*. You can also contact us to discuss math professional development needs by calling (800) 868-9092 or by sending an email to *info@mathsolutions.com*.

We're always eager for your feedback and interested in learning about your particular needs. We look forward to hearing from you.

Math Solutions®
PUBLICATIONS

Contents

Acknowledgments   *xi*
Introduction   *xiii*

1 Length   *1*

Foot-Length Rulers *1*
How Big Is a Foot? *7*
How Long a Line? *9*
How Much Is a Meter? *14*
Broken Ruler 1 *16*
Broken Ruler 2 *20*
A Life-Size Zoo *23*
Dinosaur Data *27*
Creating Benchmarks for Height *28*
Going Home *31*
Stacks of Kids *35*
Relationships in the Metric System *41*
Jim and the Beanstalk: Giant-Size Things *43*
Finger Weaving *46*

2 Area   *53*

The Mitten 1 *53*
The Mitten 2 *56*
Comparing Brownies *62*
What Do You See? *65*
Tiling a Floor *68*
Dog Yards *73*
Perimeters of 30 *78*
How Many Rectangles? *81*
Perimeters with Cuisenaire Rods *84*

Design a House 87
My Dream Bedroom 92

3 Volume 96

Scoops of Rice and Beans 96
Put in Order—Volume 99
Popcorn Containers 100
Jelly Bean Jar 104
How Do They Relate? 108
Frank's Dog Food 112
How Much Soda? 116
Cook-a-Doodle-Doo! Iguana's Mistakes 120
Filling Boxes 122
Folding Boxes 124
Maximum Box 127
Wayside School 132
Cook-a-Doodle-Doo! Great-Granny's Magnificent Strawberry
   Shortcake Recipe 145

4 Angles 149

What Is an Angle? 150
Body Angles and Simon Says 152
Hunt for Angles 155
Sorting Angles 156
Measuring Angles 159
Waxed Paper Protractors 164
Combining Angles 167
Pattern Block Angles 171
Measuring with Plastic Protractors 174
The Target Angle Game 177
Crazy Quilts 180

5 Weight 183

What Do You Know? What Can You Discover? 183
Put in Order—Mass 187
Fruit Salad 190
I See Something 193
Stuff a Bag 196
Mailing a Birthday Package 198

The Fewest Weights *202*
How Much Is a Kilogram? *205*
Metric Hunt *208*
Apple Juice Container Debate *210*
A Food Drive *213*
Heavy and Light Animals *217*

6 Time

222

Classroom Decisions *222*
Minute Experiments *224*
Time Lines of a Wonderful Day *226*
Time to Go Home *230*
TV Time! *232*
Let's Go to the Movies! *235*
The Last Day of School *238*
How Old Are You? *240*
Calendar Patterns *242*
Patterns on the Clock Face *244*
Somewhere in the World *246*

7 Temperature

249

What Do You Know About Thermometers? *250*
Temperature Scavenger Hunt *253*
Inside and Outside Temperatures *256*
Heat Experiments *258*
Too Hot, Too Cold, Just Right *261*
Packing for a Trip *263*
Patterns on a Thermometer *267*
Ice Water Investigations *270*
Color Experiments *274*
A Temperature Story *277*

Blackline Masters

279

Paper Ruler *281*
Finger Weaving Instructions *282*
Finger Weaving *283*
Centimeter Grid Paper *284*
Brownie Shapes 1 *285*
Brownie Shapes 2 *286*

Inch Grid Paper   287

Sample House Plan   288

Put in Order—Volume   289

How Do They Relate?   290

Folding Boxes A   291

Folding Boxes B   292

Folding Boxes C   293

Folding Boxes D   294

Three-Fourths-Inch Grid Paper   295

Isometric Dot Paper   296

Measuring Angles   297

Measuring Polygon Angles   298

Waxed Paper Protractor   299

Angle Estimator   300

Target Angle   301

Put in Order—Mass   302

Weights   303

Time Line Paper   304

TV Time!   305

Let's Go to the Movies!   306

Patterns on the Clock Face   307

World Time Zones   308

Temperature Scavenger Hunt   309

Inside and Outside Temperatures   310

Paper Thermometer   311

Packing for a Trip   312

Half-Inch Grid Paper   313

A Day at the Beach   314

Glossary   315

References   319

Index   321

Acknowledgments

This book, as always, is the result of the thoughts and efforts of a wide variety of people. I very much appreciate the educators who reviewed the lessons or used them in their classrooms with students: Beth Egan, Claudia Gaxiola, Cassie Gribble, Sam Luna, Suzanne McGrath, Marco Ramirez, Dora Saldamando, Yolanda Sethi, Grace Tapia-Beltrán, Olga Torres, Karolyn Williams, and Jackie Wortman. Many thanks to Doris Hirschhorn, who carefully reviewed each lesson and offered significant suggestions, and to Vicki Bachman, Ann Lawrence, and Charlie Hennessy, who co-authored the introduction with me. I appreciate both Toby Gordon and Melissa Inglis, who expertly fine-tuned the manuscript and gently shepherded it through the publication process. John Van de Walle's writings contributed to my knowledge of how children understand measurement; the world is certainly a lesser place now without his presence. I'm grateful to Marilyn Burns for her inspiration and support over the years, and the invitations she has extended to me to grow mathematically and professionally. Additionally I'd like to thank my parents for sharing with me their love of educating children, and my own two children who taught me what it means to teach. But this book is for my husband, David, who reviewed this manuscript with a scientist's eye, and who, during the writing of this book, sustained me in ways beyond measure.

Introduction

Measurement is one of the very earliest forms of mathematics. For centuries people have measured quantities to cook, to build, to make clothing, to divide land, and to keep track of time and distance. In recent years, our abilities to measure have expanded dramatically; we now measure in order to travel through space, to fabricate molecular-size devices, and to create global positioning systems.

Certainly children use measurement in their daily lives, too, as they compare heights, see how far they can run and jump, keep track of how many days until their birthdays, compare their ages, and celebrate each time they need the next shoe size. As children grow older, they may become interested in sports statistics or world records involving measurement; they may use measurement to rearrange furniture or their rooms or to build items such as birdhouses or model rockets. Clearly measurement must be an important part of the mathematics curriculum, as it helps students make mathematical sense of their lives and prepares them for their future.

Unfortunately, it is easy for teachers to become overwhelmed with the abundance of measurement objectives they are asked to address; teachers often resort to dealing with those objectives by telling students what to memorize. For students who experience this kind of incomplete instruction, measurement becomes a list of terms, numbers, and facts that they easily forget.

We too have encountered the complexities of teaching measurement in our classrooms. We know that it is very easy to become overwhelmed by all that is expected of us. But we also have experienced the joys of teaching measurement in ways that help our students make sense of the mathematics they are learning. We've seen our students come away from these lessons excited about their new and deeper understandings of measurement. We've watched our students develop confidence in their ability to use measurement to understand their world rather than struggle to simply memorize rote formulas. These are the kinds of lessons we want to share with you here.

In this three-book series, Sizing Up Measurement, we have worked to create lessons that focus on essential measurement concepts that are connected to problem-solving contexts. The lessons focus on helping students

❖ identify the attribute to be measured (for example, length or weight);

◈ know what it means to measure—comparing the attribute of the item or situation with a unit with the same attribute: lengths must be compared with units of length, areas with units of area, and so on;

◈ develop an understanding of what it means to measure using standard and non-standard units;

◈ select a system of measurement to be used—customary or metric;

◈ understand how benchmark units—such as *a centimeter is about the width of a pencil*—help determine the magnitude of specific units;

◈ estimate the result of the measurement, both before and after the act of measuring;

◈ select a measurement tool to assign a number value and determine how accurate they need to be; and

◈ keep track of results in an organized and useful way.

As you can imagine, given the grade-level spans in this series (K–2, 3–5, 6–8), the three books deal with very different levels of mathematics, but there are commonalities among them all. Each of the books includes lessons that relate to categories of measurement important for that grade-level span, and the lessons in all three books provide meaningful contexts for students to solve problems and use their mathematical skills as they develop important vocabulary related to measurement.

Before trying these lessons, it is important to consider the natural progressions in thinking that children pass through as they develop basic concepts of measurement:

When a student lays down toothpicks to measure length and leaves gaps or overlaps the toothpicks, the student is struggling with *unit iteration*. He doesn't yet understand that the distance of the units altogether should be equal to the distance being measured.

When a student thinks that, when measuring with small units, a small total should result, the student does not yet know the *inverse relationship* between the size of the unit and the number of units—small units create a larger total and large units create a smaller total.

When a student compares the length of pencils that are not evenly lined up and thinks that the pencil that sticks out is longer, the student has not yet developed *conservation of length*—the idea that a different position does not change the length.

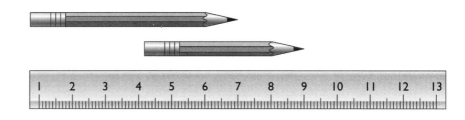

When a student knows that the marker is shorter than the pencil, and the pencil is shorter than the stick, but doesn't realize the marker therefore must be shorter than the stick, the student has yet to develop *transitive reasoning*. This is necessary in order for children to understand how rulers help us compare objects that are not side by side.

When you put a pencil against the ruler between 2 and 8, and a student thinks the pencil is 8 inches long, the student doesn't understand that the number on the ruler represents the entire distance from the "zero end" to that number.

When a student thinks an angle with longer sides has a larger measure, the student doesn't understand that the measure of an angle depends upon the spread of the angle's rays.

When a student thinks it is impossible to determine the area of an irregular polygon, the student may not understand that figures can be partitioned into shapes that have areas that she can determine.

When a student assumes that a constant perimeter always yields a constant area, the student does not understand the relationship between these two measures.

When a student depends upon a separate formula for determining the volume of each kind of prism and pyramid, the student does not understand the relationships among the volumes of such figures.

The lessons in these books are intended to provide students with opportunities to make sense of these and other critical understandings related to measurement. Through multiple experiences with length, area, capacity and volume, mass and weight, temperature, and time, students learn how to measure, compare, and order. Measurement requires estimation, making comparisons, mental math, and number sense. Students need to add, subtract, multiply, divide, and perceive numerical relationships in many different ways. Measurement is a topic that deserves attention and time in every school year. We offer these lessons in the hopes that you will use and adapt them to fit your circumstances. All students need many opportunities to build their understandings, make connections to other topics, explain their thinking and procedures, and analyze and communicate their results to others. We sincerely hope that you and your students enjoy these lessons.

VICKI BACHMAN, GRADES K–2
CHRIS CONFER, GRADES 3–5
ANN LAWRENCE AND CHARLIE HENNESSY, GRADES 6–8

CHAPTER 1

Length

Introduction

Length is an attribute that students encounter naturally in their lives. Children want to know how much taller they have grown this year, how far they can kick a ball, and how tall a *Tyrannosaurus rex* would be. The lessons in this chapter build on the understandings that students bring to school, extending them to the concepts that are important for students to learn in grades 3 through 5.

Through these lessons students develop a sense of different units of length and acquire benchmarks for them, such as "a centimeter is about the length of my little fingernail" and "a meter is about the distance from my waist to the floor." Students determine reasonable units for measuring in different situations. They estimate lengths and distances and convert between shorter and longer units. Students create, make sense of, and use measurement tools with nonstandard and standard units. These lessons help students move beyond merely learning a procedure for using a ruler—"line up the end of the ruler with one end of the object, and match the end of the object with a number." Instead they help students understand how a ruler works and how the lines, spaces, and numbers on a ruler represent distance. Through these lessons students solve problems that help them better understand both the process of measurement and the world around them.

While students' home experiences typically revolve around the U.S. customary system of units, the rest of the world uses metric units, and students must use both systems of measurement in our increasingly global society. Therefore most of the lessons in this chapter can be adapted for either system of measurement.

Foot-Length Rulers

Overview

This lesson introduces students to the concept of linear measurement. They predict the width of the cafeteria using their own feet as units and then create foot-length rulers for measuring it and other items in the cafeteria. During this lesson students learn about iteration (repeating a unit), the need for units to be the same size, the role of zero in a measuring device, and the meaning of the lines on a ruler.

Materials

◈ chart paper, about 3 feet by 4 feet, 2 sheets
◈ markers
◈ 12-inch rulers, 1 per pair of students
◈ color tiles, 6
◈ 6-foot strips of adding machine tape, 1 per pair of students (**Note:** you could also use 3- to 5-inch wide strips of paper 6 feet long.)

Vocabulary: distance, feet, foot length, inch, inverse relationship, iterate, measure, ruler, zero

Instructions
Measuring the Cafeteria with Feet

1. Prior to this lesson, tape a sheet of chart paper to the wall somewhere in the cafeteria where the students can gather and see it.

2. Explain to the students that they will measure the width of the cafeteria. Have them imagine that rulers have not been invented yet, and there is no such thing as inches or yards or meters. Tell them that a long time ago people used parts of the body to measure things. Ask them what parts of the body would be easiest to use to measure. They will likely suggest feet.

3. Now tell the students that they will use their feet to measure the distance from one side of the cafeteria to the other. Ask a student to demonstrate, with his shoes on, how he would begin. The student will most likely stand with the heel of one foot against the wall, then place the other foot right in front, with the heel of that foot touching the toes of the first foot. He will move forward, alternating feet in this way, counting as he walks across the room.

4. After a few steps, stop the volunteer and ask the class to explain why the student didn't begin measuring in the middle of the floor. (He has to cover the entire distance across the cafeteria.) Next ask the student to start over again so the class can look closely at what he is doing. Before the student begins, ask the others how they should count each time the student places a foot. Some students will think that the first foot counts as zero and the second foot

counts as one. These students are counting footsteps, not the length of each foot.

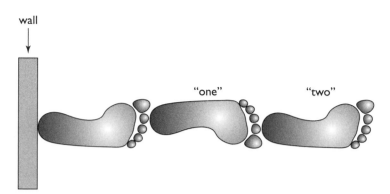

Others will understand that each foot length is counted: the first foot counts as one and the second as two.

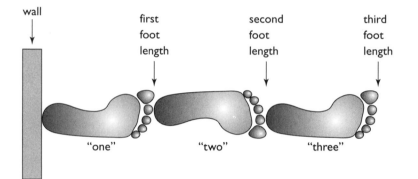

Discuss the reasoning behind each perspective. Remind the students that in order to measure correctly, the feet must cover the entire distance from one side of the cafeteria to the other.

5. Have the student begin again and take three steps. As he steps, say, "First foot length, second foot length, third foot length." Ask the students where zero is (the wall) and where one is (the end of the first foot length). These questions can be confusing to students. They will have many chances to revisit the questions throughout this and other lessons.

6. Now have the class estimate how many foot lengths it will take for the student to cross the cafeteria. Have the student find the actual number of foot lengths and write his name and the number on the chart paper.

7. Have the students predict how many of their own feet wide the cafeteria is and discuss their reasoning. For example, many students will compare their foot with the volunteer's foot and use that information to estimate a larger or smaller number.

8. Now, have the students find the actual measurement using their own feet with the help of a partner. Ask the students to write their names and numbers on the chart.

9. When everyone is ready, discuss the numbers. Ask the students why there are different numbers when the distance did not change.

10. Circle one of the larger numbers. Ask the students what they know about that person's foot. Ask the students to explain why a smaller foot would result in a bigger number. Have different students explain this important inverse relationship in their own words, giving several students an opportunity to articulate it. Then circle one of the smaller numbers and again discuss what the students know about that person's foot.

Making a Foot-Length Ruler

1. Tell the students that it takes a long time to measure by putting a foot down, then another, over and over again. Explain that a foot-length ruler would be faster to use and would be useful for measuring things where feet can't go, such as the height and width of a window.

2. Tell the students that they will work in pairs to make a foot-length ruler by marking the lengths of the feet of one of the students with lines on the adding machine tape or on a long, thin piece of paper. Ask whether it makes sense for both students' feet to be on one ruler. Discuss the importance of the units being the same size.

3. Pass out the paper and markers to the students. Explain that they will mark the end of each foot (however many will fit on the paper), and they will not use any numbers at all. As the students work, observe whether they begin with their heel at the end of the paper, whether they leave any spaces between footprints, and whether they are careful to put the next foot right against the last toe mark.

4. When everyone is ready, place three foot-length rulers on a cafeteria table and gather the students around them. Have the students compare them and tell what they notice. They will notice that the foot lengths on the different rulers are different sizes, but only slightly different. They also may notice that some rulers have different-size units on them. Discuss whether these rulers would be a good tool for measuring and have students explain their reasoning.

5. Some papers will have a small space between the last foot mark and the end of the paper. Select a foot-length ruler with an incomplete piece at the end. Ask the students to think about how they would use that ruler to measure the width of the cafeteria table, and choose one student to do this. As the student measures, have the other students explain why the volunteer is doing it that way. Discuss the following points with the students:

   • Ask, "Why didn't the volunteer begin counting with the small piece? Could she have lined up the end of the small piece with the edge of the table?" Discuss how, although that is not a standard way to use a ruler, it can be done. Talk about how they would estimate the length of the incomplete section.

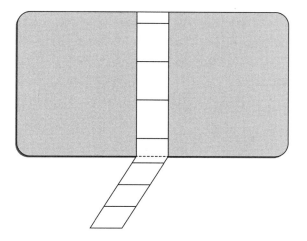

- Discuss why the volunteer didn't place the ruler on the table so the edges hung off evenly and whether she could have done that. Discuss how, although that is not a standard way to use a ruler, it can be done. Talk about how that would work.

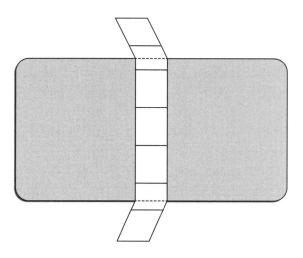

- Have the students explain what they are counting: the lines or the spaces. Have them explain in their own words that each space is the length of a foot and that each succeeding line represents another foot length.

6. Next remind the students that real rulers have lines with numbers on them. Ask the students to write numbers on their rulers.

7. Now select several foot-length rulers, some that have the numbers listed correctly and some that do not. Place them on the table and have the students compare them. The rulers that are done correctly will have the first line that completes a foot length past the edge labeled 1. Discuss what the number means: since the number is a label for the end of the foot length, it belongs at the first line.

8. Ask the students where 0 would be on their rulers. Discuss why it would be at the beginning edge of the paper.

9. Provide each pair of students with a standard 12-inch ruler. Have them look at it to see where the 0 would be. Then have the students look at the lines on their standard ruler to see what they mean. Place a standard 12-inch ruler on a table where all the students can see it. To show the repeating inches on the ruler, line up six color tiles against the ruler, beginning with the zero end. Point out that the lines on the ruler show where the color tiles end each time, just as the lines on the students' foot-length rulers show where their feet ended each time.

10. Return the students' attention to their foot-length rulers. Discuss how the students dealt with the little space left beyond their last foot length. Some may have torn it off, replicating how many commercial rulers are made. Some may have labeled the final edge with a fraction, or have used the fraction incorrectly. For example, a student may have incorrectly written:

$$1 \quad 2 \quad 3 \quad 4 \quad 5\tfrac{1}{2}$$

When you find students thinking incorrectly, ask them what each space means. Have them return to the beginning of the ruler and recount the spaces. In this case they would say, "One foot length, two foot lengths, three foot lengths, four foot lengths," and so on. Always push the students to see that the numeral represents how many foot lengths there are from the beginning of the paper.

11. Have the students write 0 on the start of their foot-length rulers and, if necessary, correct any other numbers.

Using the Foot-Length Rulers

1. Have the students help you select some things in the cafeteria that they could measure with their foot-length rulers. List these on a second sheet of chart paper. Include many things that are much longer than their rulers so that they will have to iterate their ruler. For example, you might list

   the width of the door

   the length of the stage

   the length of the cafeteria

   the length of a bench

   the length of a table

   the length of the display case

   the height of the piano

   the width of the bulletin board

   the length of the window

   the height of the menu sign

Tell the students to measure the items on the list and record their findings on a sheet of paper.

2. As the students work, observe how they use their rulers: whether they line them up correctly at the beginning, how they iterate the rulers, how they work with the fractional parts at the end of the rulers, and so on.

3. When the students have finished measuring most of the items, gather them for a discussion. Begin by asking them if they expect their answers to be the same and why. (Their foot lengths are different sizes, so the measurements will be different.) Ask them if they expect the answers to be very different and why. (The measurements should be fairly close.)

4. Now have students share their measurements for some of the items. As a group decide whether the measurements make sense. Also, ask them what they know about the foot of a person whose measurement is large. (As before, this indicates that the person's foot is small.)

5. Have the students share how they described several measurements that did not come out in whole foot lengths. Some students may use fractions of foot lengths, while others may use another body part to describe the piece, such as "a pinky."

How Big Is a Foot?

Overview

Rolf Myller's book *How Big Is a Foot?* provides the students with an occasion to think about the need for consistently sized units. The students listen to the story and then write a letter to the apprentice, explaining why the bed was the wrong size when the king used his large feet to measure the queen for a bed and then the apprentice used his smaller feet to build the bed. The students use the term *unit* and discuss the fact that, for units to have meaning, they have to be the same size.

Materials

◈ *How Big Is a Foot?* by Rolf Myller (1990)

Vocabulary: long, measure, unit, wide

Instructions

1. Show the students the cover of *How Big Is a Foot?* Have the students predict what the story might be about. If the students have already done the *Foot-Length Rulers* activity, encourage them to make a connection between the feet on the cover and the units they used in that activity.

2. Read the story to the students, up to the page with the question "Why was the bed too small for the queen?"

3. Show the students the picture on the next page, where the apprentice is sitting in jail, thinking. Explain to the students that they need to write a letter to the struggling apprentice to give him some advice. First, they need to answer the question Why was the bed too small? Then they should tell the apprentice what he should do about his problem. On the board, write:

> *Write a letter to the apprentice. In your letter include this information:*
> * *Why was the bed too small for the queen?*
> * *What advice do you have for the apprentice?*

4. When the students finish, invite them to share what they wrote. Each time a student shares, copy on the board the words the student uses to explain that the king measured the queen with his large feet, and the apprentice made the bed by measuring with his smaller feet. For example, one student might say, "Their feet were different sizes." Another student might say, "The king's feet were big and the apprentice had smaller feet so the bed didn't match." Explain that the distance that someone measures with is called a *unit*. Erase the word *feet* or *foot* in each sentence on the board and replace it with *unit*. Then with the students, reread the sentences aloud. For example, the first sentence would read, "Their units were different sizes." And the second sentence would read "The king's units were big and the apprentice had smaller units so the bed didn't match." (See Figure 1–1 for one student's letter.)

5. Have the students discuss a generalization for units, such as *When you measure, the units have to be the same size*.

Figure 1–1 *Francisco suggested that the apprentice make a copy of the king's foot size and use that to make a paper pattern for the correct bed size.*

6. Note that there are many different ways to solve a problem. Then read the rest of the book to reveal how the author decided to end the story.

How Long a Line?

Overview

Rod Clement's book *Counting on Frank* provides a humorous mathematical view of the world. In this lesson, students examine their pencil point. They predict, and then investigate, how long a line (in inches or centimeters) they will be able to draw with their pencil until it needs to be sharpened. Then, since it is difficult to visualize large numbers of small units—such as 700 inches—the students convert their measurements to feet and then to yards.

Materials

- *Counting on Frank,* by Rod Clement (1991)
- 12-inch rulers, 1 per pair of students
- yardstick
- marker
- chart paper, 1 sheet, divided into four columns and labeled as shown:

Partners' Names	Number of Inches	Number of Feet	Number of Yards

Vocabulary: estimate, feet, inches, measure, miles, strategy, visualize, yards

Instructions

Day 1: Gathering Data

1. Decide ahead of time whether you want this investigation to involve U.S. customary units or metric units, or whether you will let the students decide this question as a group. This lesson is described using the U.S. customary system.

2. Read the entire book *Counting on Frank* to the students. Enjoy the pictures and the ideas and questions that the book presents. Discuss any other ideas that come to the students as they hear the story.

3. Reread page 1. Explain that you've been wondering about a similar question: "If you and your partner used a pencil to make a long, long line, how long a line could you make before the pencil needed sharpening?"

4. Hold up a pencil. Invite the students to closely examine the pencil point and then discuss any issues that this experiment might bring up. For example, ask students how they will know when their pencil needs sharpening. The students may say that the line will get fat. Others may say that the wood will start to rub on the paper.

   Another issue is the kind of line to make. Tell the students they can choose to use rulers or draw the lines freehand.

5. Write the class criteria for this experiment on the board. Have the students estimate how long a line they think their pencil will make. Write their estimates on the board. Have the students find the shortest prediction and the longest.

6. Tell students to discuss with their partner how to share the task of making the line and how they can make a line that is easy to measure. For example, they may decide that it is easier to measure straight lines rather than lines that curve.

7. Give each pair two pieces of blank paper, leaving the rest of the paper in a pile for them to use as necessary. Make sure each pair has a pencil to work with. Tell the students that partners will take turns using the pencil to make lines on their paper until they decide that the pencil needs to be sharpened.

8. When the students are finished, have them use rulers to measure and figure out the total length of their lines. On a separate sheet on paper, have them record how they identified the length. You will observe students using different strategies. Some students will use addition, while others will multiply. The strategies students use partly depend on the kind of lines they draw: one curved, continuous line per page, as Frank does in the book, or repeating line segments. Students who make repeating line segments may need to measure one line that is the width of a sheet of paper—$8\frac{1}{2}$ inches. You may need to support them as they make sense of the fractional marks on the ruler. You may also need to provide them with help in computation as they combine halves.

9. Have the students put their names on their papers and clip them together. Save the papers for use the next day.

Day 2: Solving the Problem and Comparing Strategies

1. Return the papers to the students. Have the partners discuss what their task was and where they were in their thinking at the end of the period the previous day.

2. Ask a pair of students to share with the class how they were beginning to figure out the total length of their line. Draw lines on the chalkboard as students explain, so that their thinking is clear to the class. For example, a pair of students might show the class the line segments they drew over and over across the width of the paper. These students might say that one line is $8\frac{1}{2}$ inches long, and so two lines must be 17 inches long. Then they combined the next two lines with the first two lines, by adding $17 + 17$. Write the numbers and equations that the students used next to the lines you've drawn on the board.

3. Have other pairs of students share their strategies.

4. Now give students the opportunity to return to their task, using a strategy that makes sense to them.

5. Circulate among the pairs as the students work, offering support as needed.

6. As the students finish, have them list their names on the chart you prepared and write the total number of inches that their pencil made. (See Figures 1–2 and 1–3.)

Day 3: Visualizing Measurements and Converting Them to Other Units

1. Review the chart with the information about how long the lines were. Have the students identify the shortest line and the longest line.

2. Ask the students to try to imagine what a straight line that was 800 or 1,000 inches long would look like. Tell the students that while we might measure a piano in inches, it is easier to visualize long distances using larger units, such as feet or yards or miles.

Figure 1–2 *Jorge measured an 11-inch line, counted seventy-five lines, and used an open array to multiply. He decomposed 11 into $10 + 1$, and decomposed 75 into $70 + 5$. Jorge used the distributive property to multiply the parts, added them, and found that his lines were 825 inches long altogether.*

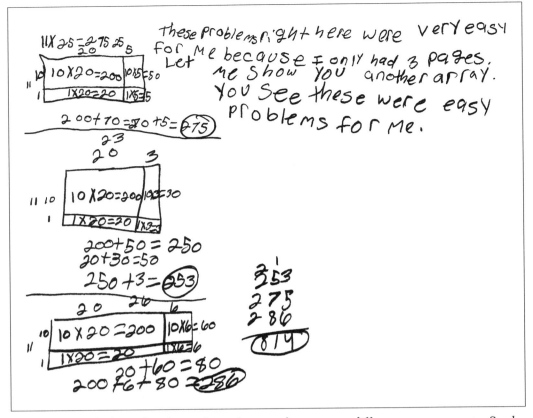

Figure 1–3 *The lines that Arminda made on each page were different measurements. So she measured the lines on each page, counted them, and used the open array to multiply. Then she added each page's total and found that her lines were 814 inches long altogether.*

3. Give a ruler to each pair of students. Have them use their ruler to estimate how many feet long their entire line is.

4. Have partners, then the whole group, discuss how they could convert inches to feet, using the example of 746 inches. Since there are 12 inches in 1 foot, many students will suggest dividing 746 inches by 12. You may choose to have students use calculators to solve this problem. Or you may encourage students to use strategies for division. For example, to find out how many 12s are in 746, a student may do the following:

$$10 \times 12 = 120$$

$$10 \times 12 = 120 \qquad 120 + 120 = 240$$

$$10 \times 12 = 120 \qquad 240 + 120 = 360$$

$$10 \times 12 = 120 \qquad 360 + 120 = 480$$

$$10 \times 12 = 120 \qquad 480 + 120 = 600$$

$$10 \times 12 = 120 \qquad 600 + 120 = 720$$

$$2 \times 12 = 24 \qquad 720 + \ 24 = 744$$

$$10 + 10 + 10 + 10 + 10 + 10 + 2 = 62 \text{ feet and 2 inches}$$

5. Have the students find the total length of their line in feet and inches and add this information to the chart. Have them see if their answer is reasonable by comparing it with their estimate, as well as with the other students' results. For example, students whose line measured the largest number of inches should also have the largest number of feet.

6. Explain that it could be even easier to imagine how many yards long their line is. Show the yardstick to the students. Have them look at their lines and estimate how many yards long their entire line might be.

7. Now have partners, then the whole group, discuss how they could convert feet to yards, using the example of 62 feet and 2 inches. Since there are 3 feet in 1 yard, many students will suggest dividing sixty-two by three. You may choose to have students use calculators to solve this problem. Or you may encourage students to use strategies for division. For example, to find out how many threes are in sixty-two, a student may do the following:

62 feet, 2 inches ÷ 3

20 yards, 2 feet, and 2 inches

$$
\begin{array}{r|l}
3\overline{)\,62\ \text{ft}} & 10\ \text{yards} \\
-30\ \text{ft} & \\
\hline
32\ \text{ft} & 10\ \text{yards} \\
-30\ \text{ft} & \\
\hline
2\ \text{ft} &
\end{array}
$$

8. Have the students find the total length of their line in yards as well as leftover feet and inches, and add this information to the chart. Have them check their answer by comparing it with their estimate, as well as with the other students' results.

9. Last, have the students remember how many yards their line is. Take them outside and hold up the yardstick so they can see it. Have the students visualize that number of yards, which is how long a line their pencil could draw before it needed sharpening.

Extension

Marilyn Burns's book *Math for Smarty Pants* (1982) has some related information that the students will find interesting. You may wish to have them investigate whether this information could be true.

- One pencil can be sharpened approximately seventeen times.
- One pencil can be used to write about forty-five thousand words.
- If you laid a year's supply of pencils end-to-end, they would circle the earth five times.
- One pencil can draw a line about $33\frac{1}{2}$ miles (56 kilometers) long.

◈ That means a year's supply of pencils could trace the distance to the moon and back about two hundred thousand times.

◈ You should be able to make about four thousand check marks with a pencil before you absolutely must sharpen it.

◈ How Much Is a Meter?

Overview

In this lesson, students identify mental images, or benchmarks, that they will use to recall the meaning of metric units. To do this, students find things in the room that are about a centimeter, a decimeter, and a meter. They make a list and sketch the items. During a class discussion, each student selects a personal benchmark for each unit that he or she wants to remember. The students compile their information into a chart that they will refer to throughout the year.

Materials

◈ centimeter cubes (or the white cubes in a set of Cuisenaire rods), 1 per student

◈ decimeter sticks (or the orange rods in a set of Cuisenaire rods), 1 per student

◈ meter sticks or 10 decimeters taped together or a string that is a meter long, 1 per student

◈ chart paper, 1 sheet

Vocabulary: benchmark, centimeter, decimeter, meter, metric system

Instructions

1. Tell the students that today they are going to learn about something that will help them remember sizes of units of measure: benchmarks. Write *benchmark* on the board. Explain that it is important to have "pictures in their heads," or ways to connect to words they hear. For example, when they hear the word *centimeter*, you want them to imagine their fingernail or something else that is a similar size. Tell the students that today they will choose benchmarks that can help them remember the length of different units.

2. Show the students a centimeter cube. Explain that each dimension of the cube is a centimeter. Write *centimeter* on the board. Have them find things on their body that are about a centimeter. They might mention things such as the width of their fingernail or the width of their eye's iris.

3. Pass out a sheet of blank $8\frac{1}{2}$-by-11-inch paper to each student and have him or her fold it in half, top to bottom. Have the students write *Centimeter* at the top of the first section. Tell them that they are going to find as many things as they can

in the room or on their body that are about a centimeter long. Explain that they will make a sketch of each item and write it its name in that section.

4. Provide each student with a centimeter cube. Ask the children to begin the investigation.

5. When the students have found enough items, bring them together for a discussion. Tape the chart paper to the board. Leave a space at the top for a title, and label the top third *Centimeter*. Have the students share what they discovered, listing several examples on the chart paper.

6. Have each student examine his or her list and select the item that he or she wants to use for a personal benchmark. Remind the students that a personal benchmark is something that is associated with that length, something that will pop into their minds when they hear the word *centimeter*. Have the students make a star beside their personal benchmark. (See Figure 1–4.)

7. Next show the students a decimeter stick. Explain that it is a unit of length called a *decimeter*. Place ten centimeter cubes against the decimeter stick to show how many centimeters long a decimeter is. Write *decimeter* on the board. Have the students write *Decimeter* in the second section of their paper, and give each student a decimeter stick. Have them find something on themselves that's about a decimeter long, and ask them to do the same investigation as they did with centimeters.

8. Add this information to the class chart in the same way as before, and have the students choose personal benchmarks for that unit.

9. Provide each student with a meter stick, a set of ten decimeter sticks taped together, or a piece of string that is 1 meter long. Have the students do the investigation once more with a meter, recording their benchmarks on the top half of the back of their paper.

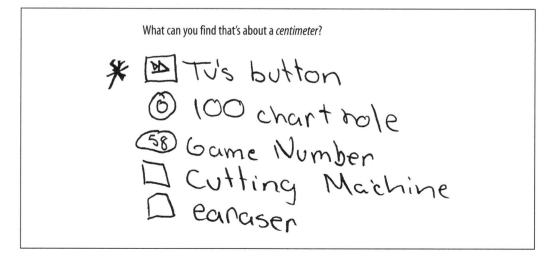

Figure 1–4 *Ashley found five benchmarks for centimeters.*

10. Record their suggestions on the chart and then review the chart together. Explain to the students that these are all units in the metric system, a system of measurement that is used throughout the world. Write a title on the chart: *The Metric System.* Have the students explain how each unit name is alike. Underline the root—*meter*—in each word. Note that *centimeter* means one-hundredth of a meter and *decimeter* means one-tenth of a meter. Explain to the students that they will learn more about these relationships during another lesson (see "Relationships in the Metric System" on page 41.)

11. Tell the students that you will leave this chart posted in the room for them to use as a reference.

Broken Ruler 1

Overview

In this lesson, students are given "broken rulers." These are paper rulers with the beginning and end sections cut off so the first number is not 1 and the final number is not 12. Students use these rulers to measure identical 3-by-5-inch index cards. Because they often misunderstand what the lines, spaces, and numbers on a ruler mean, students come up with different measurements. Through a discussion, students develop fundamental knowledge about linear measurement and what rulers represent.

Materials

◈ 3-by-5-inch index cards, 1 per pair of students
◈ paper rulers, 1 per pair of students (see Blackline Masters)
◈ 1-inch color tiles, 5 per pair of students and 8 for the teacher
◈ crayons, at least 4 of different colors per pair of students

Vocabulary: distance, inch, length, ruler, space

Instructions

1. Before class, cut out the paper rulers. Tape together the eight color tiles side by side using clear adhesive tape.

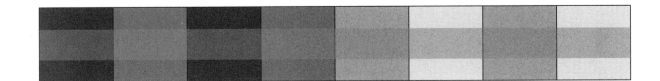

2. Show the students a 3-by-5-inch index card. Explain that each student will measure the sides of cards that are exactly the same size. Ask the students what they notice about the card's sides. The students will likely say that the top and the bottom are equal in length and that the left and right sides of the card are equal.

3. Next show the students a paper ruler. Tell the students that you are going to "break" the rulers by cutting off some of each ruler. Tell the students that the rulers are going to be broken in different ways.

4. Select a ruler. Cut off the first inch and the last inch. Cut each of the other rulers in a variety of ways, being sure to cut off at least the first three-quarters of an inch and to leave at least nine inches visible on the entire ruler.

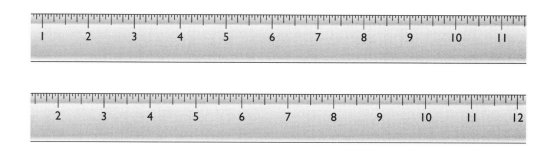

5. Have the students consider the different rulers and the index cards that they will measure. Ask the students what they think will happen when they measure the cards that are all the same using the rulers that are broken in different ways. Pose these questions: "Will the measurements of the sides of the cards be the same or different? Why?" Have the students discuss what they think. The discussion should end with consensus that since the cards are all the same, everyone should have the same measurements.

6. Next provide each pair of students with a broken ruler, an index card, and a sheet of paper on which to record their results. Tell the students to find the length of each side of the index card and record what they find out using pictures, words, and numbers. As they work on the problem, observe how the students use their ruler. You will likely see many students misinterpreting how to use the ruler. Some may simply line up the left edge of the ruler with one end of the index card and read the number that lines up with the other end. Others may count all the numbers that are visible, and still others may count the visible numbers and also count the number that was cut off from the end of the ruler. Students who have difficulty do not understand how the ruler represents space or distance. Allow the students to use the strategy that makes sense to them, but ask why they think their measurement is correct. (See Figures 1–5 and 1–6.)

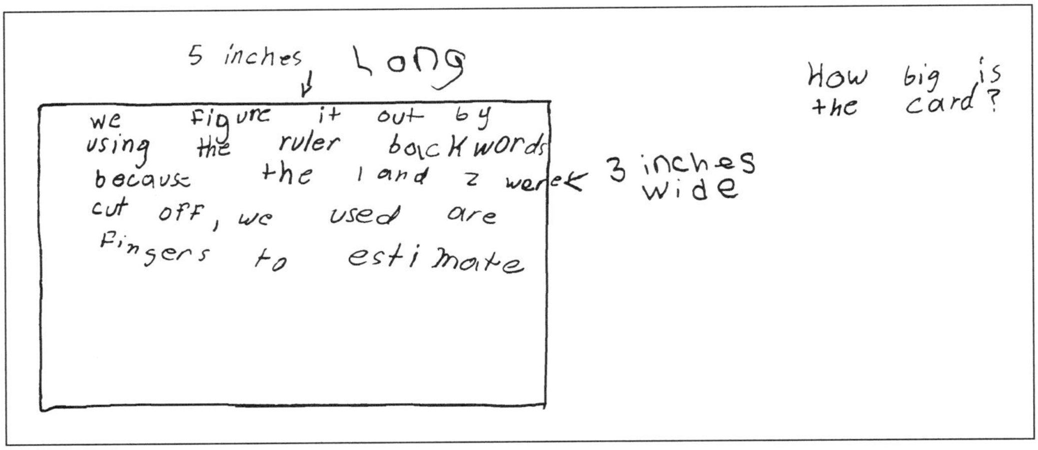

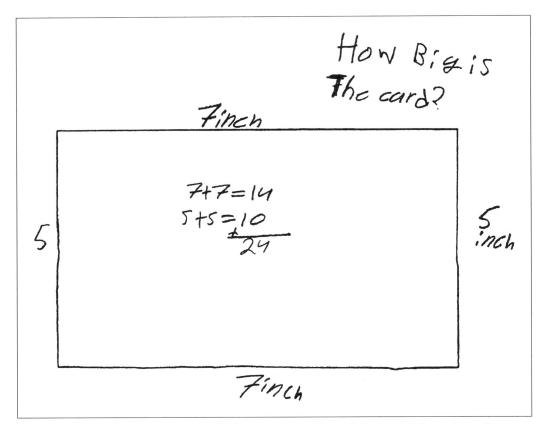

Figure 1–5 *Amanda and Liam spaced their fingers apart about an inch to remind themselves where that distance would be on their broken ruler.*

How Big is The card?

7 inch

5

7+7=14
5+5=10
+
24

5 inch

7 inch

Figure 1–6 *Carlos misinterpreted the broken ruler and simply recorded the end number.*

7. On the board, make a chart labeled *Long Side* and *Short Side*. When everyone is ready, bring the students together for a discussion. Begin by saying that you observed students thinking about their rulers in different ways. Ask several partners to share their measurements for the sides of the card and to explain how they

figured them out. List their measurements on the chart. The students are likely to identify different measurements for the same dimensions of the card.

8. Remind the students that earlier they said that there should be just one answer for each side since the cards were all alike. Ask the students to use what they know about inch benchmarks to help them understand how the ruler functions. Ask them to show with their hands about how much an inch is. Ask them what a good estimate would be for the number of inches in both the long and short sides. Then ask them to look at their rulers to see where each inch is represented. Ask the students to think about what they are counting when they use the ruler: Are they counting the numbers or are they counting the spaces or the distance between the numbers?

9. Ask the students to turn their papers over. Tell them to check their measurements for the sides of the index card again and to record on their paper what they think now and why they think the amounts are correct.

10. When the students have finished, once again bring them together to share. First have them describe how their ruler was broken, by telling which numbers are visible on their ruler. Then have them talk about what they thought about the short side of the card at first, how they used the broken ruler, and what they think now. Draw a line across the chart and add this information to show what they think now.

11. After several partners have shared, explain that it can be hard to visualize the units of space on the ruler. Hold up the strip of color tiles that you taped together before beginning the lesson. Lay the strip against the edge of an index card. Help the students see how the size of each color tile matches the inch-long space that each number on the ruler represents. Next have the partners get five loose color tiles and use them to check the measurement of their own index card. Last, ask the students to color those squares right on their broken rulers, so that adjacent squares are different colors, and the students can better visualize the spaces that the numbers represent.

12. Have the students summarize the lesson by looking at their rulers and explaining what the numbers represent. Verbalize for the group that when we measure with a ruler we are counting the units of space, not just the numbers. The numbers represent the entire length of that many units of space.

13. Collect the "broken rulers." Save them to use in the following lesson, *Broken Ruler 2*.

 **Broken Ruler 2**

Overview

In this lesson, students again confront common misunderstandings about what the lines, spaces, and numbers on a ruler mean. They use "broken rulers," as in the previous lesson, to find the length of the sides of a large index card. After a discussion, they interpret a broken ruler with larger numbers, by finding the length of a card drawn on the board, labeled with numbers 17 to 24. Through revisiting understanding introduced in the previous lesson, students solidify important ideas about measurement.

Materials

- ❖ 5-by-8-inch index cards, 1 per pair of students
- ❖ broken rulers from *Broken Ruler 1* lesson (page 16), 1 per pair of students
- ❖ 12-inch rulers, 1 per pair of students
- ❖ optional: color tiles, 1 per pair of students

Vocabulary: distance, inch, ruler, space, zero

Instructions

1. Begin by reminding the students of the lesson that they did previously with the "broken rulers." Describe the discussion and the disagreement among the students about the measurements of the small index cards. Tell the students that today they will revisit the problem with a different-size card.

2. Show the students a 5-by-8-inch index card and a broken ruler from the previous lesson. Tell the students that they will receive a broken ruler and that they will work in pairs to figure out the measurement of the short side and the long side of the new card. Remind the students that they are to record their thinking on a sheet of paper, using words, numbers, and pictures.

3. Next, ask students to individually estimate how many inches each side contains. Tell them to write their estimates on their sheet of paper. Explain that this estimate will help them verify whether their final answers are reasonable.

4. Hand out the rulers and the cards. As the partners begin measuring with their broken rulers, observe their strategies. Let them do what makes sense to them but have them explain their thinking to each other and to you. Many students, recalling their experience from the previous lesson, will use the broken ruler correctly. But some students will again simply read the end number, or count the numbers, coming up with incorrect measurements. Respond to these students by encouraging them to check their estimates to see whether their answers are reasonable. You might also ask them to use a color tile as they explain to you what the numbers on

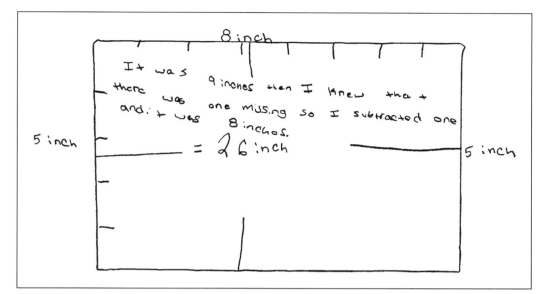

Figure 1–7 *Erin read the final number on her ruler and subtracted the inches that were missing from the beginning of it.*

a ruler represent. In addition, suggest that they check their outcomes with those of other pairs at their table. If they see a different answer, ask everyone at the table to explain how they used the ruler, and then to come to an agreement on one answer.

5. When the students finish, begin a group discussion. Tape an index card on the board and have pairs of students who used different strategies share what they think and why. When they disagree on answers, have students with both correct and incorrect answers explain their thinking using their rulers. As a class, come to consensus about strategies that make sense. Following are some successful strategies that students may use:

   - Line up the broken ruler as if it were a regular ruler, read the final number, and then subtract the inches that were cut off. (See Figure 1–7.)
   - Line up the broken ruler with any number matching the end of the card, and count each space that touches the card. (See Figure 1–8.)

6. Next, move the discussion to the part of the broken ruler that is missing. On the board, tape a broken ruler against the base of an index card. Beneath the ruler, write the numbers that are visible. Now ask the students to think about the part of the ruler that is missing.

7. Have the students tell you what to draw, as you complete the missing part of the ruler. Have the students discuss whether the number at the left end of the ruler is 1 or 0 and explain their thinking. (The answer is 0, because the ruler's left end represents the initial starting point—no distance at all.)

I know the card
is ___8___ inches wide
because I counted
with my knuckle
in the spaces.

Figure 1–8 *Raymundo used his knuckle to count the spaces.*

8. Now give the students standard rulers, and have them remeasure their cards. Again have them discuss why 0 is implied on the edge of the ruler: the 1 represents the end of the first space, the 2 represents the end of the second space, and so on.

9. For an assessment of the students' current thinking, explain that you'd like to know what each of them thinks about this problem after having had several experiences with broken rulers. Tell them that you'd like them not to talk to each other, but to write on a sheet of paper what they think and why they think that. On the board draw a rectangular card and a broken ruler underneath. Ask the students to figure out long the bottom of the card is.

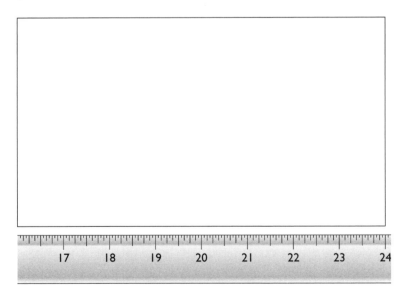

10. Again, observe the students as they work. More students should answer correctly this time (see Figure 1–9). However, you may have some students who think the

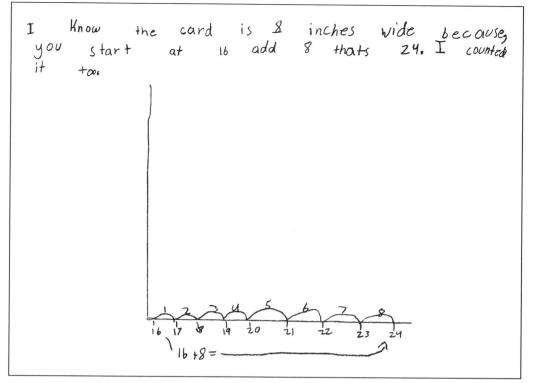

I know the card is 8 inches wide because you start at 16 add 8 thats 24. I counted it too.

Figure 1–9 *Falina counted on from 16 to 24, showing a good understanding of the meaning of a ruler.*

distance is 24 inches. Also, some students may subtract seventeen from twenty-four and determine the answer is 7 inches.

11. Collect the papers to review at a later time. Have students share their thinking with the whole group and, again, come to consensus about what the answer is and why some strategies don't work. For example, if a student subtracted seventeen from twenty-four, encourage that student to draw the part of the ruler that is missing. Then it will become more evident that the student needs to subtract sixteen, which marks the beginning measurement point of that broken ruler.

12. Again, note that when we measure from one end of a card to the other, we want to know how far it is—the distance—so we must count the spaces between the numbers.

A Life-Size Zoo

Overview

Children enjoy thinking about animals of surprising and extreme sizes, such as those described in *The Big and Little Animal Book,* by David Taylor. In this activity, the children use the measurement information found in that book to make life-size drawings of animals and write descriptive measurement labels for them. They then create a hallway display of their animals, making a life-size zoo.

Materials

◈ books or magazines that name the actual size of animals and have pictures of them, such as *The Big and Little Animal Book,* by David Taylor (1995); *Big and Little,* by Steve Jenkins (1996); *Amazing Animal Facts & Lists,* by Sarah Khan (1988); and *The Littlest Dinosaurs,* by Bernard Most (1989)

◈ butcher paper, sized appropriately for the animals the students will draw, 1 sheet per pair of students

◈ adding machine tape, for representing animals that are too large to draw on butcher paper, such as a blue whale, 1 roll

◈ meter sticks or measuring tapes, 1 per pair of students

◈ half sheets of blank paper, 1 per pair of students

◈ markers, 1 per pair of students

Vocabulary: centimeter, measuring tape, meter, meter stick, millimeter, scale

Instructions

1. Prior to the lesson, decide whether the students will do the investigation using the U.S. customary system or the metric system. This lesson is described using the metric system, but simply change the units if you prefer.

2. Read *The Big and Little Animal Book* (or another animal book with measurements). As you read, take time to let the children examine the illustrations and make sense of the book's information. For example, this book's introduction has a nice description of how length is measured and explains the advantages and disadvantages of an animal being large or small.

3. As you read, encourage the children to react to the facts presented about the animals. When a length or height measurement is given, have them visualize the size by holding their hands up or by comparing that height with something in the room or with the room itself. When the book compares a measurement with something in the children's lives, discuss whether that comparison makes sense to them. This book also has a "scale box," which presents a visual comparison of the actual size of all the animals in the book. When you and the children look at the scale box, have them consider how tall each animal would be in comparison with their own bodies.

4. Review the book to find length measurements. List the animals discussed and their measurements on the board. For example:

   blue whale's length: 33 meters

   Andean condor's wingspan: 3 meters

   poison arrow frog's length: 2 to 5 centimeters

African elephant's shoulder height: 4 meters (their tusks can be 2 meters in length)

great white shark's length: 6 meters

Madagascar pygmy white-toothed shrew's length, not counting its tail: 46 millimeters

African giant shrew's length: 140 millimeters

hairy-winged dwarf beetle's length: .25 millimeters

Goliath beetle's length: 15 to 20 centimeters

Queen Alexandra birdwing butterfly's wingspan: the diameter of a dinner plate

extinct dragonfly's wingspan: 3 times larger than the Queen Alexander birdwing butterfly's wingspan

edible crab's body shell width: 13 to 15 centimeters

giant spider crab's reach with outstretched claws: 4 meters

king cobra's length: 6 meters

5. Explain to the children that they will make life-size paper cutouts of the animals and compare them as the scale box does. Tell them that the illustrations will then be arranged in a hallway display called a life-size zoo so that other students and parents can learn about sizes of animals and how they compare with human sizes. **Note:** The rest of this activity is best done with six to eight children at a time, so that they can refer to the books' illustrations as they draw.

6. Have partners choose an animal and decide what size paper to use. If an animal is too large to fit on the butcher paper, the children can simply draw the head or tip of the tail and cut a strip of adding machine tape of the appropriate length to show how long or tall the animal really is.

7. Tell the children to use a meter stick or measuring tape, the book, and the information on the board to draw a life-size sketch of their animal with a pencil. If children find this difficult, help them in the following way: Ask the children how long their animal is, and where the animal picture would begin and end on the butcher paper. Make two marks in those places. Next help the children find a section of the animal, such as its head. Ask them what fraction of the animal the head would be, such as one-quarter of the animal or one-eighth. Have the children mark where the head would go in relation to the two marks already on the paper. Do the same with other major parts, such as the body and the tail, until they are able to continue drawing alone. Explain that when they finish their sketch, they are to outline the animal with a marker and cut it out.

8. When ready, have partners make a label for their zoo exhibit by writing the animal's name, its length, and a short description of the animal on a half sheet of paper. (See Figures 1–10 and 1–11.)

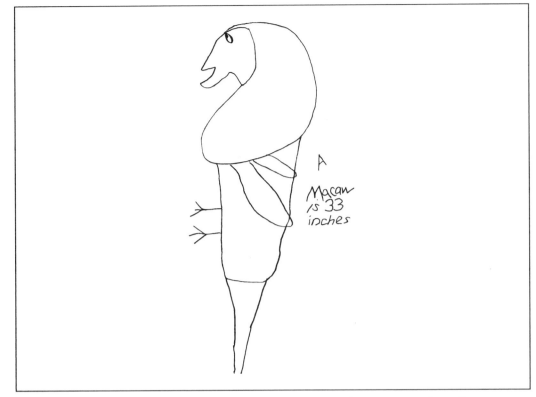

Figure 1–10 *Carlos and Amanda made a life-size macaw that was 33 inches tall.*

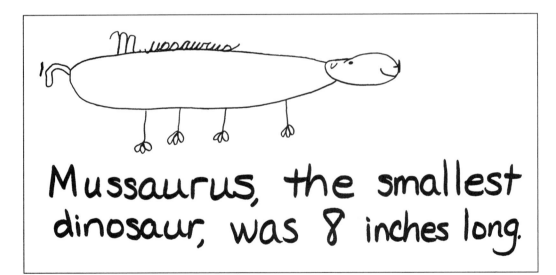

Figure 1–11 *Brittney made a life-size, 8-inch-long* Mussaurus.

9. Display the children's animals and labels in the hallway, creating a life-size zoo. If a student cut a piece of adding machine tape to show the length of the blue whale, the paper may need to wind around corners into other hallways. To encourage viewers to relate to the animals' sizes, post questions such as the following:

- Which animals are smaller than you?
- Which are half your size?

- Which are smaller than your hand?
- Which are larger than you?
- Which are twice your size?
- Which are longer than a car?

Dinosaur Data

Overview

In this lesson, students have the opportunity to react to the magnitude of very large measurements. After listening to *Patrick's Dinosaurs*, by Carol Carrick, students discuss whether the measurement data in the book can be true. They work in groups to gather information to answer the question Can it be true? They then make a display of their findings to convince others about their conclusions.

Materials

- *Patrick's Dinosaurs*, by Carol Carrick (1985)
- factual books about dinosaurs that include size information, such as *The Dinosaur Encyclopedia*, by Michael Benton (1984), or *The Kingfisher Illustrated Dinosaur Encyclopedia*, by David Burnie (2001)
- measuring tapes or yardsticks, 1 per pair of students
- 3-foot-long butcher paper, 1 sheet per group of students
- markers, enough for each group to create its displays
- optional: access to the Internet

Vocabulary: fiction, inhabit, nonfiction, typical

Instructions

1. Read the book *Patrick's Dinosaurs* to the children. Begin by showing the cover. Discuss what genre the book is: nonfiction or fiction. Note that humans and dinosaurs never inhabited the earth at the same time. Discuss how fictional books may contain some facts, but may also take poetic license.

2. As you read, encourage the students to react to the magnitude of the numbers. For example, when reading the page that describes ancient crocodiles' jaws as being "twice as big as you are," help students visualize how long that is by having a student draw a line that long on the board and then fill it in with sharp crocodile teeth.

3. As you continue to read, engage the children in discussions about whether the information in the book can possibly be true. For example, can it be true that ancient crocodiles grew three times as big as present-day crocodiles?

4. Write these questions on the board:

Can it be true that ancient crocodiles grew three times as big as present-day crocodiles?

Is it true that a stegosaurus was bigger than a car?

Could a Tyrannosaurus rex be tall enough to peek in the second-story window of a house? Would his teeth be about the size of the teeth in the picture? Would his head fit in the window in the way that the illustration shows?

Also write any additional "Can it be true?" questions that the children come up with during the discussion.

5. Write instructions for the investigation on the board:

With your group:

a. *Choose a question to investigate.*

b. *Gather information from the books in the room, do a computer search, or look in the encyclopedia to help answer your question.*

c. *You may need to measure something or make a good estimate, to make your comparison.*

d. *Make a poster of what you found out. Include the question you investigated, your findings, and a convincing argument to support your belief. Also include a picture diagram that shows the measurements that helped you make your decision.*

6. Give each pair of students a measuring tape or yardstick, butcher paper, and markers. As the students work, encourage them to measure actual items, or gather data about the size of actual items, to support their conclusions. For example, students might decide to do an online search to identify the typical size of a car, or they might measure a number of cars for homework and then determine which car would be considered typical. Students might also decide to identify the height of a second-story window by counting the bricks that they see on the exterior of a house and multiplying by the height of a brick and its mortar joint. Encourage students to solve these problems in ways that make sense to them.

7. Have the groups share what they discovered. If groups come to different conclusions about the same question, have them discuss their reasoning and ask each other questions to try to resolve the differences.

◆ Creating Benchmarks for Height

Overview

This lesson helps children create mental images for specific heights and referents for units that we typically use to measure height. Children find the heights of several people they know at school, such as the principal, the custodian, a second grader, and a kindergartner. After using a height chart to find how tall the first person is, students visually compare the height of the first person with that of the second person to make an estimate of the second person's height. The students then find the second person's actual height and place this information on the height chart and repeat the process with the third and fourth people. Later they add the heights of famous historical people and athletes to the chart.

Materials

◈ strips of 6-inch-wide paper, taped together to make 1 strip about 8 feet long
◈ strips of light-colored paper, about 2 inches by 6 inches, approximately 20
◈ collection of reference books, nonfiction books, or websites containing information about the height of famous sports figures, historical figures, or other famous people

Vocabulary: estimate, foot, height, inch

Instructions

Before Class

1. Decide whether the students will do the investigation using the U.S. customary system or the metric system.

2. Prepare the height chart. Use the markers to draw a dark line across the length of the 8-foot strip of paper. Rotate the paper to a vertical position and mark it in the units that you want your children to investigate: meters and centimeters or feet and inches. (Instead of marking the units, you may wish to simply attach a tape measure to the paper.)

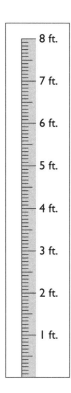

Day 1

1. Show the students your height chart and explain that they will use it to measure the height of several people at school. Have the students look at the chart and share what they notice. Have the students hold their own hands apart to show the units 1 foot and 1 inch. Make sure the students understand the abbreviations and representations for the units on the height chart.

2. Tell the students that you need help deciding how to tape the height chart to the wall. Hold it against the wall, at different heights above the floor. Tape it at a random distance above the floor. Then have groups of students discuss if it has to be moved and why they think that.

3. Ask several students to share what they think. Some students may say that the 1-foot mark should be at the floor level. Others may think that the bottom of the chart can be placed above the floor. During the discussion, ask the students where 1 foot is on the chart. Help the students see that the number 1 is not the measurement of 1 foot, but instead it indicates the end of the 1-foot distance. Ask the students to explain where 0 is on the chart. (It is implied at the bottom edge.) Since they will use the chart to measure people, they must tape the chart so the bottom edge (0) is even with the floor (where a person would measure 0 inches).

4. Now invite several people of different heights, whom the children know well, to your classroom. For example, you might invite the principal, the custodian, a kindergartner, and a second grader. Ask the first visitor to stand near the height chart.

5. Have the children estimate the person's height and then talk to their partners, explaining why they chose that estimate. Ask several children to share their estimates with the class and explain their thinking.

6. Ask the visitor to stand against the height chart. Use a marker to draw a line on the paper at that height. Write the person's name on a small strip of paper and tape it next to the line.

7. Ask the second visitor to stand back-to-back with the first visitor, away from the chart. Tell the children to use what they know about the height of the first visitor to estimate the height of the second. Again, allow the partners time to discuss their estimates, and then have a few volunteers share with the whole group. Then have the second visitor stand against the height chart. Record the person's name and height on another strip of paper and tape it to the height chart.

8. Continue the process with the other visitors, until all their names are on the height chart.

Day 2

1. Ask partners to list three to five famous athletes or historical people who are interesting to them. For example, they might write the name of a famous basketball player, an Olympic gymnast, or Abraham Lincoln.

2. Have the children use the information on the height chart, and their own background experience, to estimate the heights of these people.

3. Next have them find out the actual heights of these people. This information can be found in the reference books, nonfiction books, or websites you've gathered. On the small strips of paper, have children write each person's name and height and add these to the height chart in the appropriate locations.

4. When you are finished adding the names to the height chart, find a place to display it so that your children can review it on a regular basis. For example, you might display it in the cafeteria, the school entrance, or outside the classroom door. This will help create a mathematical environment in the school. Not only will your children continue to talk about and interact with the measurement information, but other children in other classrooms will have the opportunity to do the same.

Extensions

◈ Have the children estimate, find, and mark their own heights on the height chart. Then, using the height chart, ask them to make a list of people who are taller than they are and people who are shorter than they are.

◈ Ask the children to figure out how much they would need to grow in order to be as tall as the taller people on the chart.

 Going Home

Overview

Eve Bunting's beautiful book *Going Home* introduces this lesson by telling the story of a family returning to a village in Mexico where the children were born, a place the children no longer remember. For homework, students interview their own parents to find out where they are from. Then the students use maps to figure out the best route to travel to visit this place, estimate and compute that distance using the map's scale, and finally figure the length of time it would take to drive that distance.

Materials

❖ *Going Home*, by Eve Bunting (1996)
❖ atlas maps or other road maps that show how to get to the places the children's families are from, 5–10 (**Note:** Travel companies or websites can be good sources of maps. You may want to make copies of the maps if this option is available to you, so that more children can investigate at the same time.)
❖ maps of the city where the children live, 3 or 4
❖ atlas map of Mexico
❖ globe or world map for children who are from a faraway country
❖ ball of string
❖ 12-inch rulers, 1 per student

Instructions

Day 1

1. Read *Going Home* to the class. Enjoy the anticipation of the children in the story as they travel to a new place, how the children come to appreciate the village that is at first so strange to them, and how these migrant workers are rich in family and heritage.

2. Have the children share their memories of traveling by car to other places—their destination, how they felt as they traveled, how long the trip took, and how many miles they think they traveled.

3. Ask the children if they have used a map, or watched their family use one, to get to a destination.

4. Show the map of Mexico. (If you do not have a map of Mexico, use an appropriate map for Instructions 5 through 8, showing the children where you are from.) Find a city in the United States that borders Mexico, such as El Paso, Texas, or Nogales, Arizona, and a city that the family might have driven to farther down in Mexico. Have a child use a finger to trace the route that the family might have taken.

5. Next, examine the map's scale. Find the number of miles that the line segment represents, and use a ruler to measure that line segment. Most maps use an inch scale to represent miles and a centimeter scale to represent kilometers. Show both scales to the children, but emphasize the one that you want the children to use. (This description uses miles.)

6. Ask the children to estimate how many miles that route might be. Write their estimates on the board.

7. Next have the children explain how to identify the number of inches the route measures on the map. They may decide to use just a ruler, or use a piece of string and a ruler, or measure the distance with their fingers.

8. With the children, figure out the distance of the route, having them do the calculation. One way is to lay the string out along the route, cut off the piece of string, use the ruler to measure the string, and then multiply the number of inches times the distance per inch on the scale. For example, in one class, the string was $14\frac{1}{2}$ inches long and the scale showed 150 miles per inch. One child calculated the distance this way:

$$10 \times 150 = 1,500$$
$$2 \times 150 = 300$$
$$2 \times 150 = 300$$
$$\tfrac{1}{2} \text{ of } 150 \text{ is } 75$$

$$1,500 + 300 + 300 + 75 = 2,175 \text{ miles.}$$

9. Compare the answer with the students' estimates.

10. For homework, ask the children to interview their parents to find out where their family is from. Invite them to interpret "from" in a way that makes sense to them. It can mean where the family was from generations ago, where the parents lived before the children were born, or where they and their family lived before moving to their present city. If any families have lived in their present city for a long, long time, those students may want to find out what hospital they are "from," or the hospital where they were born.

Day 2

1. Before class, decide whether you have enough maps for the whole class to do the investigation at once, or whether the children will work one group at a time.

2. Have students share where their families are from. Write each child's name and the place of origin on the board. Tell the students that if their families are from several different places, they will choose one of those places to investigate. Tell students whose families have lived in the local area a long time that they will figure out how far from the hospital their current home is.

3. Help the children find these places on the maps. If you are using an atlas, show the children how the book is organized so that they will be able to more easily find the maps they need. Celebrate the diversity of the children's backgrounds by commenting on how fortunate they are to be able to learn so much from their

differences. Tell children who are from a distant country to use a world map scale to find the distance of a plane flight and then figure out how far a car would drive from the place the child lives now to the nearest airport.

4. Draw lines to connect the names of children who come from the same places, and ask them to use the same map. For example, in one class two children were from India, two children's families were from the community where they currently lived, two children were born in Texas, one was from Florida, eight children were born in Mexico, and five children were born in other states in the United States.

5. Tell the children who were born in areas that are on the same map that they will share a map, help each other interpret it, and work together to gather their information. Explain, however, that each student will record his or her own information.

6. On the board, list the things the students need to record:

   Starting place:

   Destination:

   Estimate of the distance:

   States, cities, or towns that the route passes through:

   Distance, including how you figured it out:

   How long you think the trip would take, and why:

   Hand out the rulers and map materials and let the students get to work.

7. When the children are finished, invite them to share what they discovered. Have the children describe the routes they investigated, showing the maps they used, and explain how they solved the problem. (See Figure 1–12.)

8. After several children have shared, have them stand in a line showing the relative distances they currently live from their families' places of origin. The children whose families' places of origin are closest to the their current homes begin the line. Children whose families are from the next closest place get in line next, and so on, so that the children end up standing in order, from those who live closest to where they are from to those who live farthest from where they are from.

9. Join the line yourself. Tell the students where your family is from and how far away that is.

10. Again comment how fortunate they are to be from different places, so they can all learn from their different experiences and backgrounds.

> Going Home
>
> Beginning place: Tucson, AZ.
> Destination: Agua Prieta.
> States or cities you'll pass through:
> Tombstone, Bisbee, Douglas and Agua Prieta.
> Estimate total Miles: 200 miles
> Total miles: 125 miles
>
>
> How long will it take: 4:00 hours
> I figuared this out by: Because I know
> that 50 miles is 1:00 hour so four 50's is
> 4:00 hours

Figure 1–12 *Oswaldo determined that if a car drove 50 miles an hour, it would arrive in Agua Prieta, 200 miles away, in four hours.*

 ## Stacks of Kids

Overview

After listening to David Schwartz's *How Much Is a Million?* children investigate how high a stack of students would be if they stood on each other's shoulders. Once they figure out the measurement of the stack in inches, and convert it to feet, the students find things in the school that are about that same length or height. (**Note:** While this investigation is described using feet and inches, it can also be done using metric units.)

Materials

❖ *How Much Is a Million?* by David M. Schwartz (1985)
❖ measuring tapes, 1 per pair of students
❖ 12 color tiles
❖ 12-inch ruler

Vocabulary: benchmark, convert, distance, estimate, feet, gap, height, inch, overlap, spaces, unit

Instructions

Day 1

1. Read the book *How Much Is a Million?* to the children. Enjoy the book's ideas, its pictures, and the mathematical discussions that it encourages.

2. Return to the first page where the author compares the height of things with stacks of children standing on each other's shoulders. Explain that the author is measuring using the unit of 1 child. Explain that they will investigate how to compare the height of things around them in "kid stacks."

3. Invite a child to the front of the room. Ask the students to explain how they could use stacks of children to measure, as in the picture. Ask what part of that child would be the unit that repeats over and over. During the discussion, remind the students that units must be the same size. As the students talk, you may find that some think they should measure from the child's head to the floor. Others may want to measure from his shoulder to the top of his foot. Encourage the students to explain to each other their reasoning, and come to an agreement about what part of the child should be measured.

4. Draw a sketch of stick children standing on each other's shoulders. Then draw parentheses that show what the students think the unit is. This way they can see whether the units repeat with no gaps or overlaps. (See Figures 1–13 and 1–14.)

5. Now ask the students to estimate how many inches it is from that child's shoulder to the floor. Remind them what an inch is by asking them to hold their fingers that far apart and, if you have already completed the *How Much Is a Meter?* activity, asking them to remember their benchmarks. Also hold up a single color tile as a reference. Write the children's estimates on the board.

6. Ask the children to help you measure that child's shoulder-to-floor length. Begin by trying to use the color tile repeatedly to cover the distance. Share that this is taking a long time, that you might be overlapping the tile distance, and

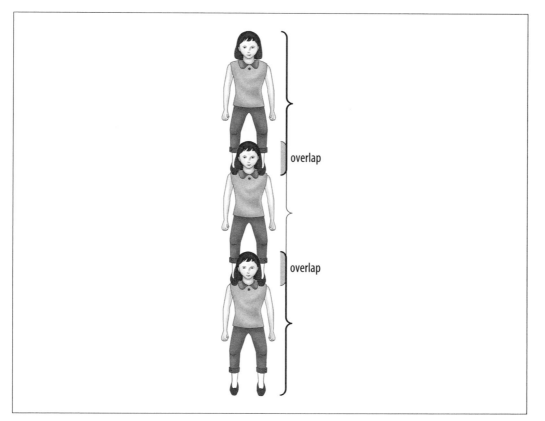

Figure 1–13 *Measuring the unit from the head to the bottom of the foot makes the units overlap.*

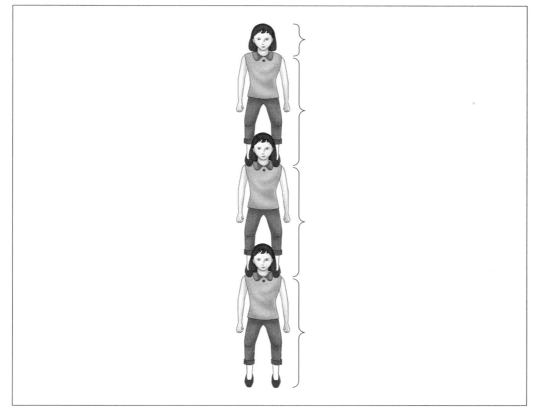

Figure 1–14 *Measuring from the shoulder to the bottom of the foot doesn't cause overlaps or gaps. But the students must remember to add the head at the top.*

that you might be leaving spaces. Ask the students to explain how else you could measure.

7. Students will most likely suggest using a tool that already has inches repeated, such as a ruler or a measuring tape. Show the students a measuring tape. Use the color tiles to remind the students where the inch distances are on the tape. Then show the students the numbers on the tape. Ask them what the *12* means: Are they counting the lines on the tape, or are they counting the twelve spaces that are the same length as the color tiles?

8. Next have two students use a measuring tape to measure the volunteer from shoulder to floor in inches. Discuss issues that come up as these students measure. For example, they may have difficulty lining up one end up of the tape with the floor, or finding where the top of the student's shoulder is. Write the student's name and measurement on the board. Now ask all the students to work in pairs to find each child's shoulder-to-floor measurement and record this information on paper.

9. When everyone is ready, have several students share their measurements.

10. Explain that it can be hard to imagine large numbers of small units, such as inches. Tell the students that you find it easier to think about feet, which are larger units. Hold up a ruler, and remind children that 1 foot is the same as 12 inches.

11. Make a T-chart on the board to show the relationship between feet and inches with the children's help:

feet	inches
1	12
2	24
3	36
4	48
5	60
6	72

Interpret the chart by having the class read, "One foot is the same as twelve inches. Two feet are the same as twenty-four inches," and so on.

12. Tell the students how tall you are in inches. Ask the students to think about how many feet you are, and how many inches are left over, and ask several students to share how they figured it out. Now have all the children figure out their shoulder-to-floor measurements in feet and leftover inches and record their thinking on their sheet of paper.

Day 2

1. Arrange the class into groups of five to seven children. Ask them to think about the total number of inches that they would have if everyone in their group stood on each other's shoulders: How high would their stack be? Ask each group to make a prediction. Then have each group share its prediction with the whole class.

2. Next have groups find the actual height of their stack. Explain that after telling each other their individual measurements, each child is to find the total distance for the group, and then group members should compare their answers with each other. As you circulate among the groups, ask whether they remembered to add in a head measurement for the child on top.

3. When everyone is ready, write the data from one group on the board, listing each child's shoulder-to-floor distance in feet and inches. Have the students in that group share how they compiled their total. For example, one group might have the following data:

   3 feet, 6 inches

   3 feet, 2 inches

   4 feet, 2 inches

   3 feet, 8 inches

   3 feet, 7 inches

   10 inches (head)

   The children could total the feet and inches this way:

   16 feet, 35 inches

   Ask them how they can use the T-chart to convert as many inches to feet as possible. The students will figure out that their stack would be 18 feet, 11 inches. Ask all the groups to convert their measurement to the greatest number of feet possible.

4. Now have the students write a list of things they think are about the same height as their stack of kids. Remind the children that they are now estimating. For example, they might say that three times the distance from the floor to the ceiling is about equal to their kid stack. Other children might say their stack is about the same height as the flagpole or six doors. Or children might think of an equivalent horizontal distance, such the distance from the cafeteria door to the stage.

5. Have groups choose an item to measure and compare with their kid stack. Once you approve of the item chosen, give each group a tape measure to help them determine

if that item is about the same height (or length) as their kid stack. (Some things cannot be measured directly, such as the height of the portable classroom. In this case the children will have to measure a part of it, for example, the door, and then estimate how many doors high the portable would be.)

6. Have the children record if that item is about the same height or length as their kid stack and how they know that.

7. When everyone is ready, have groups share what they discovered and how they figured it out.

Extension

Continue the discussion with students to see how they can use knowledge of the height of a single person to make a good estimate of something tall, such as a tree or tall building. For example, if a student is about four feet tall and he stands next to a wall, the other students might estimate that two of him would about equal the wall's height, so the wall must be about eight feet high. (See Figure 1–15.)

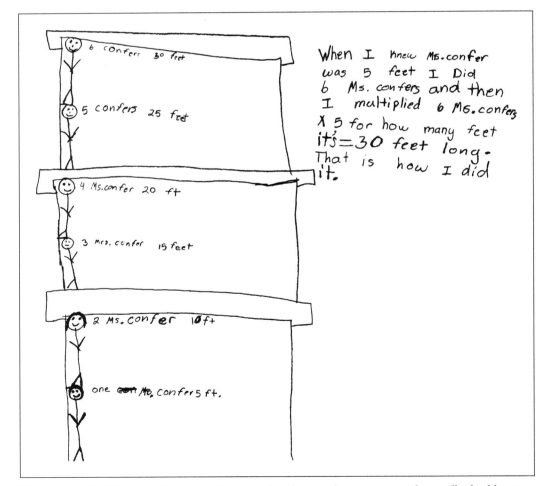

Figure 1–15 *Selena made an imaginary stack of her teacher to estimate how tall a building is.*

◈ Relationships in the Metric System

Overview

The metric system is particularly easy to work with since its units relate to each other in the same way that units in place value relate to each other: powers of ten. This activity helps make that connection for students. In this lesson, students compare centimeter cubes, decimeter rods, and meter sticks and find all ways that they can describe the relationships among these units.

Materials

◈ centimeter cubes, 10 per pair of students

◈ decimeter rods, 10 per pair of students

◈ meter sticks, 1 per each small group of students

◈ chart paper, 1 sheet

Vocabulary: centimeter, decimeter, hundreds place, meter, metric, metric system, place value, powers of ten, relationships, tens place, units

Instructions

1. Tape the piece of chart paper on the board. Write the title *Metric Relationships*.

2. Explain to the students what you mean by *relationships*. Talk about how we are related or connected to people in our families. Explain that one person can be related to different people in different ways. For example, you may be a daughter to your mother, a sister to your brother, and a wife to your husband. In the same way, a centimeter has many different relationships to other units of measure.

3. Hold up a centimeter cube and a decimeter rod so the class can compare them. Ask the children to talk to their partners about how those two units of measure, or lengths, are related.

4. Have the children share some of their statements with the class. After each child shares, ask the others whether they agree. If so, write these statements on the chart. For example, one statement might be "There are 10 centimeters in 1 decimeter." Ask a student to make a sketch on the chart to show what that relationship looks like. The sketch might look like this:

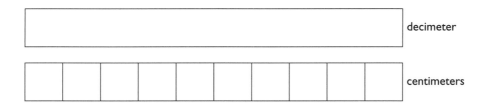

5. Ask the students to give you an example of that relationship, for instance, how many centimeters are the same as 2 decimeters. Illustrate this relationship by placing one centimeter cube on top of two decimeter rods laying end to end. A student might say that 20 centimeters equal 2 decimeters. When a child explains a relationship, add those words to the chart. Ask for another example, such as how many centimeters would be in 5 decimeters, and add students' ideas to the chart.

6. Now encourage the students to think about how they would explain the first statement in terms of fractions. You may need to restate the question, saying, "What fraction of the decimeter is a centimeter?" Again place a centimeter on top of a decimeter. Then have partners talk, ask a child to share, and write the statement on the chart. The child may say, "A centimeter is one-tenth of a decimeter."

7. Once again ask for an example of that relationship. For instance, ask what fraction of 2 decimeters is 1 centimeter. If no one knows, explain why it is one-twentieth.

8. Explain to the students that they are going to work in pairs to find as many different ways as possible to describe how metric units—meters, decimeters, and centimeters—relate to each other. Ask the children to explain the relationship in writing and include pictures as well as examples of how those relationships work. Pass out ten centimeter cubes and ten decimeter rods to each pair of students, and explain that small groups will share meter sticks.

9. As the students work, circulate to offer support. Students may explore relationships such as how centimeters relate to meters or how decimeters relate to meters. They may consider relationships in terms of fractions or multiples. Students may explore how many centimeters or decimeters are in more than one meter. Ask key questions such as: "Do you both agree that this statement is true?" and "How can you prove it?" Be sure to have students use the manipulatives to explain their thinking and make diagrams showing the relationships. If students have statements only with whole numbers, encourage them to think about how to describe those relationships in fractions.

10. When the students are finished, gather them into a group to share what they have discovered. Begin by discussing how centimeters relate to decimeters. Invite a pair of students to share a statement that they have written or a diagram that they have made. Each time a pair shares, have the other students decide whether they agree with the statement. If so, add it to the "Metric Relationships" chart. If not, the group may need to help the students revise their statement. Then do the same with how decimeters relate to meters, and then how centimeters relate to meters.

11. Sum up the relationships between the metric units by using terminology that is probably new to the students. Tell the students that when we say that decimeters are ten times larger than centimeters, and that meters are ten times larger than decimeters, the units are increasing by *powers of ten*. If the students have not yet made this observation, note that powers of ten also describe the relationship between units in place value: the tens place is ten times larger than the ones place, the hundreds place is ten times larger than the tens place, the thousands place is ten times larger than the hundreds place, and so on.

12. Finally, make the connection between the units' names and their relationships. Write *centimeter* on the board, and underline *centi*. Ask the students what that reminds them of. Next to *centi*, write *cents* and *century*. Explain that there are one hundred cents in a dollar and one hundred years in a century, just as there are one hundred centimeters in a meter. If the students speak Spanish, make the connection with the words *cien* and *ciento:* one hundred.

13. Now write *decimeter* on the board, and underline *deci*. Ask the students what that reminds them of. Next to *deci,* write *dime* and *decade*. Explain that there are ten dimes in a dollar and ten years in a decade. If the students speak Spanish, make the connection with the word *diez:* ten.

14. Post the chart on the wall. Encourage the students to refer to it when they encounter metric units at school. (**Note:** This chart is used again as a reference in the *Finger Weaving* lesson, on page 46.)

Jim and the Beanstalk: Giant-Size Things

Overview

In this lesson, the students listen to *Jim and the Beanstalk*, by Raymond Briggs. They figure out how long or tall the giant's glasses, teeth, wig, and other objects are by considering how large the boy looks next to each item in the illustrations. The students measure a typical boy and use that information to find an object's length. Then they draw the giant-size object on butcher paper as it would really look.

Materials

- *Jim and the Beanstalk*, by Raymond Briggs (1970), 1 copy per group
- measuring tapes, 1 per small group of students
- 3-foot-long butcher paper, 1 sheet per small group of students
- dark-colored markers, 1 per small group of students
- optional: pair of eyeglasses

Vocabulary: foot, height, inch, length

Instructions

1. To begin the lesson, read *Jim and the Beanstalk* to the students. Enjoy the humor in the book and the story itself.

2. Reread the book, focusing on the mathematics. As you read, encourage the students to comment on the height or length of the giant-size objects in the book, and compare the objects with the boy's height. For example, when reading the page with the giant's glasses, ask the students how long the *stem* of the glasses is. (If this word is unfamiliar to the students, you may wish to show them the stem, or earpiece, of a pair of real glasses.) Some students may look at the picture that includes the giant's measuring tape and say that the stem is 6 inches long. If this happens, have the students hold their fingers about 6 inches apart, and ask them whether the stem of the giant's glasses would be this long. Help the students understand that the giant's measuring tape is bigger than our measuring tape, so in our world, the giant's glasses would be much longer. Suggest that they compare the boy in the picture with the stem of the giant's glasses. Have the students explain how they compare. Students may say that the stem is twice the length of the boy, or that two boys would equal the length of the stem. Have a medium-size boy stand up and ask the students to visualize how much higher than him the stem would extend.

3. Continue rereading the book and having similar discussions about other giant objects, such as the giant's teeth, the saltshaker, and the wig.

4. Next, introduce the investigation to the students. Tell them that they are going to work in small groups to figure out how large some of the giant's things would be. Tell them they will figure out how tall or long an object would be in feet and inches. Remind the students that 12 inches equal 1 foot. Tell the students to measure the length of the object on a piece of butcher paper, draw an outline of the object with pencil and then a marker, and cut the object out. List on the board some of the objects that the students may select:

   the giant's gold coin

   stem of the giant's glasses

   lenses of the giant's glasses

   the giant's saltshaker

   the giant's teeth

   the giant's wig

5. On the board, write the instructions:

> *Select an object. Figure out the length of the object in feet and inches, and show your work on your paper, using words, numbers, and pictures. Measure that length on the butcher paper, and draw the giant's object that size. Then cut out your drawing.*

6. Pass out the materials and a copy of the book to each group. As the students work, provide them with additional support as needed. Some students may try to use a measuring tape to measure the size of the giant's item in the picture. Explain that they need to know the size of that item in our world, not in the picture. Tell the students that the size of a typical boy might be a reference, just as the class looked at the medium-size boy earlier to get an estimate of how big the giant's glasses would be. As the students work, observe how they use the measuring tape and how they read the measurements, as well as how they determine the true measurement of the giant's possessions.

7. When the students finish their work, begin a discussion. Invite each group in turn to hold up its paper object. Have the other students estimate the length or height of the object in feet and inches. Then have the group tell the class the actual length or height of the object and explain how the students determined that measurement. Encourage the students to respond to each other's thinking and compare how other groups' methods are similar, or different from, their methods. (See Figures 1–16 and 1–17.)

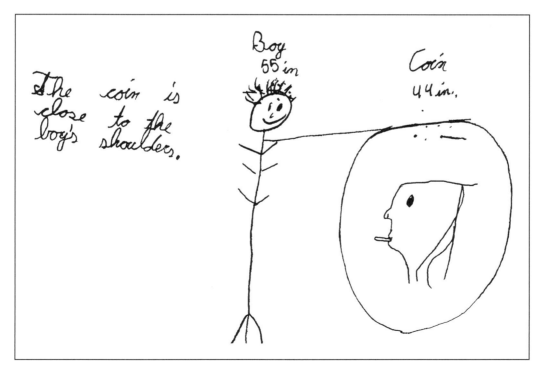

Figure 1–16 *Francisco's group decided that the coin would be as tall as the boy's shoulders.*

Figure 1–17 *Amanda and Daniel determined that the stem of the giant's glasses was as long as the two boys.*

Finger Weaving

Overview

Students enjoy learning how to weave yarn chains using only their fingers. Once students know the technique, they weave long, long chains. They wonder how long these chains are, giving them a reason to develop measurement concepts. This lesson is structured to connect metric ideas to our place-value system and is a nice follow-up to the lesson *Relationships in the Metric System* (page 41).

Materials

- ◈ skeins or balls of yarn (preferably of different colors), 1 per small group of students
- ◈ masking tape, 1 roll
- ◈ *Finger Weaving* instructions (see Blackline Masters), 1 per group of students
- ◈ *Finger Weaving* recording sheets, about 2 per small group of students (see Blackline Masters)
- ◈ orange Cuisenaire rods (these are 10 centimeters long, or 1 decimeter), 10 per small group of students
- ◈ white Cuisenaire cubes (these are 1 centimeter long), 10 per small group of students
- ◈ meter sticks, 1 per small group of students
- ◈ sticky notes, 1 per student
- ◈ clipboards, 1 per small group of students
- ◈ "Metric Relationships" chart from *Relationships in the Metric System* lesson (page 41)

Note: Decimeter rods and centimeter cubes can be found in base ten kits.

Vocabulary: centimeter, decimeter, meter

Instructions

Before Class

1. Teach yourself how to finger weave. It won't take you, or most of your students, long to learn. (See instructions in the Blackline Masters.)

2. Prepare a looped string for each child in the class, using the skeins of yarn. For each string, cut about a meter of yarn and tie a loop about $1\frac{1}{2}$ centimeters in diameter on one end.

3. Label the bottom half of each sticky note with a different letter of the alphabet. Use capital letters.

Day 1: Introducing Finger Weaving

1. Gather a small group of students, whom you will teach to finger weave. Tell these students that they will teach others in the class. Tape an instruction sheet to the board, and refer to it as you teach the students.

2. Show the students a string with a loop that you prepared ahead of time. Explain that you will teach them to finger weave chains and that as they weave, they will keep track of how long their chain is. Review the "Metric Relationships" chart from the *Relationships in the Metric System* lesson (page 41), and have the students use their hands to show you what a centimeter looks like, what a decimeter looks like, and what a meter looks like. Then use your hands to show one of those three units of measure, and have the students say the name of the unit you are demonstrating.

3. Show the students the hand position that they will use as they weave. Explain that they will keep their index finger pointed while using their thumb and three other fingers to hold the string, or grab it. Have the students put their hands in the same position and practice grabbing:

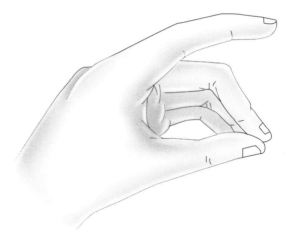

4. Now begin weaving a chain, explaining to the students what you are doing. While you weave, say the steps, "Loop the string over your finger between the string and the end of your finger, grab the chain with your other fingers, cross the string over and off your finger, grab the chain with your other fingers, and pull the chain down to form another link."

5. As you weave more links, say the words, "Loop, grab, cross over, grab, pull."

6. While you continue holding the chain that you started, invite a child to do the steps *loop, cross over,* and *pull* on your string.

7. Let the child weave several more links in the same way. Then give that string to the child, who can continue to finger weave independently. Provide that student with a copy of the instructions to refer to as necessary.

8. Get another string, begin chaining while describing the steps, and then have another student do the procedures described in Instruction 6.

9. Continue in the same way until all the students know how to finger weave. As the students run out of yarn, show them how to estimate a new piece of yarn about a meter long, cut it off, and attach it to the remaining yarn in their chain by simply tying a knot.

10. Have other students in the class join the group. Again demonstrate how to finger weave, and have the first group of students help teach the others. Have the students weave their chains for the rest of the period.

Day 2: Measuring the Chains

1. Ask students to bring their chains and gather in a circle on the rug. Choose a child's chain that is more than 2 meters long. Lay it on the floor, taping the ends down with masking tape to keep them in place.

2. Place a meter stick, a decimeter rod, and a centimeter cube on the rug. Have the students name the units.

3. Have partners explain to each other, and then to the whole class, how the units compare with each other. Have them refer to the "Metric Relationships" chart, if necessary. Students may say that a decimeter is 10 centimeters, a meter is 10 decimeters, a meter is 100 centimeters, a decimeter is $\frac{1}{10}$ of a meter, a centimeter is $\frac{1}{100}$ of a meter, and a centimeter is $\frac{1}{10}$ of a decimeter.

4. Discuss which unit the group should use to measure the chain. Try to have students who disagree convince each other why one unit is better than the other. For example, a child may say that it is ten times faster to measure in meters than to use decimeters to measure the same distance. If the group decides to use meters, continue as described in the following steps. (If the group decides to use decimeters, adapt the following steps using decimeters, and then during the discussion convert the measurements to meters.)

5. On the board draw the following chart, and explain to the students that they will fill out a similar chart as they measure.

Chain	Meters	Decimeters	Centimeters	Length in Meters	Length in Decimeters	Length in Centimeters

6. Identify the chain by folding the sticky side of sticky note A around it. Write the letter A in the first column of the chart.

7. Place a meter stick near the chain and have the students estimate about how many meters the chain measures. Write the estimate for Chain A in the Estimate column.

8. Now have a child place meter sticks end to end to find out how many meters long the chain actually is and write the number of meters in that column while the other students watch the process to see if they agree with what the child does. Talk about the decisions that the student made, such as whether or not to measure the end of the yarn that is not part of the chain (the "tail"). Leave the meter sticks in position, so the students can fill the rest of the distance with smaller units.

9. Next, have a child fill in the remaining space along the chain with as many decimeters as possible. Write that number in the Decimeter column. Leave those rods in place. Then have another student use centimeter cubes to fill in all the remaining space. Also keep those cubes in place next to the chain and record the amount on the chart.

10. Have the students examine the chart and discuss what the total length of the chain is. Discuss how the decimal point is used when measuring in meters: the decimeters go to the right of the decimal point because each is one-tenth of a meter, and the centimeters are written in the next column because each is one-hundredth of a meter. In the Length in Meters column, write the total measurement. Be sure to include the unit name, as in *2.34 meters*.

11. Emphasize the importance of the decimal point. On the board, write *234 meters* and ask the students if those numbers without a decimal point would be a reasonable measurement of the chain's length. Then add a decimal point so the measurement is 23.4 meters. Ask whether 23 meters and a fraction of a meter is a reasonable measurement.

12. Introduce the task to the students. Explain that they will work in small groups to measure their own chains, and that they will record what they find out on a group recording sheet. (You may want the students to work in the hallway if the chains are very long.) Explain that they will tape a chain onto the floor and label it with a sticky note in the same way that you did. Advise them not to stretch the chains, since some knots may come apart with too much tension.

13. Tell the students to leave the chains taped to the floor. Explain that after they measure all the chains in their group, they will measure every other group's chains, which will have been left taped to the floor. In this way, each group will measure each student's chain.

14. Divide the class into small groups. Provide each group of students with a meter stick, ten decimeter rods, ten centimeter cubes, some masking tape, one labeled sticky note for each student, a pencil, and two recording sheets clipped to a clipboard. Have them set to work measuring the chains.

15. When they are finished, gather the students on the rug in a circle near the chart on the board. Tape Chain A on the floor when everyone can see it.

16. Have the students discuss what was easy about the measuring process as well as any difficulties that they encountered.

17. Now ask the students how they would figure out the length of Chain A if they didn't have any meter sticks, but had only decimeter rods and centimeter cubes. Have partners discuss that question, and then discuss it with the class.

18. Write the students' ideas on the board. After each child responds, invite other students to answer these questions: "Are you convinced? Does the idea make sense to you?"

    Write the actual numbers in the Length in Decimeters column of the chart. (You will find that the numbers are the same, but the decimal point is moved to the right one space. However, don't tell the students this. Let them come to this conclusion on their own, by counting the ten decimeters that are in each meter.)

19. Have the students imagine that they have only centimeter cubes to measure with. Ask: "What would the length of the chain be now?" Record this information on the chart.

20. Untape Chain A and tape another chain in the center of the circle. Have the student who made the chain demonstrate measuring it, as described in Instructions 8 and 9 on page 50. Then repeat the process in Instructions 17 through 19. Do this with several more chains.

Chain	Meters	Decimeters	Centimeters	Length in Meters	Length in Decimeters	Length in Centimeters
H	12	6	1	12.61	126.1	1,261
P	1	8	6	1.86	18.6	186
Q	3	1	3	3.13	31.3	313
N	2	9	3	2.93	29.3	293

21. Ask the students to explain to a partner what patterns they see on the chart and why those patterns are there. Ask the students how these patterns connect to place value. Emphasise the fact that each place is ten times bigger than the place to its right. Explain that this is the beauty of the metric system: it matches place value. Explain further that when we change a metric measurement from one unit to another, all we have to do is move the decimal point.

22. Over the next week have the students add to their chains from time to time. After each session, have the students measure their chains in meters and then determine that same length in decimeters and in centimeters.

Area

Introduction

While the word *area* is part of students' everyday vocabulary—"I live in that area"—it has a more specific meaning in mathematics. In mathematics, *area* means the amount of space that covers a surface.

Students encounter area concepts in their lives when they wrap a gift, paint a board, or make a book cover, and they often find that an estimate is sufficient to complete their task. Finding the exact area, a skill necessary in many careers and situations, requires people to first make an estimate, to then measure precisely, and to finally check their outcome with their estimate.

In order to understand the concept of area, students must first distinguish the attribute to be analyzed. They must move their attention from a shape's linear dimension to the entire space that covers it. Students must then see the need to use square units, rather than linear units, to cover and measure this space. Students must learn to see a rectangular array in terms of its rows and columns. Additionally, students must understand that simply rearranging a shape does not change its area.

In the lessons in this chapter, students do not simply use the formula of length times width, but move beyond it to confront issues related to area measurement: Why are square units better than circular units for measuring area? Why can there be no gaps between units, and why must the units not overlap? Is there a relationship between area and perimeter? How can we find out whether different shapes are congruent? These lessons provide students with opportunities to estimate areas, to decompose areas, to describe areas in different ways, and to solve a variety of real-world problems using nonstandard and standard units.

The Mitten 1

Overview

Students explore the idea of area by using a body part, their hand, which in this lesson is called a "mitten." After tracing their mittens on a sheet of paper, students use a variety of materials to find the area of the shape, then the class discusses the advantages and disadvantages of measuring with the different types of units.

Materials

◈ containers with items that can be used to measure area, such as dry lima beans, flat plastic circles, centimeter cubes, color tiles, and interlocking cubes, 1 container of the same item per small group of students

Vocabulary: area, centimeter, enclosed figure, gaps, overlaps, square centimeters

Instructions

1. Introduce the lesson by holding your hand up vertically, fingers close together. Explain to the students that your hand is in the shape of a mitten. Open your fingers like a glove and have your students explain how this differs from the mitten.

2. Now ask a student to make a hand into a mitten. Hold your hand flat against the student's hand, and ask the other students if they can tell whether the area of your mitten or the area of the student's mitten is bigger and why they think that. Have students explain what *area* means in this instance: the space that covers the surface of the mitten. Write the word *area* on a vocabulary word chart and write the students' definitions.

3. Next ask partners to compare the areas of their mittens. Have partners share whose mitten area is larger and how they know. Record their words on the board. Again, have students explain the meaning of area.

4. Now introduce the investigation to the students. Explain that each of them will trace around their own mitten on a piece of paper. Illustrate with your own hand: On the board, trace your hand and enclose the shape on the bottom. Emphasize that it's important to make their mitten an enclosed figure.

5. Tell the students that they will select an item to use to find the size of the area of their mitten. Show the students the containers of measuring units that you have available. Explain that they will place the items inside their traced mitten until it is completely covered, count the items, and record the number, leaving the counters on top of their mitten. Tell the students that if they have to remove the items to count them, they must put them back on the mitten when they are done.

6. On the board, write the directions:
   a. *Trace your mitten.*
   b. *Use one kind of item to fill its area.*
   c. *Figure out the number of items that cover the area, and record it on your paper.*
   d. *Leave the items on your mitten.*

7. Now place one container at each table. Invite students to choose an item to use and sit at that table to do the investigation. As the students work, observe their

strategies. Watch to see if any students do not understand the concept of measuring area, leaving large gaps or overlapping counters. Also, observe how the students count the items and whether they group them by tens or use another strategy.

8. When they are ready, have students compare their areas with those of others at their table. Then on the board list the areas of two mittens of students who used different units of measure, for example:

Fernando: 64 lima beans

Mary Ann: 57 circles

Discuss whether this information makes it possible to compare these students' mittens. The students will likely conclude that they can make conjectures based on how lima beans compare with circles, but it is easier to compare when the units of measure are the same.

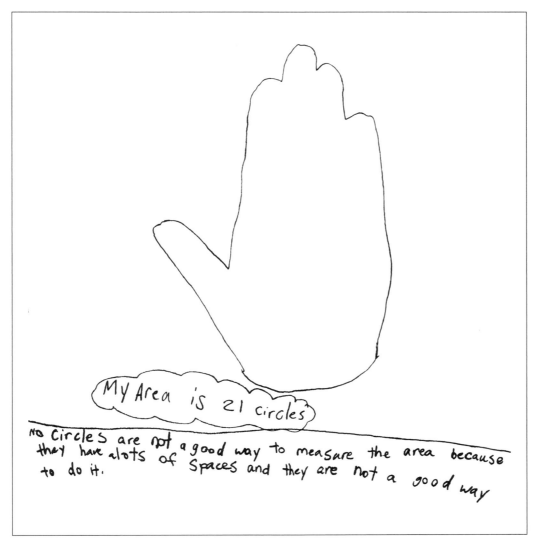

Figure 2–1 *Elena decided that circles are not a good tool for measuring area.*

9. Now have a class discussion about the items that students used to measure their mitten areas. First gather the students around the table where circles were used, and together examine a student's mitten and the circles that the student left on it. Have the students discuss whether the circles were a good way to measure the area. Some students may say that using circles was a fast way to measure, but others may note that there were spaces left uncovered between the circles. Other students may notice the gaps left on the edge of the mitten or places where the circles went outside the mitten's edge. If any students overlapped their circles, discuss how this affects the measurement. You may wish to give the example of piling the circles into a mountain on top of the mitten, asking: "Does that tell you the area of the mitten?"

10. Now move the students to a table with lima beans. Have the same discussion about the advantages and disadvantages of using beans to measure area. Do the same with the other objects that the students measured with. When the students examine the centimeter cubes, they may notice how the cubes fit together better, leaving fewer spaces uncovered.

11. Next have the students return to their own mittens and write about whether or not the item they used was a good tool for measuring area, listing the advantages and disadvantages. (See Figure 2–1 on page 55.)

◈ The Mitten 2
....

Overview
In this lesson, the students trace their mittens on centimeter grid paper and measure the area, focusing on easy ways to count the squares as well as how to deal with parts of squares. Then the students discuss what a typical mitten size would be for their class. They make a class graph and analyze it, finding the median and the mode.

Materials
◈ centimeter grid paper, 1 sheet per student (see Blackline Masters)
◈ 3-inch square sticky notes, 1 per student and 8 additional notes
◈ marker
◈ butcher paper, about 4 feet long, 1 sheet

Vocabulary: area, centimeter, gaps, median, mode, multiples, partial squares, spaces, square centimeters, subdivide, typical, units

Instructions

1. Begin by reminding the students about the previous mitten lesson they did. Hold up your hand like a glove and then like a mitten so they remember the hand position that they investigated. Have each student hold up his or her

mitten against a friend's mitten and discuss which mitten has the larger area. Refer to the definition for *area* they created on the vocabulary word chart.

2. Now ask the students to remember the items that they used during the previous lesson to find the area of their mittens. Have them recall the advantages and disadvantages of each. As the students share, illustrate what they say by sketching a mitten on the board. First draw circles inside to illustrate the gaps that circles leave. Then sketch beans inside another mitten and squares inside a third mitten. Point out how squares don't leave spaces between them, but do leave spaces next to the edge of the mitten or extend beyond the edge. Explain to the students that today they will explore another unit that might help them measure more precisely, since it will let them more easily see the parts of units.

3. Tape a sheet of centimeter grid paper on the board. Trace your mitten in its center, enclosing the bottom to make a closed figure. Tell the students that they will do the same and then find out how many square centimeters are enclosed in the mitten. Tell the students that you will be interested in the different ways they find the area, and that there are faster ways to count than by counting each square one at a time.

4. Next, focus the students' attention on the pieces of squares around the edge of the figure. Tell the students that you will be interested in hearing how they deal with these pieces and how they include them in the measurements. Remind the students to write how they figured out the total area as well as their answer.

5. Hand out a sheet of grid paper to each student and have the students begin the investigation. As they work, observe how they count the squares. Many will count by ones. (See Figure 2–2.) Other students may outline larger squares or rectangles made up of rows of square centimeters and then multiply to find the area. (See Figure 2–3.)

    As the students work, ask them to explain what they are doing and why. Also, observe how they deal with the partial squares, and ask them to explain what they are doing. Encourage the students to show on their paper how they combine the parts of squares. Remind them to show all their thinking on paper.

6. When the students finish their work, have several students share their areas as well as their strategies for finding the areas. You may wish to have a student who counted the squares by ones share first and have a student who found arrays share next. Then have students who found other kinds of arrays share, so everyone can see the different ways to subdivide the space. As students share, have them also show the different ways they represented their thinking in writing.

7. Discuss how students dealt with parts of squares. As students share, encourage the others to respond, offering their perspectives. Some students may have ignored the pieces. Note that these are part of the mitten's area, so ignoring the

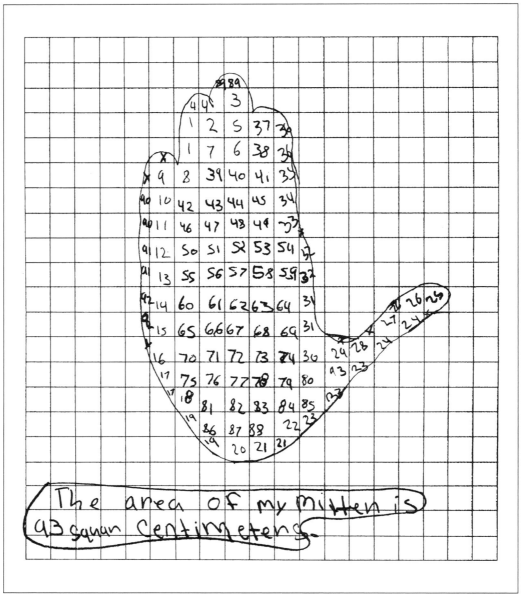

Figure 2–2 *Carlos counted each square by ones.*

pieces would make a smaller total than the actual measurement. Other students may have counted each partial square as a whole square (see Figure 2–4) or combined parts into wholes (see Figure 2–5). For example, some students may have looked for pieces that were about half and combined them into one unit. Other students may simply have estimated how the parts of squares would affect the total.

8. Now have them share their ideas about what would be a typical mitten area for the class. Explain what *typical* means—the area that is most common or is most likely to be found in a group such as this. As an example, ask: "If a new student of the same age walked into the room, what would be a reasonable guess for the area of that student's mitten?"

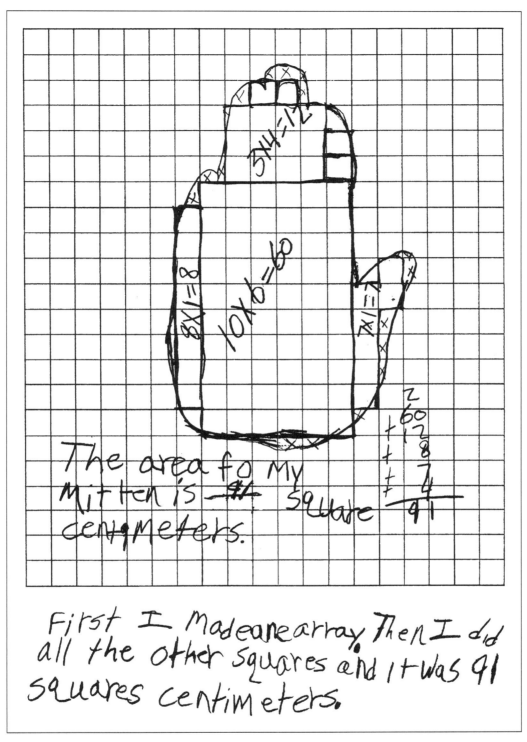

Handwritten annotations within the figure:

5×4=12

8×1=8

10×6=60

7×1=12

The area fo my Mitten is 91 square centimeters.

2
60
12
+ 8
+ 7
+ 4
91

First I madeanearray, Then I did all the other squares and It was 91 squares centimeters.

Figure 2–3 *Javier multiplied to find sections of his mitten, and then he added the sections together.*

9. Tell the students that they will organize their data on a class graph so they can better answer that question. Tape the sheet of butcher paper on the board.

10. Ask the students who they think has the mitten with the smallest area in the class. As students share, be sure that they state the unit as "square centimeters." If the

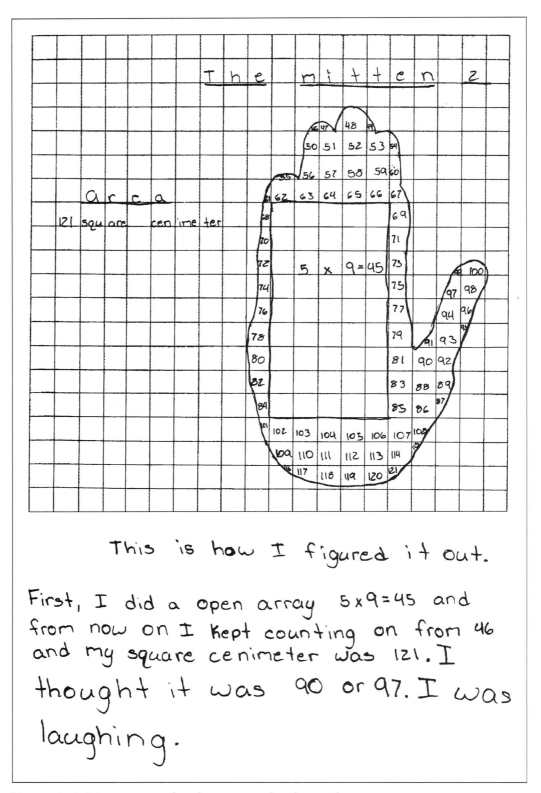

The mitten 2

area
121 square centimeter

5 x 9 = 45

This is how I figured it out.

First, I did a open array 5x9=45 and from now on I kept counting on from 46 and my square cenimeter was 121. I thought it was 90 or 97. I was laughing.

Figure 2–4 *Marcus counted each square, and each partial square, as one.*

students simply say "centimeters," have a discussion about this, noting that centimeters are a way to measure how long something is: it's a linear measure. But when you measure the area, you need to fill in a space in two dimensions: length as well as width. Tell the students that it's as if you are stamping squares all over

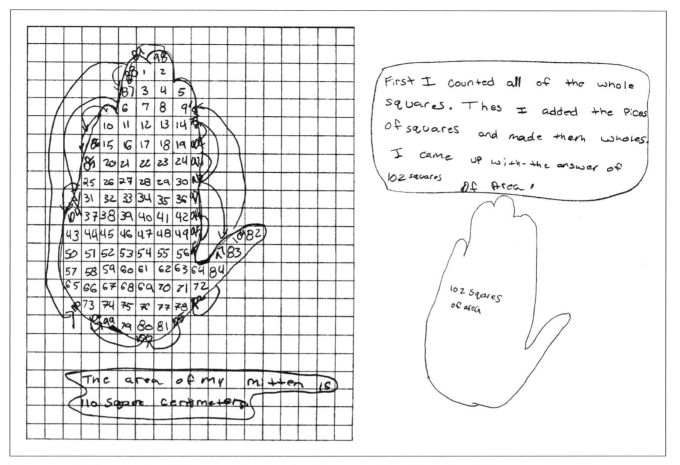

Figure 2–5 *Selena combined the parts of squares that she estimated would equal a whole square.*

the enclosed figure to fill in all the open space. When students agree on the smallest area, write that area (again labeling it *square centimeters*) on the board. In the same way, find the mitten with the largest area and write that number.

11. Make graph labels on sticky notes by using a marker to write the multiples of ten that match the students' data. For example, for a group that had the smallest area of 74 square centimeters and the largest area of 120 square centimeters, the labels would be 70, 80, 90, 100, 110, and 120. Place these labels along the bottom of the butcher paper.

12. Pass out one sticky note to each student. Ask students to write their name on their note and the number of square centimeters of their mitten in large print so it will be visible to the class.

13. Have students come up to the board in groups and affix their notes above the appropriate labels. As they affix the notes, have the students arrange each column in order, with the largest numbers at the top and the smallest numbers at the bottom.

14. When the graph is complete, have the class examine the data and tell what they notice. Write the students' summary statements on the board. When students

find the number that occurs most often, label this the mode and add information about the mode to the summary statements.

15. Ask the students if they had to choose one value that best represented the whole class, what it would be. Have a discussion about their ideas about a typical mitten area for the class. Students may refer back to the mode—the area that more students had than any other area.

16. Students may also discuss the middle, or median, number. Have two students find this number. A systematic way to do this is for one person to point at the largest number while the other person points at the smallest number. Then have them touch the second largest number and the second smallest number, then the third largest and third smallest number, and so on. They continue in this manner until both are touching one number (if the total number of responses is an odd number) or until they are touching adjacent numbers (if the total number of responses is even). Add information about the median to the summary statements.

17. Now revisit the idea of the typical mitten area for the class. Have the students discuss if a new student joined the class what area they predict that student would have. They may think about this in terms of a range of reasonable areas. If so, add this information to the summary statements.

18. Last, explain that visitors to the school are often interested in knowing about the students, so you will tape the graph to the wall in the hallway. Tell the students that a graph must have a title to inform the reader about the topic, in the same way that a book has a title. Discuss with the class what an informative title might be, and write the best suggestion at the top of the graph. Then tape the graph on a wall near the school entrance.

Comparing Brownies

Overview
In this lesson students examine different-shape "brownies" and decide how their areas compare: Is one larger or smaller, or do they all have the same area? The students cut or fold the shapes to determine the answer. As they partition the brownies into smaller pieces, students develop ideas about equivalence and conservation of area.

Materials
◈ *Brownie Shapes* worksheets, 1 of each per pair of students (see Blackline Masters)
◈ clear adhesive tape or gluesticks, enough for the class to share

Vocabulary: area, convincing argument, equal, equivalent, narrow, rectangle, wide

Instructions

1. Provide each pair of students with a copy of each *Brownie Shapes* worksheet. Explain to the students that each shape represents a brownie.

2. Ask the students to discuss, and then explain to the class, how the shapes of the brownies are different. As the students share their thinking, encourage the use of mathematical vocabulary such as *narrow* instead of *skinny* and *wide* instead of *fat*.

3. Introduce the problem to the students. Explain that you'd like them to work in pairs to decide how the brownies compare in area. Ask the following questions to help the students understand:

   • Is one brownie larger than the others? Would you have more brownie to eat if you selected that one?
   • Is one brownie smaller than the others? Would you have less brownie to eat if you selected that one?
   • Are any brownies medium size?
   • Are any brownies equal in size?

4. Write the questions on the board. Invite the partners to discuss their predictions.

5. Next explain that the partners must agree with each other about the answer to each question. Tell the students that after they determine the answer, they are to write a convincing argument for what they think. Since you want the students to focus on the concept of area as covering space, tell the students that they can fold the paper, or they can cut and tape the paper, but they may not use anything else to solve the problem. (Do not allow the students to measure with rulers or cover the area of a brownie with items. This lesson encourages them to look for units within the shapes themselves or subdivide and recombine the areas to find equivalent pieces.)

6. As the students work, observe their strategies. For example, you may find that some students fold the shapes into smaller rectangular regions of the same size and count them, thereby finding that the areas of the shapes are equal. Other students may cut the shapes apart and rearrange them into the other shapes. As the students work, encourage them to explain what they are thinking. Use mathematical terminology as you discuss the brownies, such as *rectangle*, *equivalent*, and *area*. Remind the students that they need to convince others in the class that they are correct.

7. When the students have finished, lead a group discussion. Begin by rereading the questions that they were to investigate. Have pairs of students share what they think and why. As the students talk about a brownie, encourage them to refer to its area. For example, when the students say that a "brownie is bigger," you might

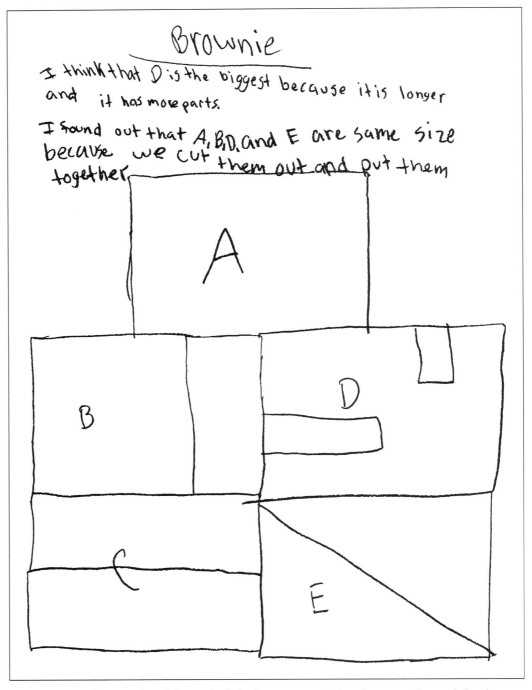

Figure 2–6 *Elena predicted that D had the largest area. After she cut and traced the shapes, she discovered that the brownies have the same area.*

say, "So you think the brownie's area is larger." If a student says, "The brownies are the same size," you might say, "So you think they are equivalent in area."

8. After each pair presents its findings, ask the other students whether they are convinced. Encourage the students to question each other and come to an agreement as a group. Also encourage the students to compare the different ways that they subdivided the same shape. (See Figure 2–6.)

What Do You See?

Overview

In this lesson each student creates a shape with an area of 30 square inches. Together the class examines one shape and shares different ways to see the parts inside the shape, while the teacher uses numbers and equations to record each different way. Then students write an equation showing how they see their own shape. They exchange shapes and share their thinking.

Materials

❖ inch grid paper, 1 sheet per student (see Blackline Masters)

Vocabulary: area, equations, square inches

Instructions

1. Begin by introducing the task. Tell the students that they are going to create a shape, look at its area, and use numbers to describe the area in different ways.

2. Show the students a sheet of inch grid paper. Explain that they will each make a shape with an area of 30 square inches and then write their name next to the shape. Tell the students that they must draw on top of the grid lines when they make their shape. Also explain that the lines must form a single shape that would stay together if the shape were cut out. To make this clear, on the board, draw some shapes that follow the rules and some shapes that do not:

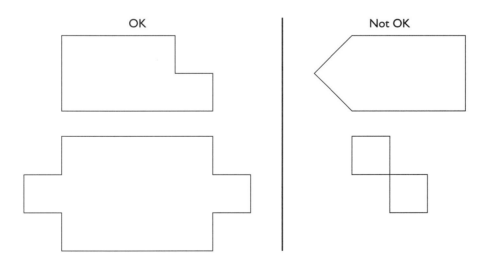

3. Hand out the grid paper and set students to work. When everyone is finished, collect the shapes that the students have made. Post one on the board for the class to examine.

4. Gather the students near to the board so they can easily see the shape. Ask them to verify that its area is 30 square inches.

5. Ask the students to share how they know that the area is 30 square inches. Explain that for this lesson, they may not count by ones, but must instead describe the smaller rectangles that they see inside the larger shape. Record what one student says using numbers and equations. A student might see the shape in this way, and you could record like this:

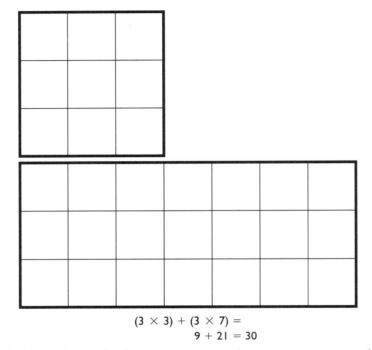

$$(3 \times 3) + (3 \times 7) =$$
$$9 + 21 = 30$$

6. Next ask the students whether someone sees the arrangement in a different way. You may want to rotate the shape on the board to give the students a new perspective. Another student might see the shape this way:

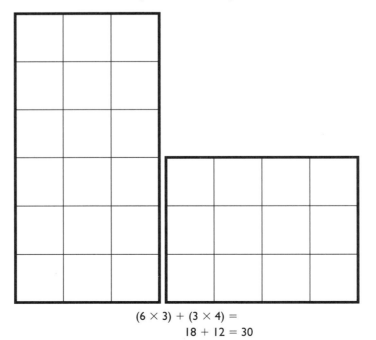

$$(6 \times 3) + (3 \times 4) =$$
$$18 + 12 = 30$$

7. Choose another shape and repeat the process. Ask the students to explain what smaller rectangles they see inside the larger shape, and record each different way that they see it.

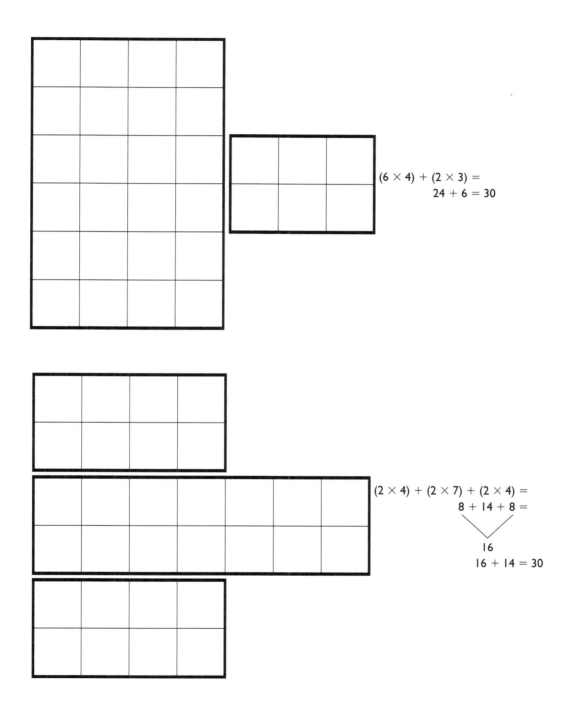

$(6 \times 4) + (2 \times 3) =$
$24 + 6 = 30$

$(2 \times 4) + (2 \times 7) + (2 \times 4) =$
$8 + 14 + 8 =$

16
$16 + 14 = 30$

Repeat the process as necessary, depending on students' experience with seeing parts within shapes and describing those parts with equations.

8. Ask students to write an equation that describes how they see the chunks inside their own shape. Circulate among the students and have them explain how their equation matches how they see the parts. (See Figure 2–7.)

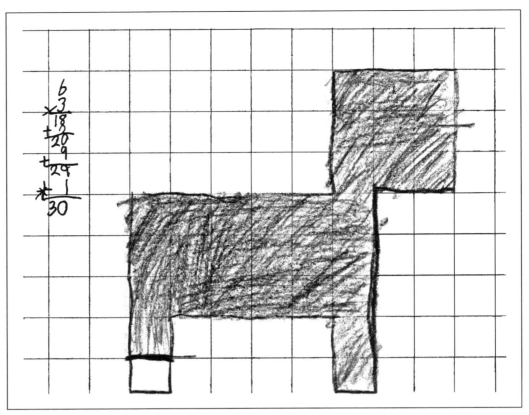

Figure 2–7 *David created a dog shape and found the areas of each of its smaller sections.*

9. Now have partners exchange shapes. Ask the students to read their partner's set of equations and try to understand how that person interpreted the parts in the shape. Have the students talk to each other to see if they are correct.

10. Have the students rotate their partner's shape, look at the parts in a new way, and write a set of equations that show a new way to see the shape's chunks.

11. Finally, ask the students to return the shape to the person who created it. Have them read the equations that their partner wrote for their shape and try to interpret how that student saw the parts inside the arrangement. Ask the partners to talk to each other to see whether they correctly interpreted each other's thinking.

◆ Tiling a Floor

Overview

In this lesson, students develop the ability to decompose areas as they design a hallway for a tile company. An imaginary homeowner wants the tiles in her 4-by-6-foot hallway to be arranged in two rectangles, one red and the other blue. The students record their designs on grid paper and write equations to describe the smaller rectangular areas within the large rectangle. Then students write a note to the homeowner explaining which arrangement they recommend.

Materials

◈ centimeter grid paper, 2 sheets per student (see Blackline Masters)
◈ transparencies of centimeter grid paper, 2
◈ overhead pens, 1 red, 1 blue, 1 black
◈ optional: chart paper

Vocabulary: _____ feet by _____ feet, area, decompose, dimensions, horizontal, narrow, orient, orientation, rectangle, region, rotated, rows, square feet, vertical, wide

Instructions

1. Tell the students to imagine that they work for a tile company, designing tile floors. Explain that they are to design a hallway floor with red and blue tiles in four rows of six tiles each. Tell the students that homeowner wants the tiles arranged in exactly two rectangles: one red and one blue. The students' task is to figure out all the possible designs.

2. Show the students an overhead transparency of centimeter grid paper. Tell the students that each square centimeter on the grid represents a square foot in the real hallway. Outline the 4-by-6 hallway on the grid paper, as shown. Point out the four rows with six tiles in each row.

3. Now have the students look at the room they are presently in and visualize the space that a 4-by-6-foot space would take up. (Some floor tiles are 1 foot square, which can help students make this comparison.)

4. Next have the students refocus on the rectangle you drew on the transparency and determine how many square feet are in that hallway altogether. Have the students share how they figured it out. Some students may count by ones, some may talk about four rows of six tiles or six columns of four tiles, and some students may simply multiply four times six. If students do multiply, have them explain how the four matches the rectangle and how the six matches the rectangle, and why multiplying makes sense (this will encourage the students to articulate the four rows of six or the six columns of four).

5. Now explain to the students that to start their task, they must draw the hallway horizontally as you have done, because that is how it is oriented within the house.

6. Tell the students that in their hallway tile design, the rectangles can be wide or narrow, but the hallway needs to have exactly two rectangular areas. On the board write:

> *Design tile arrangements for a hallway that measures 4 by 6 feet.*
>
> *Find all the ways that the hallway can be tiled. The tile arrangement must have exactly <u>one red rectangle</u> and <u>one blue rectangle</u>.*
>
> *How many different designs can you make that follow that rule?*

7. Do one example together. Ask the students to tell you how the floor could look. On the overhead, divide the hallway as they suggest. Use red and blue overhead pens to indicate the colors of the tiles. This will help the students compare arrangements at a glance. Check to see that the design follows the rules. As you do so, explain that you are "decomposing" the area into two smaller areas. Ask the children to describe the dimensions for each region, and write the equations that stand for those regions. Remind the students that the parentheses help the reader understand that one pair of numbers belongs to the red area and the other pair belongs to the blue area. For example:

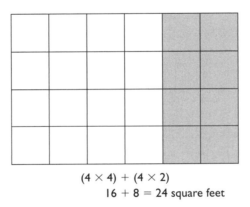

(4 × 4) + (4 × 2)
16 + 8 = 24 square feet

8. Next ask the students to tell you another way that the hallway area could be divided into two rectangles. Ask them to tell you a way that it could have horizontal rectangles. Again draw their suggestion on the transparency, and write the equations that describe how the area is decomposed.

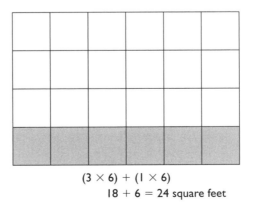

(3 × 6) + (1 × 6)
18 + 6 = 24 square feet

9. Ask the students how many different arrangements they think are possible to create. Make sure that the students remember the criteria: they must have two rectangular areas, and the hallway must always be oriented horizontally. Tell the students that it's OK to have opposite patterns; for example, in the previous illustration, the 3-by-6 rectangle could be on the bottom instead of the top. Explain that the arrangement would look different to the homeowner if he walked in a door on one side.

10. Hand out the centimeter grid paper and have the students begin the investigation. Encourage them to work in partners or as a small group, but have each student record each arrangement. As the students work, make sure that they follow the criteria that the homeowner has given. Ask them to tell you how they know the design they are working on is different from the others that they have designed. Also ask them to show how the equation they wrote matches the drawing they made. (See Figure 2–8.)

11. When the students finish working, gather them for a discussion. First ask the students how many different arrangements they found. Write the numbers on the board.

12. Next have the students share the different designs that they discovered. As each student describes a design, draw it on the second overhead transparency of centimeter grid paper and write the equation that the student shared. You may instead wish to record on chart paper or a whiteboard using colored pens

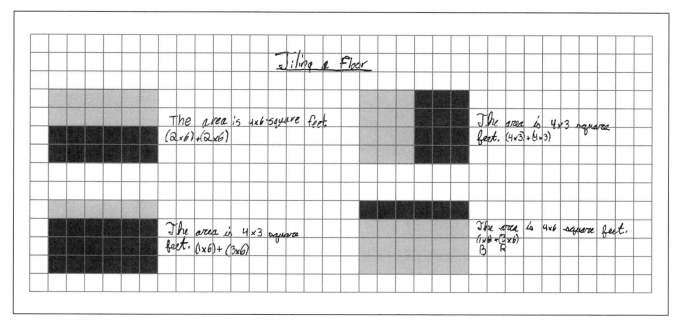

Figure 2–8 *Four of the ten different tile arrangements that Fernando found.*

and by drawing open arrays. Open arrays do not have the interior squares drawn:

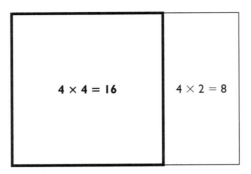

13. Have the students share the strategies they used to find new arrangements, such as making "opposite" designs (designs that are a reflection of each other) or working with the numbers sequentially (e.g., decomposing the 6-foot dimension into 1 + 5, 2 + 4, 3 + 3, 4 + 2, and 5 + 1). As each student presents, have the others decide whether each design fits the homeowner's criteria, whether the arrangement is different from the ones already presented, and whether the equation matches the drawing.

14. When all the different designs have been found, ask the students to discuss which design they would recommend to the owner. Then have them write a note to the owner sharing their recommendation, and the reasons they think that would be the best design. (See Figure 2–9.)

Dear Mr. House;

I recommend that you build a 4 x 6 but split it up like This. I'd like to build one like that if I were you. You need to buy 12 red tiles and 12 blue. Each tile will cost 2 dollars so if You Moltyply it's 48 dollars.

Sincerely,

Architect

Figure 2–9 *Hannah recommended a 2 × 6 red section and a 2 × 6 blue section.*

 **Dog Yards**

Overview

In this lesson students design different rectangular dog yards using exactly 36 feet of fence. They identify the total square feet in each arrangement and then choose the arrangement that they think would make the best dog yard.

Materials

◈ centimeter grid paper, 2 sheets per student (see Blackline Masters)
◈ transparency of centimeter grid paper

Vocabulary: area, criteria, dimension, feet, length, perimeter, rectangle, square, square feet, width

Instructions

1. Begin by telling the students that they are going to design different kinds of dog yards. Tell the students that the dog yards must be rectangles and can be thin rectangles or wide rectangles. Remind the students that a square is a special kind of rectangle and is acceptable. Draw different examples of shapes that are OK and shapes that are not OK.

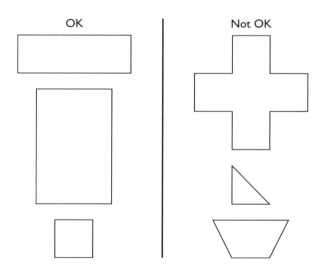

2. Place a transparency of centimeter grid paper on the overhead. Explain to the students that they have thirty-six foot-long pieces of fencing to put together to make a dog yard. Draw a line on the grid paper to show that a line segment represents a foot-long piece of fencing. Draw a line six segments long and

explain that this piece of fencing is really 6 feet long. Label that side with the number 6.

3. Explain that the next side of the dog yard is going to use ten pieces of fencing and will be 10 feet long. Draw that side on the grid paper and label that side with the number *10*.

4. Draw the opposite side ten segments long, and draw the final side of the rectangle six segments long, labeling each side with its length.

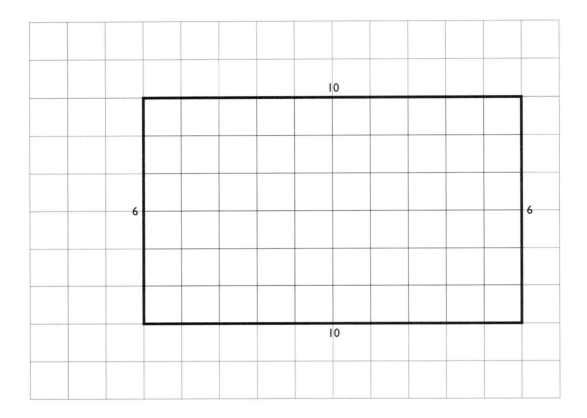

5. Ask the students to check whether the shape is a rectangle. Have them explain how they know it is. For example, they might say that the opposite sides are the same length and that each corner is a right angle.

6. Next ask them whether you used exactly 36 feet of fencing. They may say that you used only 32 feet, because 10 + 10 + 6 + 6 = 32.

7. Have the students give you a suggestion about how you can change the dog yard. For example, they might say to extend the 10-foot sides so they are 11 feet long. Do what they say, and have the students check the total amount of fencing to see

if that yard uses exactly 36 feet of fencing. If it doesn't, have the students tell you how to revise the yard until it meets the criteria. When you do find a rectangle that is 36 feet around, use the word *perimeter*, saying, "The perimeter of the dog yard is thirty-six feet." Write the word *perimeter* on your vocabulary word chart, and have the students explain in their own words what it means.

8. Now tell the students that they will investigate how many different ways the yard could look, but still be a rectangle made from all 36 feet of fencing. Have them use grid paper to find all the possible shapes, labeling each rectangle with the length of each side. Tell the students to show with numbers how they know that they have used exactly 36 feet of fencing. Write the instructions on the board:

   a. *On grid paper, draw all the possible dog yards that can be made from exactly 36 feet of fencing. Remember, each dog yard must be a rectangle.*
   b. *Label the length of each side.*
   c. *Write an equation to show the total length of the perimeter.*

9. Hand out the grid paper. As the students work, ask several students to prove to you that their shape meets the criteria. Encourage them to use strategies for adding numbers or multiplying in ways that support developing number sense. For example, if a child uses a formula or a traditional procedure, you may wish to ask him to show an additional strategy for calculating. For example, if a student writes:

$$
\begin{array}{r}
1 \\
17 \\
\times\ 2 \\
\hline
34
\end{array}
$$

you might help her think about 17 as $10 + 7$. Then she may be able to mentally compute:

$$2 \times 10 = 20$$
$$2 \times 7 = 14$$
$$20 + 14 = 34$$

10. After the students work for a while, have a short whole-group discussion. Ask different students to share two or three possible arrangements. On the board, draw the arrangements by drawing rectangles without outlining each individual interior square. Label each side and have the group figure out mentally whether the arrangement uses exactly 36 feet of fencing.

11. Next ask the students to continue finding all the possible arrangements for the dog yards. Explain that after they have found all the possible ways, they should figure out the total area of each arrangement. Explain that the area is each square foot of space that the dog gets to play on. Tell the students that after they have found the area of each dog yard, they must decide which dog yard would be best for a dog and write what they think and why.

12. Bring the students together for a final discussion. On the board draw one arrangement, the 7-by-11 dog yard. Have students share how they figured out the total square feet of that yard. Some students may count each square by ones. Others may be able to count by sevens or by elevens. Remind the students that they can also break apart that area into smaller areas that are easy to think about. For example, a student may count the 11-foot rows by tens and then count the ones that are left over, for example, 10, 20, 30, 40, 50, 60, 70, 71, 72, 73, 74, 75, 76, 77. Or they might multiply one area, multiply the other area, and add the parts together. Show how the array would be broken apart by drawing this diagram:

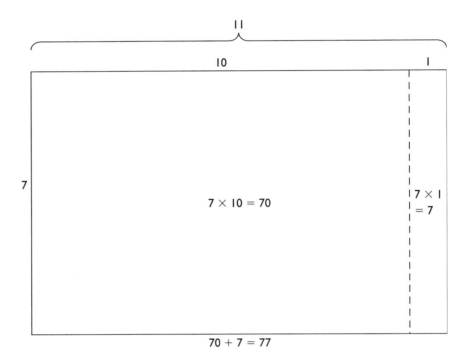

13. Ask the students to share their arrangements, beginning with the widest rectangle. On the board, draw a T-chart and record the students' information:

length in feet	width in feet	total square feet
1	17	17
2	16	32
3	15	45
4	14	56
5	13	65
6	12	72
7	11	77
8	10	80
9	9	81

14. Ask the students why they can't have a length of 10. They will say that the arrangement is a duplicate.

15. Have the students look at the T-chart to see what they can say about the arrangements that have the largest areas and the arrangements that have the smallest areas. The students may say that the largest area arrangements are "fattest" or "the most square." This is an important idea, one that architects use to maximize room space for the fewest materials and least cost.

16. Ask the students to share which area they would recommend as the best and why they made that decision. (See Figure 2–10.)

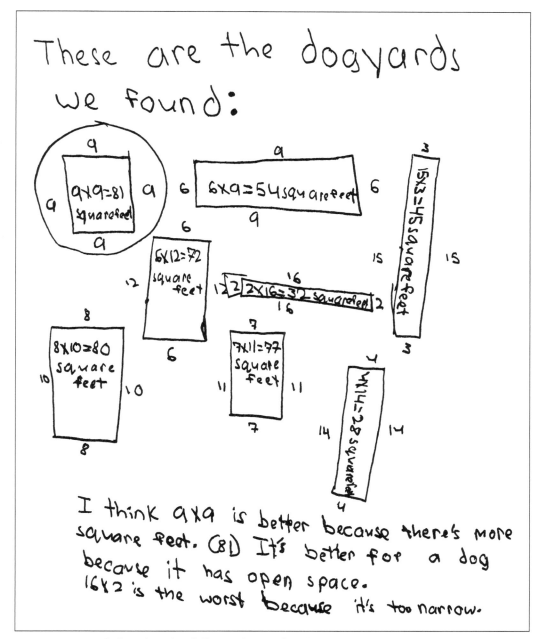

Figure 2–10 *Shakira found 8 different dog yards. She recommended the 9 × 9 foot one.*

 **Perimeters of 30**

Overview

In this lesson, students draw on centimeter grid paper as many different polygons as possible that have a perimeter of 30 centimeters. In small groups, they find the polygons with the largest area and the smallest area, cut them out, and post them on a class chart. The students describe the characteristics of polygons with the largest and smallest areas and come up with an explanation of why those characteristics produce that kind of polygon.

Materials

- ❧ chart paper, 2 sheets
- ❧ centimeter grid paper, 2 sheets per student (see Blackline Masters)

Vocabulary: area, centimeter, perimeter, polygon, square centimeter, units

Instructions

1. Write the word *Area* on one sheet of chart paper. Ask the students to talk in pairs and then share with the class what the word means. As students share, write their words on the chart to serve as a reference as they work. They may say things like "the space something covers" or "the top of something" or "the inside." Next ask students for examples of things that they see that have area, and list these items on the chart. Students may list things such as the wood panel on a wall, the white space on a whiteboard, or the surface of the rug. Make sure the students understand that area describes flat shapes rather than three-dimensional shapes. Explain that when we measure area, we use square units, such as square centimeters or square inches. Write those units as well as their abbreviations, *cm*^{2} and *in.*^{2}, on the chart. Tell the students that when we measure with square units it's as if we are stamping little squares all over a space so we can see how many squares will cover that space.

2. Follow the same procedure with perimeter. The students may describe it as the "distance around" or "the edge" or "the outside." Write their descriptions on the same piece of chart paper as well as examples, such as the stripe around the outside of a basketball court, or the baseboard around a floor, or the red strip around the edge of the rug. Explain that when we measure perimeter, we are looking at length and we use units such as centimeters or inches. Write those words and their abbreviations on the board.

3. Draw a 4-by-5 array on the board:

Ask the students to tell you the area of the shape and how they figured it out. Students will share strategies such as counting each square, as well as additive strategies such as $5 + 5 + 5 + 5 = 20$ if they see rows or $4 + 4 + 4 + 4 + 4 = 20$ if they see columns. They may also use multiplicative strategies such as $4 \times 5 = 20$. Write what the students say as equations. Next to the rectangle write $A = 20$ *square units*.

4. Now draw a line on the board to show the unit of the perimeter. Tell the students that this line could be like the fence for a dog yard, or the distance a bug has to walk as he walks around the rectangle. Have the students find the perimeter of the 4-by-5 rectangle and share how they figured it out. Students will share strategies such as counting each unit, as well as additive strategies such as $4 + 5 + 4 + 5 = 18$, or multiplicative strategies such as $(2 \times 4) + (2 \times 5) = 18$. Write what the students say as equations. Emphasize that to find the perimeter of the rectangle, they have to count each side of the exposed corners. Next to the rectangle, write $P = 18$ *units*.

5. Show the students centimeter grid paper and tell them they will be using metric units, centimeters, for this investigation. Explain that they will make as many different polygons that they can that have a perimeter of 30 centimeters. On one piece of paper, draw a nonrectangular polygon with a perimeter of 30 centimeters. As you draw it, count each segment in the perimeter. You may need to edit your shape, if you find that its perimeter is not exactly 30 centimeters. Explain to the students that they may also find it necessary to erase and change their polygons until they have the required perimeter. Tell the students that the lines they draw must be on top of the grid lines, and they may not draw diagonally across the squares. Remind the students that polygons are closed figures with no empty spaces in the center.

6. Explain to the students that they must find both the perimeter and the area of each polygon that they draw and write both inside the polygon, using the abbreviation for each kind of unit, as you did with the rectangle.

7. As the students do the investigation, make sure that they are counting perimeters correctly by including all exposed sides of the squares and that they are writing the units correctly. Also ask the students which is the largest area that they have found so far and which is the smallest area that they have found. (See Figure 2–11.)

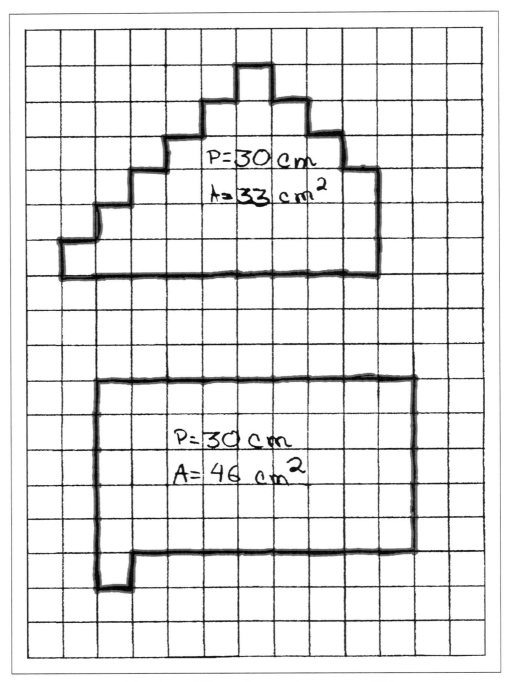

Figure 2–11 *David found two different shapes with perimeters of 30 centimeters.*

8. After the students have had time to make a large assortment of polygons, ask them to look at the polygons made by others in their group and find the polygon with the smallest area and the polygon with the largest area. Have them cut those polygons out.

9. On the second sheet of chart paper, draw a line down the center and label the columns *Smallest Area* and *Largest Area*. Have the students post the two polygons from each table in the appropriate spaces.

10. Ask the students to focus on the polygons and individually think about what the polygons in each column have in common. Next have the students find words that describe how the polygons in each category are different. Write those words at the bottom of each section. Ask the students to explain why polygons with large areas are "fat" or "square" or "wide," and why polygons with small areas are "thin" or "wiggly" or "have stair steps." The students may talk about polygons with small areas as having more exposed sides and polygons with large areas as having fewer exposed sides.

How Many Rectangles?

Overview

In this lesson, the students work in pairs to find how many rectangles with perimeters of 40 centimeters they can make. They draw each rectangle, writing equations to prove the perimeter is 40 centimeters. The lesson ends with a group discussion in which students use patterns in the dimensions to find all possible rectangles. They record on a chart that highlights two procedures for identifying perimeter, one that uses addition and another that uses multiplication.

Materials

◈ centimeter grid paper, 2 sheets per student (see Blackline Masters)

Vocabulary: centimeter, length, pattern, perimeter, rectangle, width

Instructions

1. Show the students a sheet of centimeter grid paper. Tell the students that they will do a partner investigation. They will find as many rectangles as possible that have a perimeter of 40 centimeters.

2. To clarify the task, draw a rectangle on the board. Have the students explain what a rectangle is. Be sure they note that rectangles have four sides and that opposite sides of rectangles measure the same. Remind the students that a square is a special kind of rectangle, one with all four sides that measure the same. Draw several kinds of rectangles on the board, thin ones and wide ones. Tell the students that they will draw their rectangles on the lines of the centimeter grid paper.

3. Explain to the students that each time they find a rectangle with a perimeter of 40 centimeters, they should write the dimensions of each side as well as number sentences that prove that the perimeter totals 40. (See Figure 2–12.)

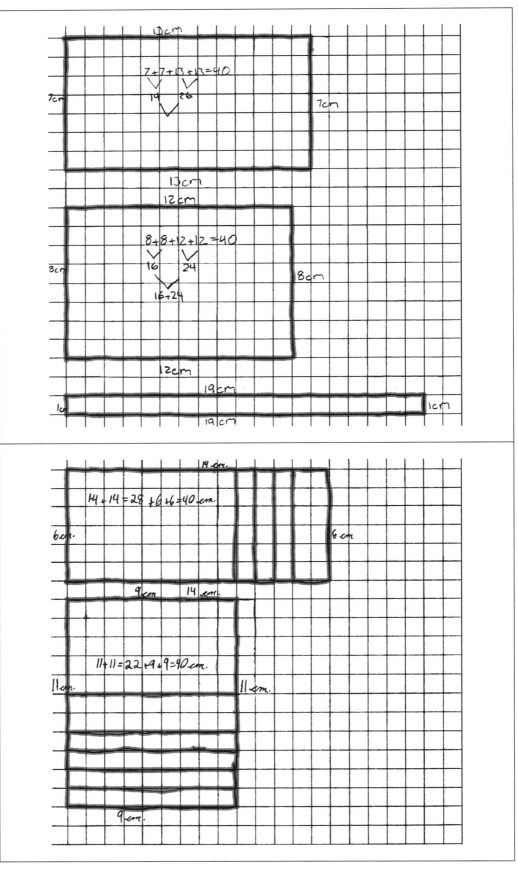

Figure 2–12 *Ramon and Jorge found five different rectangles with perimeters of 40.*

4. Before the students begin the investigation, ask them to predict how many rectangles with a perimeter of 40 are possible to make. Write their predictions on the board.

5. Pass out the grid paper. As the students work, check to see that they are identifying perimeters correctly, and that they are counting each exposed side of the corners. Have students explain why this is necessary.

6. When the students have found many different rectangles, bring them together for a group discussion. Make a chart on the board, and ask the students to make a similar chart on a sheet of paper. Label the chart. Draw a rectangle next to the chart to show the students what *width* and *length* mean.

Width	Length	Perimeter Equations	Total Perimeter

7. Ask the students what rectangles they found with the narrowest width. Fill in the chart with the information that the students share. Then have the students share the next widest rectangle. Continue in the same way with other rectangles.

8. Soon the students will recognize the pattern in the rectangle dimensions and will be able to identify any rectangles that have not been found. Ask the students to explain why that pattern exists, so that they understand that when a centimeter is added to each width, it must be subtracted from each length to maintain the same perimeter. Ask the students to explain why there is no length of 20, so that they can articulate the limit caused by the impossibility of having a rectangle with a width of 0. At the end of the discussion the chart will look like thus:

Width	Length	Perimeter Equations	Total Perimeter
1 + 1	19 + 19	(2 × 1) + (2 × 19)	40 centimeters
2 + 2	18 + 18	(2 × 2) + (2 × 18)	40 centimeters
3 + 3	17 + 17	(2 × 3) + (2 × 17)	40 centimeters
4 + 4	16 + 16	(2 × 4) + (2 × 16)	40 centimeters
5 + 5	15 + 15	(2 × 5) + (2 × 15)	40 centimeters
6 + 6	14 + 14	(2 × 6) + (2 × 14)	40 centimeters
7 + 7	13 + 13	(2 × 7) + (2 × 13)	40 centimeters
8 + 8	12 + 12	(2 × 8) + (2 × 12)	40 centimeters
9 + 9	11 + 11	(2 × 9) + (2 × 11)	40 centimeters
10 + 10	10 + 10	(2 × 10) + (2 × 10)	40 centimeters
		4 × 10	
11 + 11	9 + 9	(2 × 11) + (2 × 9)	40 centimeters
12 + 12	8 + 8	(2 × 12) + (2 × 8)	40 centimeters
13 + 13	7 + 7	(2 × 13) + (2 × 7)	40 centimeters
14 + 14	6 + 6	(2 × 14) + (2 × 6)	40 centimeters
15 + 15	5 + 5	(2 × 15) + (2 × 5)	40 centimeters
16 + 16	4 + 4	(2 × 16) + (2 × 4)	40 centimeters
17 + 17	3 + 3	(2 × 17) + (2 × 3)	40 centimeters
18 + 18	2 + 2	(2 × 18) + (2 × 2)	40 centimeters
19 + 19	1 + 1	(2 × 19) + (2 × 1)	40 centimeters

9. Compare the number of possible rectangles with the predictions that the students made.

◈ Perimeters with Cuisenaire Rods

Overview

In this lesson, students place a set of Cuisenaire rods together on grid paper and trace around them to create different polygons. They find the perimeter of each of these polygons and then make more polygons with the shortest and longest perimeters that they can. During a group discussion, the students come up with different ways to explain how to arrange rods to make short perimeters and long perimeters.

Materials

◈ sets of Cuisenaire rods containing 1 red, 2 light green, and 1 purple rod, 1 set per student

◈ centimeter grid paper, 1 sheet per student (see Blackline Masters)

Vocabulary: area, centimeter, linear, longest, perimeter, polygon, shortest, square centimeter

Instructions

1. Gather the students around you. Tell them that they will be doing an area and perimeter investigation.

2. Show the students the set of Cuisenaire rods that they will use: one red rod, two light green rods, and one purple rod. Tell the students that the rods are to be placed on the centimeter grid paper following two rules:

   a. The rods must touch in such a way that if you were to trace around the shape and cut it out, the pieces would stay together.

   b. The rods must be placed within the lines on the centimeter paper.

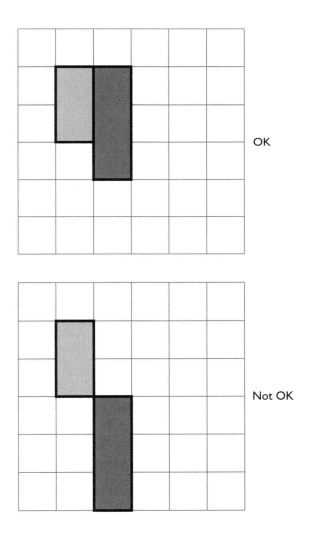

OK

Not OK

3. Place all four rods together in an arrangement that follows the rule. Show the students how to trace around the perimeter of the rod combination to create a polygon. Remove the rods from the paper.

A = 12 square centimeters
P = 16 centimeters

Ask the students to help you find the area of the polygon and to explain their thinking. Write the area near or inside the polygon, by writing A = *12 square centimeters* or the abbreviation *cm²*. Ask the students why we use the unit square centimeters rather than just centimeters. Remind the students that square units allow them to measure the space that the polygon covers.

4. Next ask the students to figure out the perimeter of the shape. Ask why it makes sense to use a centimeter as a unit of measure instead of a square centimeter. (A centimeter is a linear unit that allows students to measure how long something is, rather than a two-dimensional shape that lets you measure the area.) Write the perimeter near or inside the polygon: *P = 16 centimeters* or *P = 16 cm*.

5. Now tell the students that they are to find different arrangements for the rods, following the rules. Ask them to find arrangements with the shortest perimeter possible and the longest perimeter possible.

6. Hand out the Cuisenaire rods and the grid paper. As the students work, watch to see that they are counting the perimeter correctly. For example, some students have trouble remembering to count each exposed side of the corners. Ask students—both those who do it correctly and those who do it incorrectly—to explain their thinking. Ask students whether they think they have found the polygons with the shortest and longest possible perimeters and have them explain their reasoning.

7. When the students have created many different shapes and have covered much of their papers with polygons, gather them for a discussion. Ask them what is the same about each polygon (the area) and what is different (the perimeter).

8. Ask the students to share the polygons that they found with the shortest perimeters. List those perimeters on the board until the group agrees which is the shortest one of all. Draw grid lines on the board and draw that polygon along the lines. Have the students make sure that the identified perimeter is correct.

9. Do the same to find the polygon with the longest perimeter. Ask the students to explain how the shapes are different. Ask them how they would tell someone else to arrange the rods to get the longest perimeter and the shortest perimeter. For example, students might say, "Shapes with long perimeters are thin," or "Shapes that have short perimeters are fat." Write different students' explanations as summary statements on the board.

Design a House

Overview
Pretending to be architects, students work in groups to design a floor plan for a client who wants rooms of specific areas. They use centimeter grid paper to make a floor plan of the house and write a letter to the client informing her of the total square feet in the house, the length of the exterior walls (perimeter), and why the client should consider their particular design.

Materials
◈ centimeter grid paper, 4 sheets per small group of students (see Blackline Masters)
◈ rulers, 1 per small group of students
◈ 3-foot-long butcher paper, 1 sheet per small group of students
◈ sample house plan, 1 per student (see Blackline Masters)

Vocabulary: area, centimeter, dimension, distance, linear feet, perimeter, square centimeters, square feet

Instructions

1. Begin the lesson by explaining to the students that mathematics is a tool used in all careers, and that today they will use mathematics in a real-world situation. Tell the students that they will become architects and work in groups to create a house design for a client, Dr. Mendoza.

2. Tell the students that architects make floor plans that show a contractor how a house must be built. Pass out copies of the sample house plan to the students.

Explain to them that the house in the picture is not for Dr. Mendoza, but it shows how a floor plan matches a house. Ask the students to talk in their groups about how the floor plan compares with, or matches, the picture of the house and what things they notice on the floor plan.

3. Have the groups share what they noticed. For example, they might say that the picture is a side view of the house and the floor plan shows the layout of the house as seen from above. Or they might say that the house and the floor plan are rectangles. The students might also talk about where the living room is in the picture and on the floor plan. Point out to the students how the windows in the kitchen are shown on the floor plan. Then have them find windows in other rooms. When the students talk about the front door, have them find how that door is shown on the floor plan and then find other doors in the house. Note that folding doors are represented differently than hinged doors.

4. Now have the students consider the flow, or how people move from one part of the house to another. Have them imagine walking in the front door and figuring out how they would get to the master bedroom or how they would get from the kitchen to the bathroom. Help the students understand how the hallway helps people move from one area to another, but explain that having many hallways adds to the cost of the house. Tell the students that as they design Dr. Mendoza's house, they will need to consider how to make it convenient for people to move from one part of the house to another, but it will be important to consider cost as well.

5. Next, discuss how the area of a house is measured—in square feet. Draw a square on the board, and label each side one foot in length. Show the students that when one dimension is a foot long and the other dimension is a foot long, the area that is identified is literally the shape of a square, which is why we call it a "square foot." Show the students the abbreviation for square foot: $ft.^2$ Also show the students the symbol architects use for square feet: ⊠.

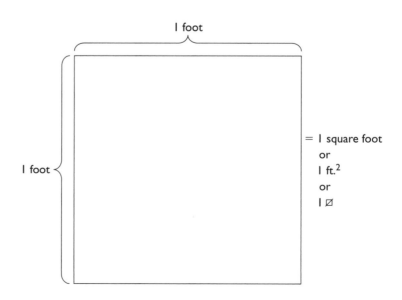

6. Last, discuss how the size of the rooms is labeled on the floor plan. Note the abbreviations for the size of the master bedroom: 13′4″ × 13′4″ means 13 feet, 4 inches by 13 feet, 4 inches. Have the children find the area of the master bedroom and then compare it with the size of their classroom to get a sense of what the area looks like. (Some classrooms have floor tiles that are about a square foot, which can help the students get a sense of the size of that area.) On the board, write the following: *12 ft. × 12 ft. = 144 ft.²* and *12′ × 12′ = 144 ft.²* Tell the students that they will label each room with its name and the total square feet in the room. If the room is not a rectangle, they must label the dimensions of each side.

7. On the board list the criteria that Dr. Mendoza has for her house:

- *It must be a single story.*
- *It can be any shape that uses whole square feet.*

   Show the students the centimeter grid paper that they will use to design their houses. Explain that each square centimeter represents an entire square foot and that they must draw along the lines, never between the lines.

- *The rooms can be any shape, but they must have the square footage that Dr. Mendoza requested.*

8. On the board, write the square foot requirements that Dr. Mendoza has for her house.

living room: 240 square feet (240 ft.² or 240 ▱)

dining room: 120 square feet: (120 ft.² or 120 ▱)

kitchen: 100 square feet (100 ft.² or 100 ▱)

bathroom: 60 square feet (60 ft.² or 60 ▱)

master bedroom: 120 square feet (120 ft.² or 120 ▱)

bedroom 2: 96 square feet (96 ft.² or 96 ▱)

bedroom 3: 84 square feet (84 ft.² or 84 ▱)

9. Tell the students that hallways can be added, but no additional rooms. Each time they add a hallway, they must label its dimensions and total square feet.

10. Explain to the students that after they draw the rooms, they will cut them out. Then they will arrange the rooms in a way that they think is best. Remind the students of the criteria they must consider: convenience, attractiveness, and cost. Tell the students that as they arrange the rooms, they must make sure that the square feet are aligned from room to room. On the board, sketch two grids that are aligned and two grids that are not aligned.

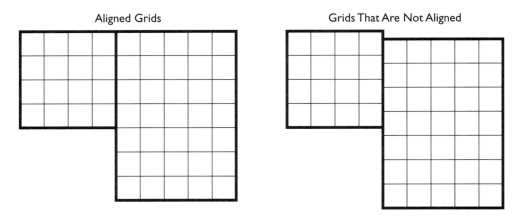

Aligned Grids   Grids That Are Not Aligned

11. Tell the students that they will tape or glue the rooms onto butcher paper. Add this information to the directions on the board:

   • *Draw the rooms and cut them out.*
   • *Arrange the rooms so the grids are aligned. Choose the arrangement you think is the best. Consider convenience, attractiveness, and cost.*
   • *Glue your arrangement onto butcher paper.*

12. Last, explain to the students that after they complete the house design, they will write a letter to Dr. Mendoza, persuading her that she should consider this design for her family. Brainstorm with the students things that might convince her. The list may include things such as how attractive the design is, the flow from one room to the other, and cost. Tell the students that the letter must include the total area in the house, how they know the area of each room is correct, how they figured it out, as well as the length of the exterior walls (the perimeter) of the house. On the board write:

   • *Write a letter to Dr. Mendoza. Include*
        the total area of the house and how you figured it out
        the total length of the exterior walls (perimeter) and how you figured it out
        why she should consider your design

13. Hand out the materials. Have the students work in groups to design their houses. As students work, clarify misunderstandings such as what dimensions are and why area is listed in square feet and dimensions in linear feet.

14. Toward the end of their first day's work, ask the groups to share their initial designs with each other and ask each other questions to help them refine their designs.

15. On the second day, have students continue working on their designs.

16. When the students complete their designs, have the groups present their floor plans to the class. After each presentation, have the others ask questions to clarify information. Then ask questions yourself, as if you are Dr. Mendoza, to understand the design and to compare the relative merits of each floor plan. (See Figures 2–13 and 2–14.)

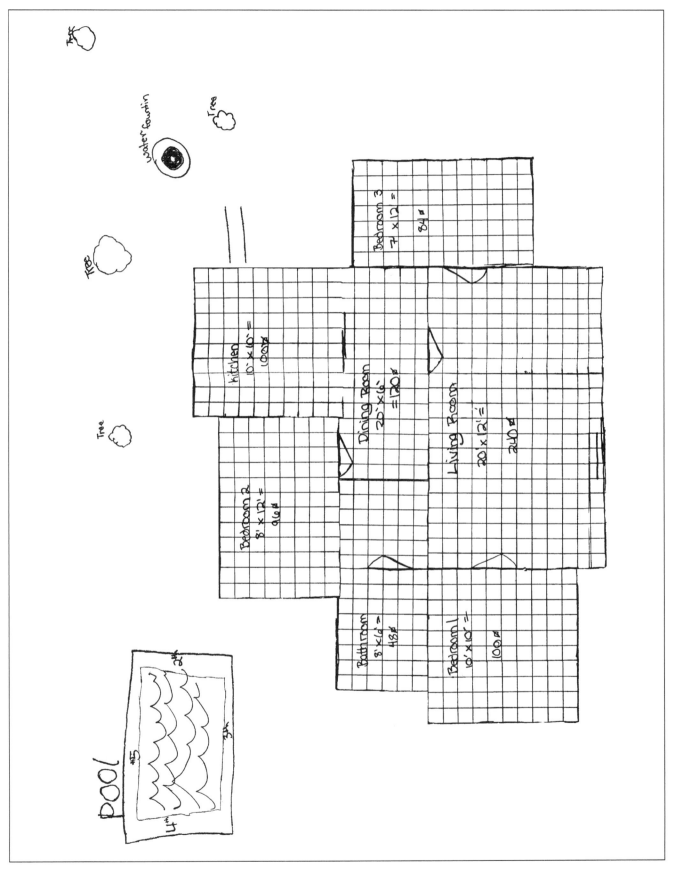

Figure 2–13 *Susanna and Joaquin eliminated hallways from their house design to decrease building costs.*

Dear, Dr. Mendoza

We are finished with your house. The area of the house is 7880. The exterior wall is 1180. This is a good house becuase its big and has a lot of rooms. and becuase it has a big living room. We did not put hall ways becuase hall ways coast money so thats a good thing. It is attractive becuase the shape and how it looks. It is Convenient becuase you can get easily to the Kitchen to the living room.

Figure 2–14 *Susanna and Joaquin explained to Dr. Mendoza why they selected that floor plan.*

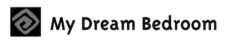

My Dream Bedroom

Overview

In this lesson, students design the bedroom of their dreams. They use a single sheet of centimeter grid paper, imagining that each square centimeter represents a square foot. The students imagine pieces of furniture that they would like to have and draw them on the grid in a reasonable size and arranged in a reasonable manner.

Materials

◈ centimeter grid paper, 1 sheet per student (see Blackline Masters)

Vocabulary: dimensions, estimate, feet, foot, length, reasonable, square foot, strategy, width

Instructions

1. Explain to the students that they will have a chance to design the bedroom of their dreams. Show them a sheet of centimeter grid paper. Explain that each square represents one square foot. Tell the students that their design must fit on one sheet of grid paper.

2. Tell the students that as they design their dream bedroom, they must not think in terms of toys or games or things they will put in their room. Instead they must think about spaces or places, or structural things such as bookshelves and furniture that they would like. List some things they may want to put inside their room, such as a bed, a bookshelf, and a computer table. You may wish to include more-inventive things such as a whirlpool, a slide, and a secret place to read.

3. With the class, find the length and width of the largest room that can fit on the grid paper. On the board list those dimensions, writing them in complete words as well as in abbreviations, which the students may choose to use:

   18 feet by 24 feet
   18 ft. × 24 ft.
   18' × 24'

4. Next have the students relate those dimensions to the dimensions of their class-room. Have them make a good estimate of that length and width to visualize the space they would have in their room.

5. Now have the students figure out the total area of that space. They should first estimate and then use pencil and paper to find the total. Students may use repeated addition, such as adding twenty-four eighteen times. Or they may multiply using the standard procedure. Or they may multiply using number relation-ships. For example, they may find 18×25 by thinking of quarters, and come to 450. Then they may subtract 18 from that amount, because it really is 18×24, and come to 432. Another strategy they might use is to make an open array.

	20	4
10	$10 \times 20 = 200$	$10 \times 4 = 40$
8	$8 \times 20 = 160$	$8 \times 4 = 32$

$$200 + 160 = 360$$
$$360 + 40 = 400$$
$$400 + 32 = 432$$

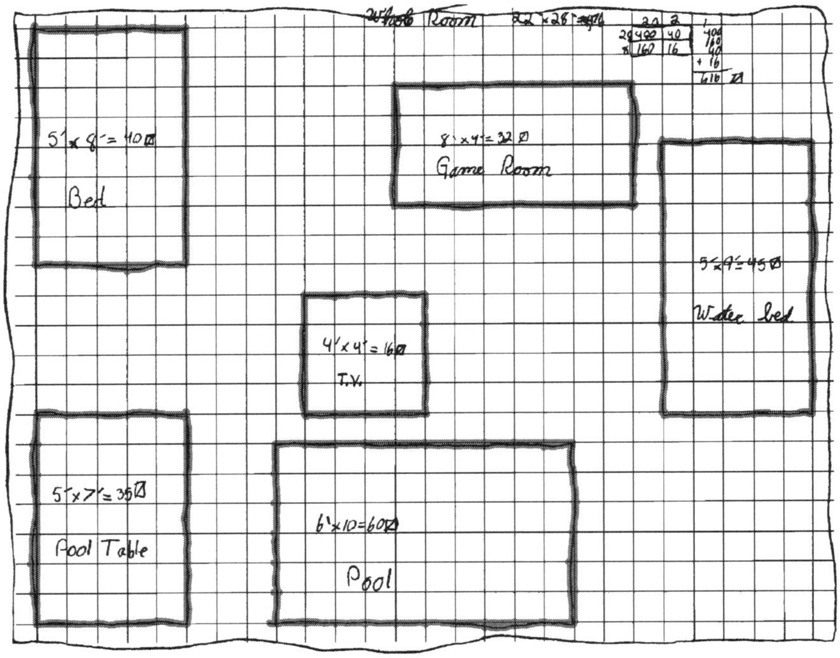

Dear Mom,

My dream bedroom's dimensions are 22'×28'=616. It has a bed. It's dimensions are 5'×8=40, a games room (it's dimensions are 8'×4'=32), a water bed (it's dimensions are 5'×9'=45), a T.V. (it's dimensions are 4'×4'=16), a pool table (it's dimensions are 5'×7'=35), a pool (it's dimensions are 6'×10'=60). If you do give me all of this I will stop bothering you, I will stop teasing my brothers. Please could I have it I would do anything. Please could I have it?

P.S. Sign ☐ Yes or ☐ No

Figure 2–15 *Jonathan included a pool in his dream bedroom design. He used the symbol for* square feet *that architects use* (⧄).

6. Explain that as they design their bedroom, they must find the dimensions, or the length of the sides, for each item they put in their bedroom. They also must record the area of each item. Remind the students that area is measured in square feet, and they may use the abbreviation ft.^{2} or the symbol that architects use, $\square$. As the students design, they will need to imagine the actual size of the pieces of furniture to determine whether the sizes are reasonable. Explain that they must also leave reasonable spaces between the pieces of furniture so they can easily walk around them.

7. Let students start their designs. As they work, encourage them to articulate how they know the items they are choosing are of a reasonable size. Watch to see what computational strategies they use and whether they use them with confidence or require support.

8. When the students finish, have several volunteers share their designs with the whole group. As students share, occasionally make a diagram of a piece of furniture on the board, including a grid within to show the area. Ask the students to share what the total area is and describe the strategy they used to find it. Some students may count by ones. Others will use addition, and still others will multiply. (See Figures 2–15 and 2–16.)

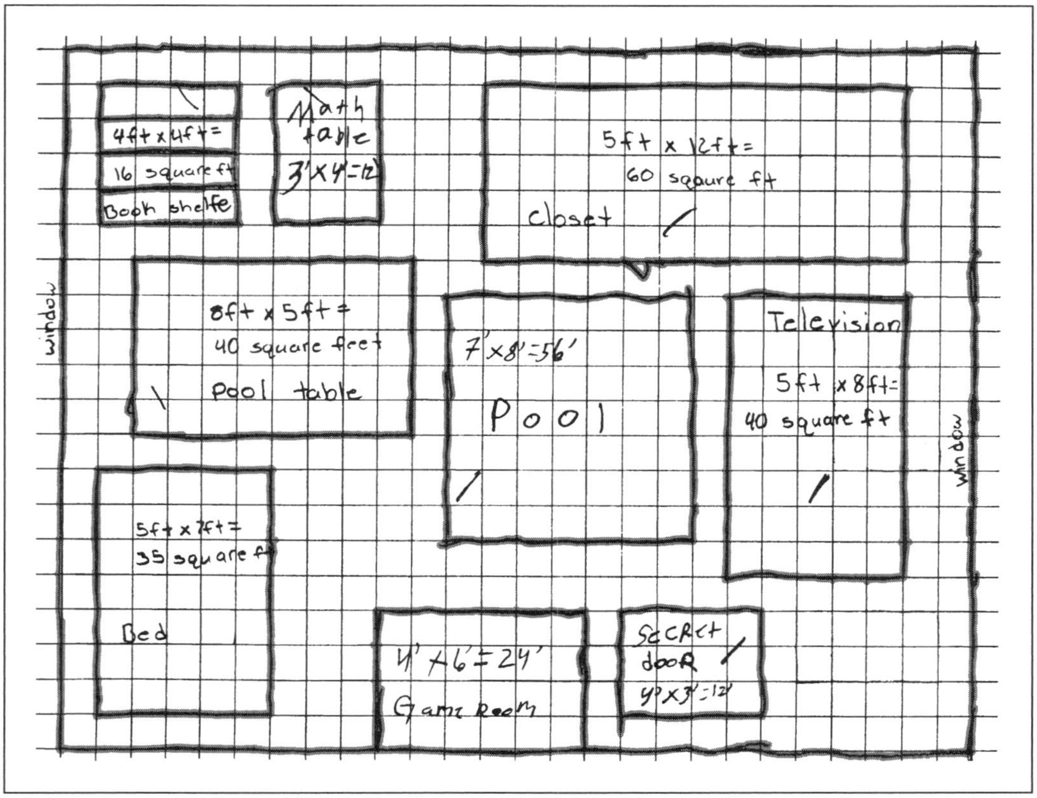

Figure 2–16 *Amanda's dream bedroom included a math table, a pool, and a secret door.*

Volume

Introduction

While length is one-dimensional and area is two-dimensional, volume describes the space of a three-dimensional object or region. Because of its additional complexity—length, width, and height—measurement of volume is more difficult for students to visualize and conceptualize.

Nonetheless, students bring many intuitive understandings about volume to school, ideas that can be capitalized upon in the classroom. At home children want to be sure that they got the same amount of soda as their sibling, and they invent ways to find out. Students have a sense of the size of a liter bottle of water, and many have used measuring cups in the kitchen. Furthermore, many students have played with blocks, putting them together to create three-dimensional figures.

The lessons in this chapter develop understandings about units of capacity, which are typically used to measure liquids. Students estimate and identify the capacity of jars and standard measurement units. They develop ways to compare and order the volumes of a variety of containers. Students create containers, explore how standard units are used to measure volume, and identify how standard units relate to one another.

Through these lessons, students also learn to organize their thinking about volume and to see the volume of rectangular prisms, such as boxes, as layers of rectangles. Students use cubic units to measure a variety of rectangular prisms and investigate problems that encourage them to discover a variety of volume relationships.

◈ Scoops of Rice and Beans

Overview

In this lesson students explore the meaning of volume. They predict, and then find, the number of scoops of rice that will fill a jar. Using that information, students then predict the number of scoops of beans that will fill the same jar. After finding this number, they explain the reason for their results and use that information to explore other jars in the same way.

Materials

◈ clear jar, about 24 ounces, such as a spaghetti sauce jar

◈ rubber band, large enough to fit around jar

◈ jars or containers, different sizes and shapes than the 24-ounce jar, 4

◈ small scoop or quarter-cup measuring cup

◈ container of rice, about twice as much as will fill the largest jar

◈ container of beans, about twice as much as will fill the largest jar

◈ container of sand, about twice as much as will fill the largest jar

◈ container of water, about twice as much as will fill the largest jar

Vocabulary: difference, prediction, range, rim, scoop, volume

Instructions

1. Ahead of time, place the rubber band around the jar to designate the half-full level. Show the students the empty 24-ounce jar. Have the students discuss what aspects of the jar can be measured. The students may mention height or weight, as well as how much it can hold.

2. Tell the students that together with you they will explore how much the jar will hold, or its volume, by filling it with the rice. Write the word *volume* on the board. Explain that when you fill the jar, you will fill it right to the top of the rim. Show the students the part of the jar that is called the rim.

3. Show the students the scoop or measuring cup that you will use. Ask the students to predict how many scoops will fill the jar. Label a section of the board *Rice* and then list the students' predictions. Circle the smallest prediction and the largest prediction. Write the word *range* on the board, have the students figure the difference between the smallest and largest predictions, and record the number.

4. Use the scoop to fill the jar halfway with rice to the rubber band level. Have the students count the scoops as you do so.

5. Invite the students to make new predictions based on the count so far. Again write the predictions on the board and find the range of these new predictions. Ask the students to compare this range with the previous range and explain why the second range is smaller. Because the students now have information about how many scoops filled the jar halfway, their predictions will be closer to the actual count.

6. Finish filling the jar with level scoops of rice while the students count. Write the total scoops on the board, for example, *about $12\frac{1}{2}$ scoops of rice.*

7. Now empty the rice into its original container. Hold up the bag of beans and tell the students that you will use the same jar and scoop and do the same thing with the beans that you did with the rice.

8. On the board, draw a line separating the information about the first experiment from this new version. Label this section *Beans*. Ask the students to predict individually how many scoops of beans will fill the jar. On their own sheet of paper, have them write their prediction and explain why they think that.

9. Have students who predicted a larger number of scoops of beans than scoops of rice explain to the class why they think there will be more scoops this time. Their explanations may refer to the different way beans pack together from rice, leaving spaces between the beans. Accept each student's reasoning. Next have students who think the number will be smaller explain their reasoning. Last ask the students who think the number will be the same explain their thinking.

10. Fill the jar with level scoops of beans, and have the students count the scoops as you do so. Many students will be surprised when the half-way count matches the previous half-way count, and when the totals are also the same.

11. Write the total scoops on the board. The fact that the number of scoops of beans is the same as the number of scoops of rice will likely confuse many students.

12. Have the students discuss why the numbers are the same. Some students will understand that the jar holds the same number of scoops, regardless of what material the scoop holds. They may say, "A scoop is a scoop is a scoop." This idea may make sense to the other students, but they still need to construct the concept for themselves by actually doing the experiment. Ask the students what they think would happen if you used the scoop to fill the jar with water or sand or any other material.

13. Place the scoop, the collection of empty jars and the containers, and the containers of rice, beans, sand, and water in a station or learning center where the students can investigate volume for themselves. Over the next several days, have the students choose a new jar and do the same experiment as the one you modeled, predicting the number of scoops of different materials that will fill the chosen jar.

14. After all the students have had an opportunity to do the same experiment with the jars in the learning center, have another class discussion. Hold up a new jar and the scoop. Ask the students to consider an experiment with sand and beans: Will the jar hold more scoops of sand than beans, fewer scoops of sand than beans, or the same number of scoops of sand and beans? Have the students share what they think now and why. Then test their predictions by filling the jar with each material.

◈ Put in Order—Volume

Overview

In this lesson, groups of students discuss the meaning of volume. Then they place containers on a table in order from what they believe is least volume to greatest volume. The students verify their predictions by pouring rice from container to container. Then they verify once again by using a scoop to measure the amount of rice that each container holds.

Materials

- ◈ sets of 7 containers of various shapes and sizes that are not easy to compare visually, for example, a paper cup; a half-pint milk carton; a square storage container; a cottage cheese container; a long, thin toothpaste box; a narrow, and tall jar; and a wider and shorter jar, 1 set per small group of students
- ◈ permanent marker
- ◈ *Put in Order—Volume* recording sheets, 1 per student (see Blackline Masters)
- ◈ tubs of rice with more than enough rice to fill the two largest containers, 1 per small group of students
- ◈ sets of 2 cards, 1 labeled "Least Volume," the other labeled "Greatest Volume," 1 set per small group of students
- ◈ nonstandard scoops or quarter-cup measuring cups, 1 per small group of students

Vocabulary: greatest, height, least, length, prediction, scoop, volume, width

Instructions

1. Before class, use a permanent marker to label the containers in each set from A to G in random order (that is, do not label them according to capacity).

2. Show the class the sets of containers. Explain to them that they are going to explore the volume of the containers. Write *volume* on your vocabulary word chart. Have the students share their definitions for *volume*, and record them on the chart. They may say "how much something holds" or "how much you can put inside something."

3. Hand out a set of cards and a set of containers to each group. Give each student a recording sheet. Have the students tape the card labeled "Least Volume" on one end of their work space and "Greatest Volume" at the other end. Explain that they will visually predict how the containers' volumes compare and then place the containers on their work space in order from least volume to greatest volume. As the students work, listen to their discussions. Encourage the students to explain why the order makes sense to them. Have them be specific about the attributes of the

containers that they think are important, such as height, width, or length. Ask the students to write their predictions by writing the letter sequence on their recording sheets in the first section.

4. Next show the students the rice that they will use to check the order of their containers. Give each group a container of rice but do not give them any measuring device at this time. This will encourage the students to pour rice into one container until it is full and then pour the rice into another container to compare their volumes. Continually comparing in this way focuses the students on transitivity, the idea that if A is more than B, and B is more than C, then A is more than C. Observe the students to see if transitivity is obvious to them. Have the students write the order that they discovered on their recording sheets in the second section and then compare the results with their predictions. Discuss with the students how they know their order is correct.

5. Now show the students the scoop that they will use for the next step. Hand out the scoops and tell them that they will use the scoop as a measuring tool to identify the actual volume of each container. In the third section of the recording sheet, have the students write the order of the containers and the measurements that they actually discover. Then have them compare these results with their answers when they poured the rice from container to container. As the students work, observe to see whether they understand that the unit must be the same each time—do they know that the rice should always be scooped evenly with the top of the scoops? Also observe how they deal with parts of scoops.

6. When the groups finish, begin a class discussion about what they discovered. Have the groups share which containers' volumes were easy to predict and which were more difficult, and encourage the students to explain what caused this. For example, a student may say that since a container was short, he thought its volume would be less than a taller container, but the shorter container was also wider, and that made the difference.

Popcorn Containers

Overview

In this lesson, the students consider information in Tomie dePaola's *Popcorn Book*: the fact that 293 kernels of ancient popped popcorn were found in a bat cave. Students estimate the volume of that amount of popcorn and then make containers that they think will have that volume. After sorting the containers according to their shapes, students test their containers by pouring 293 kernels of popcorn into each one. They then sort the containers again according to whether they were much too large, much too small, or about the right size.

Materials

- *The Popcorn Book,* by Tomie dePaola (1984)
- popcorn kernels, 1 cup
- plastic food storage bag
- 5-ounce paper cups, 1 per student
- rulers, 1 per pair of students
- salt, $\frac{1}{2}$ teaspoon

Vocabulary: cone, cube, cylinder, dimensions, estimate, rectangular prism, sample, volume

Instructions

1. Prior to the lesson, pop the popcorn and count out 293 pieces. Put them in a plastic food storage bag, and hide them from the students until the final part of this lesson. Divide the remaining popcorn in half. Use one half to fill the small paper cups with 10 pieces each. Salt the other half for students to eat after the lesson.

2. Read *The Popcorn Book* to the students. When you get to the page that talks about the pieces of popcorn found in the New Mexico rock shelter known as Bat Cave, hold up a piece of popped popcorn.

3. Tell the students that 293 popped, loose kernels like the one you are holding were found in that cave, and that they are believed to be the oldest kernels ever found.

4. Explain to the students that they will make a container out of blank $8\frac{1}{2}$-by-11-inch paper that they think will *just* hold 293 pieces of popped popcorn with the popcorn coming up even with the top of the container and not extending above the sides. Tell the students that you will give them each ten pieces of popped popcorn to help them estimate the size of the container. Explain that they need to look closely at their pile of popcorn and use what they see or know about its volume to make a container of the right dimensions.

5. Tell the students that they can use tape or staples to put their container together and they can make folds or cut the sheets of paper in any way. Remind them that they should try to make a container with a top that holds *just* 293 pieces of popcorn. Remind the students that the popcorn is to be even with the top and not extend above the sides.

6. Write on the board:
   a. *Make a container with a top that is just the right size to hold 293 pieces of popcorn. Use your sample of popcorn to help you estimate.*
   b. *Write an explanation of why you think your container holds 293 pieces of popcorn. Be sure to use what you know about the pieces of popcorn in your small cup to explain your reasoning.*

7. Pass out the small cups of popcorn, paper, and scissors. Have rulers, tape, and staplers available for the students who choose to use them.

8. As the students work, make sure that they use their sample of popcorn to help them determine the dimensions of the container that they want to make. Continue asking questions such as, "How does your sample of popcorn help you think about the size of container that you need?" and "Why do you think that your container will hold the right amount of popcorn?"

9. As the students write, read what they have so far. Ask them questions to clarify their writing. Explain that the reader will need to understand how they used the popcorn sample to figure out the size or dimensions of the container.

10. When they have finished the task, gather the students for a discussion. Place the containers where everyone can see them. Have students sort the containers according to their shapes. As they sort the containers, have the students describe the containers' characteristics. Help the students use appropriate mathematical language. The containers may be cone shaped, cylinders, cubes, or rectangular prisms.

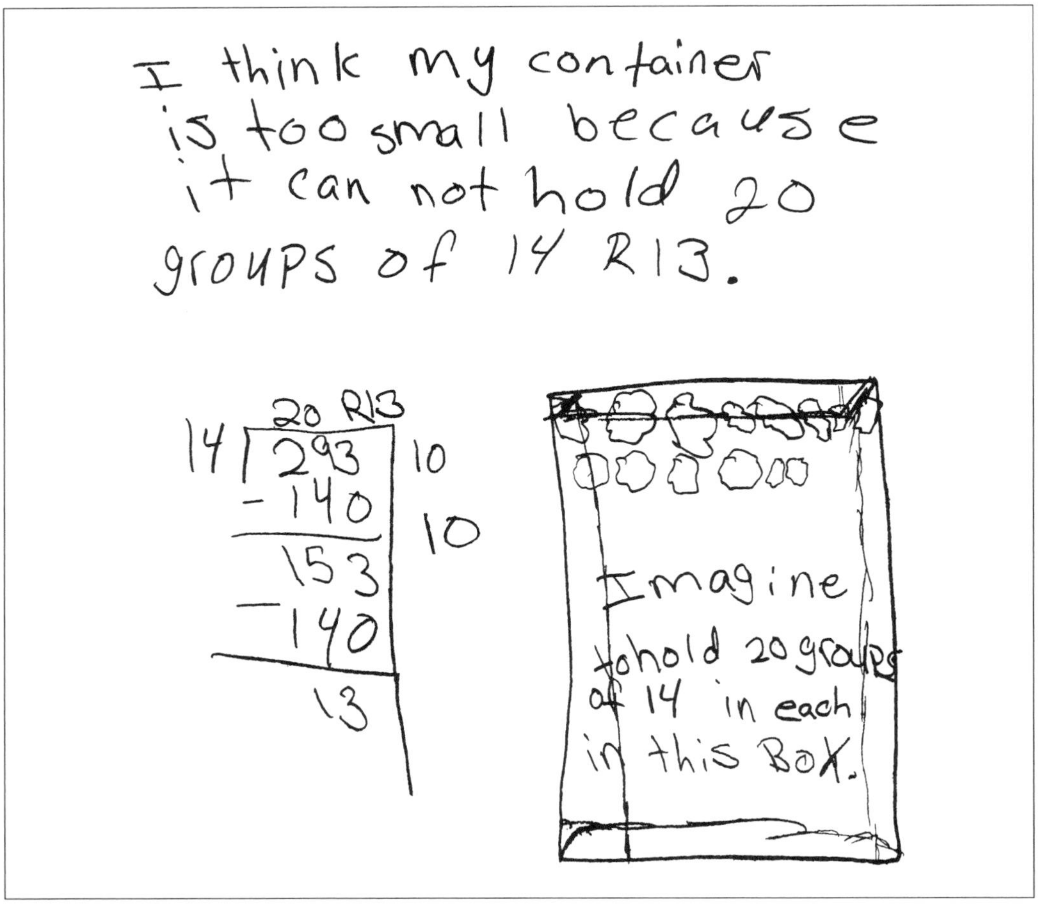

Figure 3–1 *Kyle estimated that his container wouldn't hold 293 kernels of popcorn. He divided 293 by his sample size of 14, and found that he would need room for twenty groups of his sample size.*

11. Ask several students to read how they determined the size of a container that would hold 293 pieces of popcorn. Have the students explain what they counted or measured and how they used that information to determine the dimensions of their containers. Invite the other students to respond to the reader. (See Figures 3–1 and 3–2.)

12. Bring out the bag of 293 pieces of popcorn. Have the students one at a time pour the popcorn into their container to find out whether it is much too large, much too small, close to the right volume, or just right. Then have them sort their containers accordingly.

13. Have the students who made the "just right" and "close" containers explain their strategies for determining the dimensions of the containers.

14. Last, invite the children to eat the reserved popcorn.

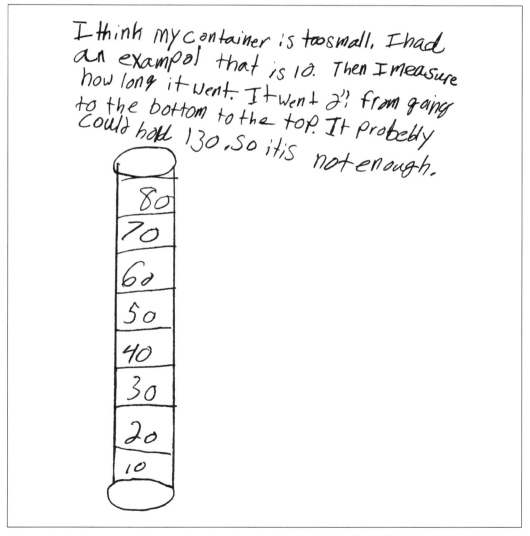

I think my container is too small. I had an exampol that is 10. Then I measure how long it went. It went 2" from going to the bottom to the top. It probebly could hold 130. So it is not enough.

Figure 3–2 *Juanita explained why she thought the container she made was too small.*

 **Jelly Bean Jar**

Overview

This lesson invites students to investigate whether a statement in Rod Clement's *Counting on Frank* is true: Are there 745 jelly beans in the average candy jar? The students estimate the number of jelly beans that will fill a jar and then use the number of jelly beans in one scoop and the number of scoops in a jar to make a closer estimate. Last, the class counts the jelly beans and finds out how far off the estimates were.

Materials

- ❖ *Counting on Frank*, by Rod Clement (1991)
- ❖ collection of clear empty jars, 4 or 5
- ❖ container of jelly beans, enough to fill the largest jar
- ❖ paper towels, 1 per small group of students
- ❖ measuring cups, measuring spoons, and scoops in a variety of sizes, at least 1 per small group of students.

Vocabulary: average, scoop, volume

Instructions

1. Read *Counting on Frank* to the students. If you are reading the book to the students for the first time, read the entire book and enjoy the quirky boy and the investigations that he does with his dog, Frank.

2. Then return to the last page, where the boy, his dad, and Frank are flying to Hawaii, and the boy has a large jar of jelly beans on his lap. Reread the sentences "There are seven hundred and forty-five jellybeans in the average candy jar. I thought everybody knew that!"

3. Tell the students that it's important to think for themselves and evaluate whether statements, even strongly worded statements such as that one, are true. Invite the students to share their reactions. Some students will focus on the word *average*. Write it on the board and ask the students to explain what it means. Some may know about the concept of averaging numbers. Let them know that there are also more general definitions for *average*. On the board, write synonyms for *average* such as *usual, normal, typical*, and any others students might mention.

4. Discuss what an average jar of jelly beans would look like. Show the students the collection of jars. Then have them look closely at the picture of the huge jar on the boy's lap. It is not a typical size for a jar of jelly beans from the store. Have the students discuss, and come to consensus about, which jar from your collection they would expect to find at a store selling jelly beans.

5. Now invite the students to consider whether that jar's volume is really 745 jelly beans. Write *volume* on the board, and remind the students that it means how much the jar can hold. Fill the "typical" jar with jelly beans.

6. Provide each group with a paper towel and place ten to twenty jelly beans on the towel for the students to examine. Ask students to predict how many jelly beans are in the jar you filled. Hold the jar up so each group can see it as they discuss their predictions. Individually, have students write their prediction along with their reasoning on a sheet of paper. Ask several students to share their thinking with the class.

7. Next show the students your collection of scoops, small measuring cups, and spoons and your container of jelly beans. Tell the students that in groups they will figure out a plan for arriving at a good estimate of the number of jelly beans that would fill the jar without having to count all the jelly beans. Tell the students that their group plan must specifically identify what they will do first, second, third, and so on. For example, a group might decide to use a measuring cup, count the jelly beans that fill it, and then find out how many of that measuring cup would fill the entire container. Then they would multiply that number by the number of beans in one cup. Another group might count the jelly beans in a scoop, find the number of scoops in half the jar, multiply the beans in one scoop by the number of scoops, and then double that number.

8. Invite the groups to select a measurement tool and begin writing. As the students work, have them share their plans with you, both orally and in writing. Push for specificity and clarity, so that a reader can understand exactly what they will do.

9. When the groups finish writing their plans, have each group share its plan with the class. Invite different groups to respond with questions. As the students share, have groups consider how their plans are similar and how they are different, and whether the different plans will produce the same answer.

10. Now place the measurement tools and the jar of jelly beans at a table. Over the next day, have the groups take turns carrying out their plans. As the students complete each step, have them write their results. Remind the students not to count each jelly bean.

11. When all the groups have made a good estimate of the number of jelly beans that would fill the jar, begin a class discussion. Have the groups share their information and react to other groups' results. Discuss whether the information was about the same or different for groups that used different-size measuring tools. Also discuss whether some tools were easier to use than others. (See Figures 3–3 and 3–4.)

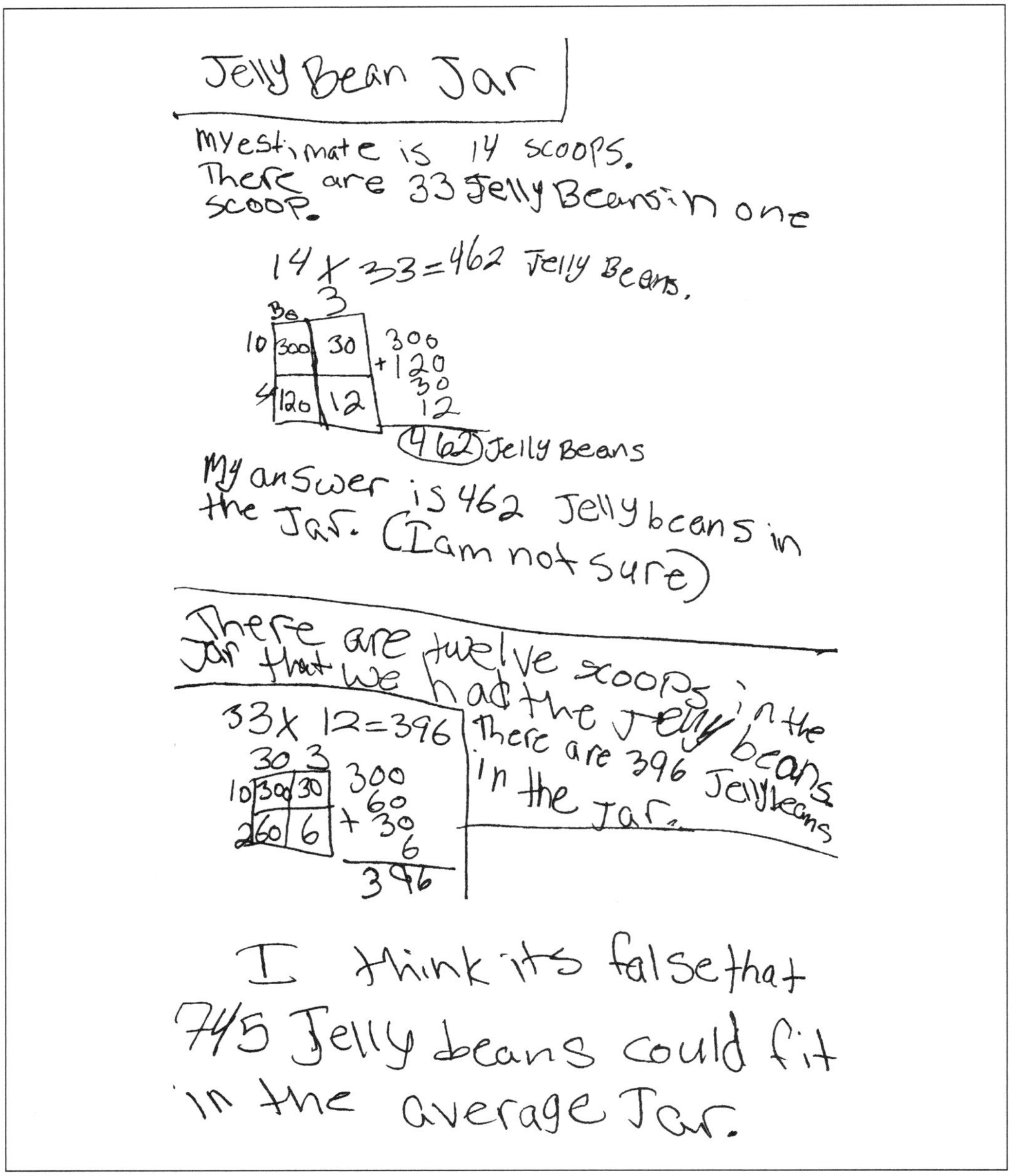

Figure 3-3 *Carrie counted 33 jelly beans in one scoop. She estimated there might be 462 jelly beans in the jar. When her group actually counted the number of scoops of jelly beans, she decided that only 396 jelly beans could fit in the average jar.*

12. End the lesson by asking several students to actually count the jelly beans, and then have groups compare the count with their estimates. As a class, come to consensus: Is Frank right? Are there 745 jelly beans in the average jelly bean jar?

Extension

◈ Repeat the investigation with other containers. Each time, have the groups write plans for estimating the number of beans in the jar and then carry out their plans. Discuss the group's results and then count the beans in the jar. The students should use what they have learned about the volume of previous containers to predict the volume of the new container.

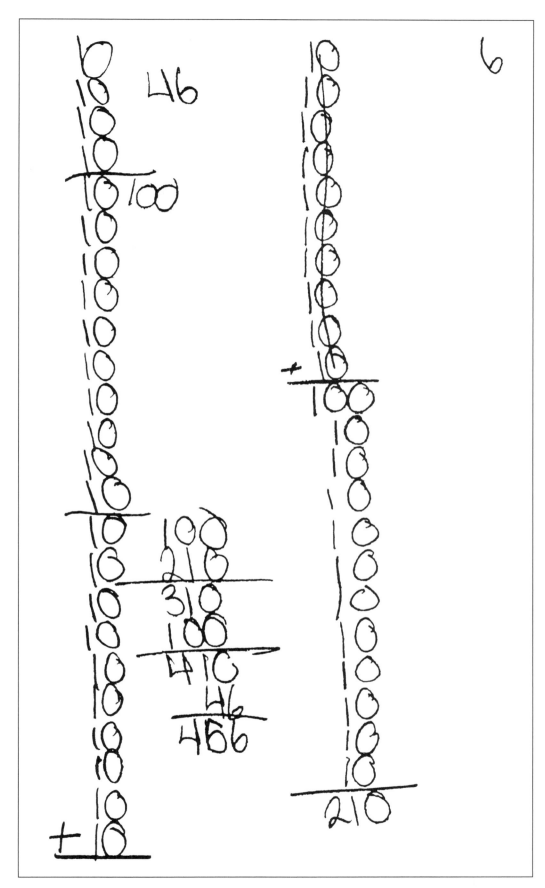

Figure 3–4 *Trenton counted by tens to figure out how many jelly beans the jar could hold.*

 **How Do They Relate?**

Overview

This small-group lesson introduces students to the customary units (ounce, cup, pint, quart, gallon) used in the United States to measure the volume of liquids. Students examine empty grocery store containers that hold standard volumes, estimate their capacities in relation to each other, and test their predictions.

Materials

◈ empty containers, 1 each that holds a cup (e.g., an 8-ounce paper cup), a half-pint (e.g., a school milk container), a pint (e.g., a whipping cream container), a quart, a half-gallon (e.g., a milk carton), and a gallon (e.g., a plastic milk jug)

◈ permanent marker

◈ 3-by-5-inch index cards, 6

◈ large pitchers, 2

◈ funnel

◈ *How Do They Relate?* recording sheets, 1 per student (see Blackline Masters)

◈ Chart paper, 1 sheet

Vocabulary: cup, customary unit, double, gallon, half-gallon, half-pint, pint, powers of two, quart, unit, volume

Instructions

1. Before class, prepare the containers. On each container, draw a "full" line on the outside with a permanent marker. You can use a 1-cup measuring cup and water to find where this mark belongs. The half-pint container holds 1 cup, the pint holds 2 cups, the quart holds 4 cups, the half-gallon holds 8 cups, and the gallon holds 16 cups. Also, fill one large pitcher with water and leave one empty. Arrange these materials on a table where you can work with a small group of students.

2. Gather a small group of students around the table. Tell them that they will investigate the volume of containers, or how much containers can hold. Write the title *Volume—Customary Units* on a sheet of chart paper. Remind the students that in the United States we encounter two different systems of measuring: customary units, which are used only in the United States, and metric units, which are used

in the rest of the world. Tell the students that today they will be exploring customary units of measurement.

3. Place the containers randomly in a row in the center of the group. One at a time, examine the containers with the students. Discuss how the container shapes are the same and how they are different. For each container, name the customary unit and, if there is a label, find the unit name. Then write the unit on an index card and place the card in front of the container. Ask the students to think about their refrigerator at home, or times they went grocery shopping, and tell what food items they think come in those units. As students share, encourage them to use the name of the unit.

4. Ask the students to agree on how to place the containers in consecutive order, from the smallest to the largest capacity. Encourage them to use the names of the units as they work. Have the students explain why the order they chose makes sense. Have the students order the index cards to match the containers. (**Note:** The cup and the half-pint hold the same amount.)

5. Tell the students that they will take turns to find out how the containers actually relate to each other. Provide each student with a *How Do They Relate?* recording sheet. Hold up the half-pint container and the cup container. Ask a student to find out how their volumes compare. The student will likely fill one container with water and pour it into the other container, showing that the two containers have the same volume. (If necessary, use the funnel to facilitate pouring.) Have the students fill in the number 1 in the first space on the recording sheet.

6. Next have the students predict, and then use water to verify, how the other containers compare. Each time have them record their information on their recording sheet:

Comparing Volume Units, Small to Large

__1__ cup = 1 half-pint

__2__ half-pints = 1 pint

__2__ pints = 1 quart

__2__ quarts = 1 half-gallon

__2__ half-gallons = 1 gallon

7. Now hold up the plastic gallon milk jug. Tell the students that you will have them use what they know so far to figure out how the other units of volume relate to a gallon. Have the students refer to their recording sheet, using its information to figure out logically the relationship between the smaller units and the gallon. For example, a student might say that she knows that 4 quarts equal 1 gallon because 2 quarts make a half-gallon and 2 half-gallons make a whole gallon and two times two is four. When the students have made their predictions, have a group discussion about their answers, and then have them pour water in the containers to verify their answers:

Comparing Volume Units to a Gallon

__2__ half-gallons = 1 gallon

__4__ quarts = 1 gallon

__8__ pints = 1 gallon

__16__ cups = 1 gallon

8. Tell the students that they will make a paper model to illustrate how units of volume relate to a gallon. Provide each student with a blank sheet of $8\frac{1}{2}$-by-11-inch paper. Explain that the whole paper represents the whole gallon. On the chart paper labeled *Volume—Customary Units*, tape the whole paper and write *gallon* and *1* beneath. Now fold another paper in half so the short edges meet, and have the students do the same with their papers. (**Note:** Some teachers call this the "hamburger fold" to distinguish it from the narrow "hot dog fold.") Tell the students to refer to their charts, to see that 2 half-gallons equal 1 whole gallon. Unfold the sheet of paper, tape it to the chart, label it with the unit name, and show the students how multiplication and powers of two describe how half-gallons relate to a whole gallon.

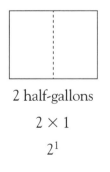

2 half-gallons

2×1

2^1

Pause to let the students see how the paper model represents this idea, and then hold up the half-gallon container next to the gallon container so the students can make a visual comparison of the containers.

9. Continue folding sheets of paper as in the following diagram, each time having students fold their paper in the same manner and allowing them time to understand how the units relate. When you finish, have them describe how the numbers increase. Students will likely say that the units double each time. Tell the students that this pattern can also be described using multiplication and powers of two.

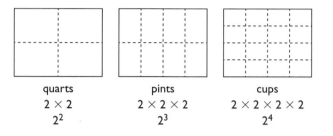

quarts	pints	cups
2×2	$2 \times 2 \times 2$	$2 \times 2 \times 2 \times 2$
2^2	2^3	2^4

10. Now tell the students that they will work in pairs to figure out other ways the containers relate to each other. Have them refer to the questions in the bottom section of their recording sheet:

How many cups equal 1 quart?

How many pints equal 1 gallon?

How many cups equal 1 half-gallon?

How many pints equal 1 half-gallon?

How many half-pints equal 1 gallon?

Explain that they will first make predictions by using the information on their recording sheet and, if necessary, the folded paper poster. (**Note:** Students can see the answers more easily on the poster. Using only the information on their recording sheet is more difficult, since it requires students to use transitive reasoning: "If a cup is the same as a half-pint, there are two cups in a pint. And if there are two pints in a quart, then there are four cups in a quart.")

11. Ask the students to write their predictions and reasoning on the other side of their recording sheet, explaining their thinking using words, numbers, and pictures or diagrams. Then have a group discussion to come to consensus about the answers.

12. Last, invite the students to use the containers and the water to verify any predictions upon which the students disagree.

 **Frank's Dog Food**

Overview

In this lesson, students investigate the truth of a statement in Rod Clement's *Counting on Frank*. They figure out whether 47 cans of dog food actually *do* fill a shopping bag and then how many bags it would take to hold 110 cans of dog food.

Materials

- ❧ *Counting on Frank,* by Rod Clement (1991)
- ❧ plastic grocery bags, 1 per small group of students
- ❧ 15-ounce cans of dog food (or, if you prefer, other cans of the same size), 6 per small group

Vocabulary: addition, array, dimensions, division, height, layers, length, multiplication, random, subtraction, volume, width

Instructions

1. Begin by reading *Counting on Frank* to the students. Enjoy the boy's intriguing questions and encourage the students to respond to them.

2. Review the page where the boy shops for dog food with his mother. Read the statement, "It takes forty-seven cans of dog food to fill one shopping bag, but only one Frank to knock over one hundred and ten!" Ask the students to tell what type of measurement that statement addresses. Write the word *volume* on the board. Ask the students to explain to each other what volume means. They will likely say that volume refers to how much something can hold or how much space is inside something.

3. Tell the students that they will work in small groups to investigate whether the author's statement is true about how many cans of food will fill one shopping bag and also determine how many shopping bags it would take to hold 110 cans of dog food. On the board write:

   - *Is it true that it takes 47 cans of dog food to fill one shopping bag? If not, how many cans does it take to fill one shopping bag?*
   - *How many shopping bags would it take to hold 110 cans of Frank's dog food?*
   - *Explain in writing how you solved these questions. Use words, numbers, and pictures or diagrams to show your reasoning.*

4. Ask the students to discuss what they know that will help them solve the problem and what they need to know. Have the students share their answers to these

questions. The students may suggest they need to know the size of a typical plastic grocery bag and discuss their experiences with putting cans into grocery bags. They may also discuss how large cans of dog food are, or they may talk about the operations or calculations they think they will need to do.

5. To solve the problem, the students will need to know how big the cans of dog food are. Show the students the cans that you have, and if they are not cans of dog food, explain that the cans in the picture appear to be about this size. Tell the students that each group will have only six cans to work with and they will have to use them in some way to figure out how many cans would fit in the entire bag. The students will also need to know the size of a shopping bag. Show them the plastic grocery bags that they will use to solve the problem.

6. Hand out the materials. As the students work, observe the strategies that they employ. Since they do not have enough cans to actually fill a bag, they will need to use what they know to figure out what they don't know. Some students may look at the volume of the six cans and then estimate how many times that amount would randomly fit in the bag. Some students may form the bag into a rectangular shape and use the cans to outline the dimensions of a bottom layer, then estimate how many layers can fit into the bag. Watch to see how the students record this multidimensional idea. They may easily draw an array but have difficulty showing the layers.

7. Once the students figure out how many cans fit in a bag, they need to use that information to figure out how many bags the boy would need to hold all 110 cans of dog food. Observe whether the students recognize this as a division problem, use repeated subtraction to solve it, or use some other strategy.

8. When the students finish, have them present their solutions to the class. During the discussion, highlight how they solved the problem, as well as how they represented their thinking. Different groups may identify different numbers of cans that can fill the bag. For example, one group may say that a 2-by-3 array would fit in the bottom, and with three layers there would be eighteen cans in a bag. Another group may say that twelve cans fit in the bottom layer, and with three layers there would be thirty-six cans in a bag. For each example, sketch a three-dimensional figure on the board and label its dimensions of length, width, and height: *2 cans long × 3 cans wide × 3 cans high = 18 cans* or *2 × 3 × 3 = 18*. After all the groups have shared, have them see how the different ways are related. The students may identify a method for finding the total volume of any rectangular prism: length times width times height.

Some groups may present a random method for filling the bag, with the cans lying in different directions. They may use repeated addition or multiplication by visualizing a single group of cans and estimating how many times that group would fit into the bag.

9. To get a closer estimate of the total number of cans that would fill the bag, put the cans from all the groups in a bag. Fill the bag in two ways: (1) randomly, finding the total number of groups, and (2) placing an orderly array on the bottom of the bag and stacking layers of that array one on top of another. Decide which method holds more cans.

10. Finally, have the groups share how many bags they would need to hold 110 cans of dog food. Again, the students will identify different solutions, depending on how many cans they said would fit in a bag. And, again, they may use different operations to solve the problem. Some students will use repeated subtraction or division. Still other students may repeatedly add, or multiply, the number of cans that fit in a single bag until they come close to 110.

11. Discuss how the students dealt with any remainders. Some may put the remaining cans in an additional bag. Some may decide to carry the remaining cans in some other way. Other groups may disregard the remainder or simply call it a remainder and not deal with it at all. Bring these students back to the context, and have them think of what they would do in this real-world situation. (See Figures 3–5, 3–6, and 3–7.)

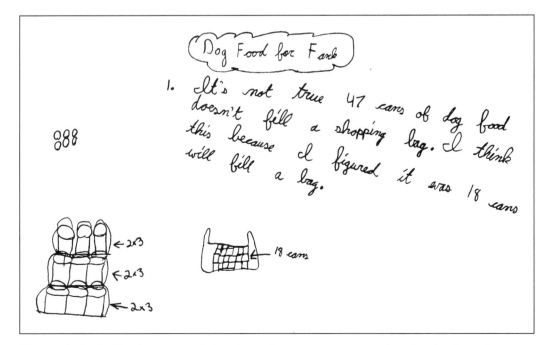

Figure 3–5 *At first Jorge struggled to draw the can arrangement, but then he drew them in layers.*

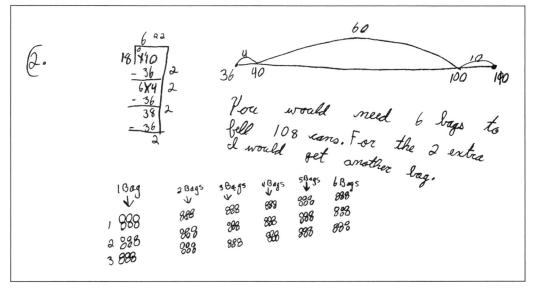

Figure 3–6 *Jorge recognized the question about 110 cans as a division problem. He investigated how many 36s are in 110 by using partial quotients. Jorge wasn't confident with the procedure for subtracting with regrouping, so he checked with the open number line.*

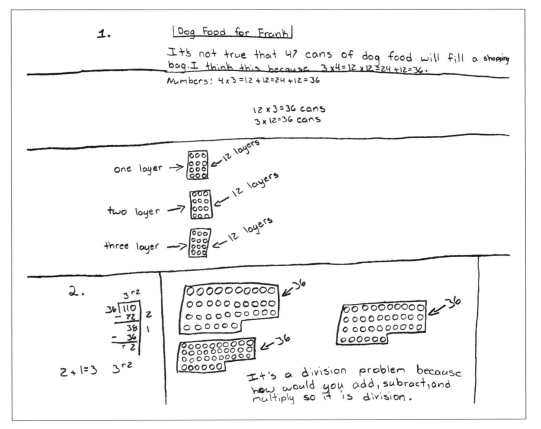

Figure 3–7 *Ramon disagreed that 47 cans of dog food would fill a shopping bag. His paper showed confusion about the term layers. While he recognized the second problem as a division problem, Ramon lost sight of the bag context and said the answer was 3 r2.*

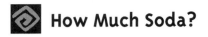 **How Much Soda?**

Overview

This lesson invites students to figure out the volume of soda that they drink in a year. Students make estimates, using standard units of measure such as gallons or cups, as well as a large, nonstandard volume unit that they can easily visualize, a bathtub. The students use the "Volume—Customary Units" information about unit relationships to help them convert from ounces or cups to gallons. Then the students figure out what that number of gallons would look like if it were poured into bathtubs. Last the students compare their result with national data about a typical American.

Materials

◈ "Volume—Customary Units" chart from *How Do They Relate?* (if students have done that lesson), page 108

◈ gallon container

◈ can of soda

◈ paper cup, 8 ounces or a similar volume

Vocabulary: convert, days, division, estimate, fluid ounces, gallon, half-pint, multiplication, operation, ounces, remainder, visualize, volume, weeks, year

Instructions

1. Prior to the lesson, hang up the volume chart from *How Do They Relate?* as a reference, if the students have done that activity. If the chart is not available, list the following facts on the board:

   4 cups = 1 quart
   4 quarts = 1 gallon

   Begin a discussion by inviting the students to think about the volume of soda that they drink. Have the students try to estimate how much soda they drink in a year. (If a student doesn't drink soda, have him think about a friend or family member who does drink soda.) Show the students the gallon container. Ask the students to think about themselves: Do they think they drink that amount of soda in a year? Do they drink enough soda to fill an entire bathtub? Less than a bathtub? More than a bathtub?

2. Now turn the discussion to the volume of one drink of soda. Show the students a can of soda and a paper cup. Ask the students to think about whether they usually drink soda in a cup or in a can. Tell the students how many ounces of soda the cup holds. Have the students read the information on the can to find its volume in fluid ounces. The idea of fluid ounces may be new to the students. They may also

be confused as they remember measuring weight with ounces. Tell the students that it's true that we measure weight in ounces. Then explain that *fluid* ounces are used mostly to measure the volume of liquids, and that we often simply call them ounces. On the board write this information:

1 cup = 8 fluid ounces or ounces (fl. oz. or oz.)

1 can = 12 fluid ounces (fl. oz. or oz.)

3. Discuss how the volume of a can relates to the cup. (A can equals $1\frac{1}{2}$ cups.) Ask the students to label a sheet of paper with the name of the investigation—*How Much Soda Do I Drink?* Tell them they will figure out how much soda they drink on a typical day, or if they prefer, how much soda they drink in a week. You may need to help the students understand what *typical* means: that some days or weeks they may drink more soda, but they need to estimate an ordinary, or usual, amount.

4. Next ask the students what other information they need to know in order to make a good estimate of how much soda they drink in a year. Depending on how they approached the first question, they will say "how many days in a week," "how many weeks in a year," and/or "how many days in a year." Elicit that information from the students and list it on the board:

1 week = 7 days

1 year = 52 weeks

1 year = 365 days

5. Model one way to find out how much soda a person drinks in a year by working with the students to figure how much soda you drink in a year, or how much a soda drinker you know drinks in a year. For example, if you drink about one cup a week, have the students remember how many weeks are in a year, and they'll know that makes 52 cups in a year. Explain that it's hard to visualize 52 cups, but it's easier to imagine that same quantity in gallons, so help them find out how many gallons a year that would be. They might refer to the "Volume—Customary Units" chart, and see that there are 16 cups in a gallon. The student might repeatedly add sixteens: 16 cups, 32 cups, 48 cups, which is 3 gallons with 4 cups left over. The students might recognize the leftover 4 cups as $\frac{1}{4}$ gallon, which would give you a year's total of $3\frac{1}{4}$ gallons of soda. However, if you begin by saying that you drink about a can of soda a week, you'll likely convert the cans into cups, perhaps by saying that each can is equal to $1\frac{1}{2}$ cups of soda, and continuing to figure from there.

6. Ask the students to figure out how much soda they drink in a year and then compare their information with another student's to see if their answers make sense and to check their work. Encourage the students to use the information on the "Volume—Customary Units" chart and the facts on the board.

7. As the students work, watch to see whether they correctly use the relationships between the units. Also observe whether they use the operation of multiplication or whether they use addition, a correct but less efficient operation. Encourage the students to use computation strategies that make sense to them. Some students may use open arrays to solve the problem, others may use strategies such as splitting numbers, and others may use the traditional procedure. If the multiplication process is out of reach of some students, you may wish to offer them a calculator so they can participate in this investigation.

   Observe whether students spontaneously convert their answers into larger units, as well as how they check to see whether their answers are reasonable. Some students may compare their daily or weekly information to see whether their final answers have a similar relationship. Other students may simply check to see whether their answers are similar.

8. When most of the students are finished, invite several students to share how they solved the problem and what they discovered. Remind the students that it is very difficult to visualize, or make sense of, a large number of ounces or cups. If any students reported their final answer in cups or ounces, have the class convert the answer into gallons.

9. The students will likely come up with a number between 25 and 100 gallons. Tell the students that in 1998, the Beverage Marketing Corporation reported that Americans consumed 56 gallons of soft drink per person per year. Ask the students to compare their information with that piece of data.

10. Last, tell the students that it is even hard to visualize that large number of gallons. Explain to the students that the volume of a typical bathtub is about 25 gallons. Ask the students to figure about how many bathtubs of soda they drink in a year. Again, since this is an estimate, have them report their information in whole bathtubs if their answer is close to a multiple of twenty-five, or report their information in whole numbers and a half or a quarter of a bathtub. (See Figures 3–8 and 3–9.)

11. Discuss the students' responses to this amount. Ask: "Is it a large amount or a small amount? Is this a healthy choice?" You may wish to extend the investigation to find out how much sugar this adds to students' diets annually. If so, cans of soda report the amount of sugar in a single can, and students can use this data, along with the information from the preceding investigation, to figure out the answer.

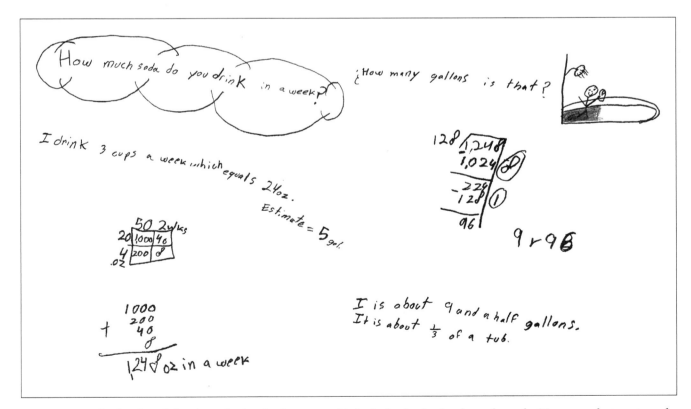

How much soda do I drink in a Year?

In everyday I drink 3 cups of soda

Estimatetion:

$$\begin{array}{r} 32 \\ +32 \\ \hline 64 \\ 32 \\ 96 \\ 32 \\ \hline 128 \end{array}$$

In four days I drink 1 gallon
I think I drink about 50 gallons
In year?

$$4\overline{\smash)365}$$ 91 r 1
-320 80
45 10
40
5 1
4
1

I drink about 91 gallons in a year.

How many Bath tubs is that?

$$25\overline{\smash)91}$$ 3 r16 I drink about 3 bathtubs.
-50 2
41 1
25
16

Figure 3–8 *While Anita estimated that she drank about 50 gallons of soda each year, she discovered that she actually drank about 91.*

How much soda do you drink in a week?

¿How many gallons is that?

I drink 3 cups a week which equals 24 oz.

Estimate = 5 gal.

50 2w/ks
20 1000 40
4 200 8
.02

1000
+ 200
40
8
1248 oz in a week

$$128\overline{\smash)1,248}$$
1,024 8
224
128 1
96

9 r 96

I is about 9 and a half gallons.
It is about ⅓ of a tub.

Figure 3–9 *Carlos found that he only drank about one-third of a bathtub of soda each week. He correctly interpreted 9 r96 as about $9\frac{1}{2}$ gallons.*

Cook-a-Doodle-Doo! Iguana's Mistakes

Overview

Students enjoy hearing *Cook-a-Doodle-Doo!* by Janet Stevens and Susan Stevens Crummel. In this book, Iguana has many silly misconceptions, some about volume. When the students hear that Iguana measures the amount of flour with a ruler, they investigate why this is not a reliable way to measure volume. When they hear that Iguana thinks that you should cut a third off a measuring cup to measure two-thirds of a cup, the students create their own liquid measuring cups from different-shape containers. The students then make generalizations about liquid heights in narrow and wide containers.

Materials

- ❧ *Cook-a-Doodle-Doo!* by Janet Stevens and Susan Stevens Crummel (1999)
- ❧ 12-inch squares of waxed paper, 1 per small group of students
- ❧ flour, at least 1 cup per small group of students
- ❧ rulers, 1 per small group of students
- ❧ empty transparent cylindrical containers of a variety of heights, each of which holds at least 3 cups, 1 per small group of students
- ❧ fine-width permanent black markers, 1 per small group of students
- ❧ $\frac{1}{3}$-cup measuring cups, 1 per small group of students
- ❧ containers of water, half-gallon or more, 1 per small group of students

Vocabulary: estimate, height, inch, measure, measuring cup, narrow, one-third, ruler, two-thirds, volume, wide

Instructions

1. Begin this lesson by reading *Cook-a-Doodle-Doo!* to the class. Enjoy the fictional story with the students, its references to *The Little Red Hen,* and its wordplay. Each time Iguana says something silly, invite the students to explain his mistake. Focus especially on how Iguana measures the flour, where he looks for the teaspoons and tablespoons, how he measures the milk, and how he keeps track of the baking time.

2. Now read the story a second time. This time as you read, discuss with the students the informational text in the sidebars.

3. Return to the page where Iguana measures the flour. Tell the students that you want to better understand what Iguana was trying to do. Ask the students

whether this was a good way to measure the flour. Have the students discuss whether it is better to measure flour with a ruler or with a measuring cup and why. Provide each group with a sheet of waxed paper and a ruler. On each sheet of waxed paper, pour out about a cup of flour in a pile. Ask the students to estimate the height of their pile of flour and then measure it. Write their measurements on the board.

4. Discuss with the students why the different measurements resulted, and why height is not a reliable measure of volume. Reread the next page, where Rooster measures the flour with a metal measuring cup. Then have the students return the flour into its original container by lifting the waxed paper and pouring it back.

5. Next turn to the page where Iguana suggests measuring two-thirds of a cup of milk by cutting a third off a measuring cup. Turn the page and read Rooster's solution of using a liquid measuring cup.

6. Explain to the students that they will make their own liquid measuring cups. Show the students the set of empty transparent containers that you have available. Tell the students that each group will fill a $\frac{1}{3}$-cup measuring cup with water, pour it into a container, and use a permanent marker to mark its height. Have them repeat the process until the container is almost full. Then tell the students that they will label the lines that represent full cups: *1 cup, 2 cups*, and so on. On the board write:

   a. *Fill your $\frac{1}{3}$-cup measuring cup with water.*
   b. *With a marker draw a line to indicate that height.*
   c. *Continue doing this until your container is almost full.*
   d. *Empty your container into the sink or back into the original container of water.*
   e. *Label the lines that indicate each cup: 1 cup, 2 cups, 3 cups, and so on.*

7. Give each group a container of water, a measuring cup, an empty container, and a marker. As students work, ask them to explain what different lines represent, for example, $1\frac{1}{3}$ cups, $2\frac{2}{3}$ cups, and so on. When the students finish, gather in a central area and ask them to place their containers in the center where all the students can see them. Fill each container with water to show 2 cups. Ask the students what they notice about the containers. They will say that the height of the water level is different in the containers. Invite the students to discuss with a partner why this is the case.

8. Now have students share their theories. Write the students' ideas on the board. For example, they might say:

- A group made a mistake when they marked the lines.
- Skinnier containers have higher water levels.
- That container has a shorter water level because it's fatter.

9. Next ask the students how they can prove whether these theories are correct or incorrect. For example, for "A group made a mistake when they marked the lines," students could suggest that you empty that container and use the $\frac{1}{3}$-cup measuring cup to refill it, checking its markings. For the theory "Skinnier containers have higher water levels," they might want to sort the containers by width to see whether it is true. For "That container has a shorter water level because it's fatter," the class could line up the containers by water level, from lowest to highest, and see whether the containers are also ordered from narrowest to widest.

10. Last, ask the students why some restaurants prefer to serve drinks in narrow glasses. The students may conclude that drinks look nicer that way, or they may decide that many people think that higher levels of liquids indicate more volume, and a restaurant that does this might sell more drinks and earn more money.

◈ Filling Boxes

Overview

In this lesson, students work in pairs to figure out the volume of boxes without tops. Having only a set of twenty wooden cubes to use to find the volume, students must move from filling and counting by ones to considering how to use dimensions such as length, width, and height, or layers, to estimate the total volume. After pairs make their estimates, students fill the boxes to find their actual volumes.

Materials

◈ collection of different-size empty boxes with no tops, more boxes than there are pairs of students (see Instruction 1)

◈ $\frac{3}{4}$-inch or 1-inch wooden cubes, 20 per pair of students

◈ Containers to hold cubes, 1 per pair of students

Vocabulary: bottom, corners, dimensions, edges, estimate, height, layer, length, rectangle, rectangular prism, square, volume, width

Instructions

1. Prior to the lesson, collect a set of boxes. Candy boxes or half-gallon milk cartons cut to 6 to 8 inches in height work well. Label each box with a large capital letter to distinguish one from another. Make sure there are more boxes than pairs of students.

2. Show the students your collection of boxes. Tell the students that they will investigate the volume of each box, using cubes as a unit of measure. Show the students the wooden cubes and the capital letters that label the boxes.

3. Ask the students to describe the shape of the boxes. Write their descriptive words on the board, such as *rectangle, rectangular prism, square, corners, edges, long, thin, tall, height, length,* and *width*. As you write, refer to the actual boxes to make sure that the students understand the meaning of the words.

4. Ask each pair to get a container of cubes and select a box to investigate. Tell the students that they must first make an estimate of the box's volume by simply looking at the box and talking about what they notice about the box dimensions, before putting any cubes in the box. Explain to the students that when the cubes fill the boxes, they must come up as even to the top as possible but not extend beyond the top of the box. Have each student write his or her estimate on a sheet of paper.

5. Next ask the students to work together to use their set of cubes to figure out the actual volume of their box. Tell them to discuss what they think and try to agree on the volume, if possible. Have the students write what they think the volume is and how they figured it out, using words, numbers, and pictures or diagrams.

6. Observe the strategies that the students use to solve the problem. Since they have a limited number of cubes, they will need to fill part of the box and use that information to decide the volume of the entire box. Also, since the cubes would not fill the boxes exactly, even if students had enough cubes, observe how they deal with the extra spaces.

7. When pairs finish, have them select a new box or exchange boxes with another pair and repeat the activity again and again. Remind them to label each set of data with the letter on the box.

8. When the students have explored many boxes, have them return the boxes and cubes. Begin a whole-group discussion. Select a box that most groups have

explored. Ask students to tell the volume they identified and why they believe that volume to be correct. On the board write words and equations that describe how the students thought about the parts of the box. For example, a student might say that she filled in the width and length of the box and found it to be 6 by 6 cubes, which would make 36 cubes in the entire bottom. Then the student might have stacked 3 cubes to find the height of the box, which would make 3 times 36, or 108 cubes in the entire box. In this case you might write:

Bottom (length times width): $6 \times 6 = 36$ cubes

Height: 3 cubes

Volume or total: $3 \times 36 = 108$ cubes

9. Ask other students who investigated that same box to share what they think. Write their thinking on the board. It is important to realize that some students will see the bottom of the box as repeated rows, and those students might have figured this way:

$6 + 6 + 6 + 6 + 6 + 6 = 36$ cubes

$36 + 36 + 36 = 108$ cubes

Accept what the students see, and show them how to record it.

10. Have a student completely fill the box with cubes, placing them inside the box as evenly as possible, making sure that the cubes do not extend above the top of the box. Find out which group's estimated volume came closest to the actual volume.

11. Repeat the process with other boxes.

◈ Folding Boxes

Overview

In this lesson, students look at a box pattern and predict how many cubes will fill it when it is taped together to make a box with no top. They write their prediction, cut out the pattern, tape the edges, and then fill the box with cubes connected together. Students then write number sentences that describe how they see the volume of the box. In a group discussion, the students share their number sentences and consider how three different dimensions—length, width, and height—can describe a three-dimensional shape.

Materials

◈ *Folding Boxes* patterns 1 of each sheet (A–D) per pair of students (see Blackline Masters)

◈ clear adhesive tape, 1 roll per small group of students

◈ $\frac{3}{4}$-inch Snap Cubes, about 35 per pair of students (or Unifix cubes or $\frac{3}{4}$-inch wooden cubes)

◈ $\frac{3}{4}$-inch grid paper, 1 sheet

◈ marker

Vocabulary: bottom, height, layer, length, prediction, rectangular prism, three-dimensional shape, volume, width

Instructions

1. Tell the students that they will fill boxes today to explore volume. Write *volume* on the board and have the students tell you what the word means. Write a definition for *volume* that the students agree upon, such as "how much something holds," or "how much space something takes up."

2. Show the students a box pattern. Explain to the students that they will look at the pattern and estimate how many cubes it will hold when the sides are folded to make a box.

3. Tell the students that they will then cut out the pattern and tape the sides together to make the box. Then they will fill their box with cubes connected together and find out how many cubes will fill the box. Show the students two cubes and how the cubes connect tightly together.

4. Model your instructions. Hold up the pattern for Box A, still flat. Write *Box A* on the board, and tell the students that on a sheet of paper they will write the name of the box that they are investigating. Ask the students to predict how many cubes will fill the box made with this pattern, and why they think that is a reasonable prediction. Encourage the students to use the numbers of squares that they see to help them make a prediction. Write *Prediction* on the board, along with several students' predictions, explaining that they will also record their prediction for each box. Next to each prediction, write the word *cubes* after the number. Remind the students that they must include the unit of measure, because otherwise a reader might think that 14 beans would fill the box, or 14 elephants, or 14 cubic centimeters.

5. Then show the students how they will cut out their pattern and then tape the edges together. Explain that they need only a little tape to attach the sides. Begin to fill the box you have made with Snap Cubes, connecting the cubes as you put them in the box. Do not fill the box completely. Tell the students that they will find the volume of the box. On the board write *Volume:* _____ *cubes.* Explain that they will write the number that they find in the blank. Again remind the students to write the unit that they are using to measure.

6. Next tell the students that they will write a number sentence that represents the number of cubes in the box. On the board write *Number sentence*. Explain that they can use addition or multiplication or anything else that represents how they see the volume.

7. Show the students the other box patterns that they will investigate. Distribute the materials. Invite pairs of students to choose a pattern and begin their investigation.

8. As the students work, circulate to watch how the students make their predictions. Encourage them to not merely guess, but to use the numbers of squares to help them decide on a reasonable number. When the students find the actual volume, have them compare it with their prediction. If the volume varies significantly from their prediction, have them think about why that is the case. Have students also explain to you how their number sentence matches the way they saw the volume.

9. When the students complete their investigations, bring them together for a group discussion.

10. Show a flat pattern of Box B. Have several students share their predictions for the volume of that box, why that prediction made sense at first, and what they found out. Encourage the students to explain why we can't simply count each square in the grid—that the edges and corners of the box use up two or three of the squares.

11. Next cut out the pattern, tape the box together, and fill it with connected Snap Cubes. Remove the rectangular prism of cubes from the box.

12. Have the students share the number sentences that they used to describe how they saw the volume of the box. For each number sentence, show where the numbers are in the actual prism. For example, if a student says $3 \times 4 = 12$, show the students that the 4 represents one layer of four cubes and the 3 shows that there are three layers of cubes. Write all the number sentences that the students share, because students may see the volume in a variety of ways.

13. Place the rectangular prism on the chalk tray or a table. Label for the students the dimensions that volume usually refers to: length, width, and height. Write each term on the board, and show that dimension on the rectangular prism.

Length: 2 cubes

Width: 2 cubes

Height: 3 cubes

14. Show the students a number sentence that describes your rectangular prism using all three dimensions: $(2 \times 2) \times 3 = 12$. Again show the students how each number describes a dimension of your rectangular prism. Explain to the students that shapes that have all three dimensions are called three-dimensional shapes. Draw a two-dimensional shape on the board, such as a square. Tell the students that this shape has the dimensions of length and width, but no height, so it is called a two-dimensional shape.

15. Repeat this process (Instructions 10 through 14) for each of the remaining box patterns. Each time have the students share how their predictions did or did not match the actual volume, and how they can now look at a pattern and predict the volume. Also, each time, share the students' number sentences that describe the volume as well as the standard way that volume is described using three dimensions.

16. End the lesson by drawing a new box pattern on the board:

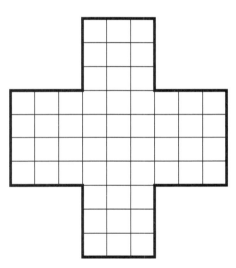

Ask the students to discuss, and then share, how they would predict the volume of that new pattern. Write their predictions on the board. Then use a marker to outline the pattern on the piece of $\frac{3}{4}$-inch grid paper. Then cut it out, tape the edges, and fill the box to find out what the volume actually is.

Maximum Box

Overview

In this lesson, students take a 20-by-20-centimeter square and cut smaller squares out of the corners. Then they fold the sides up and tape them, creating a box without a lid. The students find the volumes of the different boxes that they make. During a discussion, the students combine their information to make a chart that shows which box has the largest volume.

Materials

◈ 1-centimeter cubes, 20 to 30 per pair of students
◈ 1-inch cubes, 24
◈ centimeter grid paper, 1 sheet per student (see Blackline Masters)
◈ clear adhesive tape, 1 roll per small group of students
◈ butcher paper, about 3 feet by 4 feet long, 1 sheet

Vocabulary: array, centimeter, cube, dimensions, height, high, layer, length, long, rectangle, volume, wide, width

Instructions

1. Prior to the lesson, cut a 20-by-20-centimeter square out of centimeter grid paper.

2. Tell the students that they will investigate volume today. Have the students explain to each other, and then to you, what volume means.

3. Gather the students close to you so they can see. Using the 1-inch cubes, make a prism. Begin by building the bottom layer three inches wide and four inches long. As you build, describe the array that you are creating, and write on the board: *3 inches wide by 4 inches long*. Next, add another identical layer to the prism, and describe what you are doing. Add to the description on the board: *by 2 inches high*. Have several students explain how the phrases on the board describe your arrangement. Then ask a student to say a number sentence that describes what you built and write the equation on the board. Have several other students describe with numbers and operations what they see. Explain how the numbers fit the dimensions in your prism. Following are some number sentences the students might say:

$$(3 + 3 + 3 + 3) \times 2$$
$$(3 \times 4) \times 2$$
$$(4 + 4 + 4) \times 2$$

   Make sure that all students understand how to describe the prism as a bottom layer that is a rectangle and then layers of that rectangle. On the board draw two 3-by-4 rectangles with an arrow between to show the layers of your prism.

4. Next, show the students a 20-centimeter square of grid paper. Explain that each pair of students will receive a piece of paper like this one. Tell the students that they will work together to cut a square out of one corner and then cut a same-size square out of each of the remaining corners. Demonstrate by cutting a 2-centimeter square out of each corner of your grid. Then show the students how to fold up the sides and secure the corners with tape to make a box.

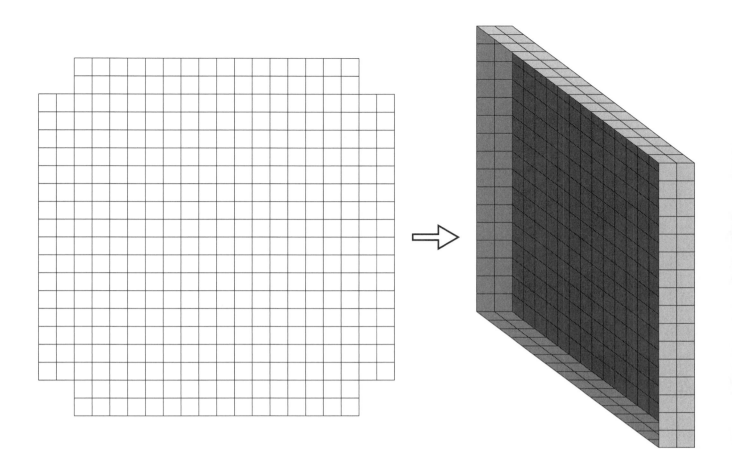

5. Fill in one of the dimensions with sixteen 1-centimeter cubes, so the students can see the bottom layer. Ask the students to think about how that information might help them make an estimate of the box's volume. Then have the students discuss in pairs, and then with the whole group, how they would find out the actual volume. As students explain their thinking, ask them to describe the box in terms of the dimensions of the bottom layer and how many layers this box will contain.

6. Write the assignment on the board:

Work in pairs to do the following:

a. *Cut out a 20-by-20-centimeter square from your sheet of grid paper.*

b. *Cut out the square assigned to you from each corner.*

c. *Fold up the sides of the box and tape the corners together.*

d. *Estimate the box's volume, and write it on your paper.*

e. *Find the volume of your box.*

f. *On your paper, describe your box and how you found the volume. Use words, numbers, and pictures.*

g. *If you have time, investigate another box.*

7. Next identify the corners that different students will cut out. Ask the students what size squares can be cut out to make different kinds of boxes. On the board, write the different squares that the students say:

Corners to Cut Out:

$1 \times 1 \ cm$

$2 \times 2 \ cm$

$3 \times 3 \ cm$

$4 \times 4 \ cm$

$5 \times 5 \ cm$

$6 \times 6 \ cm$

$7 \times 7 \ cm$

$8 \times 8 \ cm$

$9 \times 9 \ cm$

If the students say that you can cut out 10-by-10-centimeter corners, try to do this, demonstrating why this is not possible; no squares would remain to make a box.

8. Ask the students to predict which box will have the largest volume and why. Put a star next to each corner that they predict will create the largest volume. For example, many students predict the 1-by-1 corner will create the largest volume, because the fewest squares are removed. Remind the students to write the volume in cubic centimeters, because volume measures the entire space taken up by the centimeter cube. On the board write *cubic centimeters* along with the abbreviation cm^3.

9. Have partners choose a box to investigate. Make sure that each box size is assigned, and that partners or students at each table make the same-size box so that they can check each other's work.

10. Provide the students with centimeter cubes to help identify the dimensions, and pass out the centimeter grid paper and tape.

11. As students finish, ask them to compare their information with that of others who made the same-size box to correct any errors. (See Figure 3–10.)

12. When the students complete the investigation, tape the butcher paper to the board and gather the students for a group discussion.

13. With the students' help, tape the boxes onto the butcher paper in order, beginning with the box with the 1-by-1-centimeter corners removed. (Tape

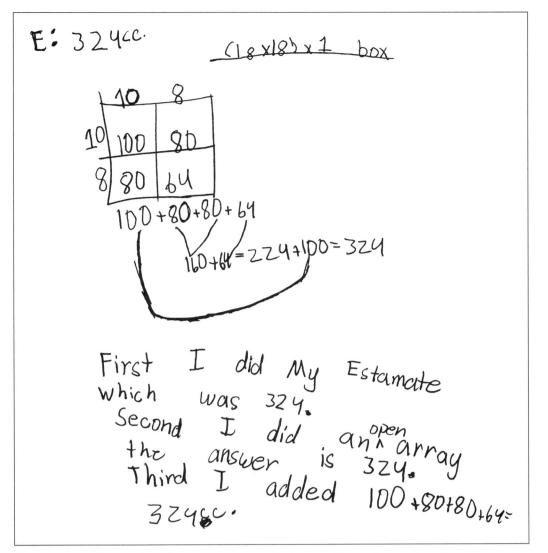

E: 324cc.

(18×18)×1 box

10   8

10 | 100 | 80
8 | 80 | 64

100+80+80+64

160+64=224+100=324

First I did My Estamate which was 324. Second I did an open array the answer is 324. Third I added 100+80+80+64= 324cc.

Figure 3–10 *Rather than doing an estimate, Carlos quickly used mental math to come up with the answer. He recorded his thinking using an open array, splitting the numbers into their place-value components.*

the boxes to the paper in such a way that you can look into the open boxes.) Begin the discussion by having the students describe how the boxes visually change. For example, many students notice that the boxes become narrower but taller.

14. Next, have the students who made each box explain the dimensions of one layer and then the number of layers and the total volume. For example, the box with 2-by-2-centimeter squares removed would be described this way: 16 long × 16 wide × 2 high = $(16 \times 16) \times 2 = 512$ cm^3. Add this information below each box. The completed chart will look like this:

Corners Cut Out	Dimensions	Volume
1 × 1 cm	(18 × 18) × 1 cm	324 cm^3
2 × 2 cm	(16 × 16) × 2 cm	512 cm^3
3 × 3 cm	(14 × 14) × 3 cm	588 cm^3
4 × 4 cm	(12 × 12) × 4 cm	576 cm^3
5 × 5 cm	(10 × 10) × 5 cm	500 cm^3
6 × 6 cm	(8 × 8) × 6 cm	384 cm^3
7 × 7 cm	(6 × 6) × 7 cm	252 cm^3
8 × 8 cm	(4 × 4) × 8 cm	128 cm^3
9 × 9 cm	(2 × 2) × 9 cm	36 cm^3

15. Have the students examine the data and draw conclusions about which box has the largest volume. Discuss whether their data match their predictions. Have the students discuss why they think the volumes for the boxes increase and then decrease.

◈ Wayside School

Overview

In this lesson, students are introduced to a humorous children's book series, Wayside School. They hear about, and then visualize, an imaginary school built thirty stories high with one classroom on each story. The students discuss the advantages and disadvantages of a school built this way. They build different possible rectangular arrangements for schools with four classrooms, and then eight classrooms, and optionally may learn how to record what they find on isometric dot paper before recording on a chart. The students then investigate how many different ways Wayside School, with its thirty classrooms, could be arranged.

Materials

◈ *Sideways Stories from Wayside School*, by Louis Sachar (1998)
◈ Multilink cubes, 30 per small group of students and 30 for the teacher
◈ optional: isometric dot paper, 2 sheets per student (see Blackline Masters)
◈ optional: transparencies of isometric dot paper, 4

Vocabulary: array, chart, configuration, dimensions, horizontal, isometric dot paper, rectangle, rotate, row, story, vertical

Instructions

1. If possible, read the short chapter book *Sideways Stories from Wayside School* to your students prior to teaching this lesson. If this is not possible, incorporate the book as it is presented here.

2. Before class, connect your thirty cubes into a tall tower. Place the cube tower nearby, for use later in the lesson. Place thirty cubes at each student's work space.

3. Begin the lesson by introducing the following scenario to the students. Have students imagine their classroom, with the classroom next door right on top of it, and another teacher's classroom on top of *that* classroom, and another classroom on top of *that* classroom. Tell them that you are going to read a passage from a funny book with silly, imaginative situations that they can continue reading at a later time, a book about a school that has only one classroom on each floor, but has thirty classrooms right on top of each other.

4. Read the first page of *Sideways Stories from Wayside School* to the students, ending with the sentence "They have an extra-large playground." Invite the students to discuss the advantages and disadvantages of a school arranged in this manner. They may wonder how the people get from one classroom to another, or they may comment on how great it would be to have such a large playground. Tell the students that they will have the opportunity to enjoy reading the entire book at a later time, but right now they will investigate the unusual configuration of the school.

5. Reread the sentence that describes how the school is arranged: "It was supposed to be only one story high, with thirty classrooms all in a row. Instead it is thirty stories high, with one classroom on one story." Show the students your cube model of Wayside School—thirty cubes arranged in a tall, vertical column.

6. Clarify the term *story* by having the students explain what it means. They will likely use synonyms such as *floor*, *level*, and *layer*. During the lesson, use the term that is most familiar to your students. Hold your hand flat at each floor that has one classroom, so the students can see what you mean by each floor.

7. Hold up a Multilink cube, and explain to the students that the cube represents a room in the school. Now connect four Multilink cubes in a row, hold the tower vertically, and ask the students to imagine that it is a very small Wayside School with only four classrooms, with one classroom on each floor. Have students use multilink cubes to build an identical school.

8. Now, if you wish to have the students record the arrangements by drawing, provide each student with two sheets of isometric dot paper. If not, skip the drawing steps in the rest of the lesson. On an isometric dot paper transparency, show the students how to record the cube arrangement. Have the students record the arrangement on their own papers.

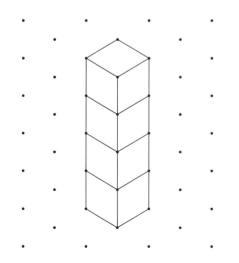

9. Now show the students a different building that arrangement could make, by rotating it horizontally so that it has one floor that is four rooms long, and ask the students to rotate their buildings in the same way.

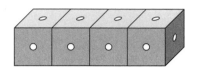

10. Again, you may wish to show the students how to record this building on the isometric dot paper transparency, and have them record it on their dot paper.

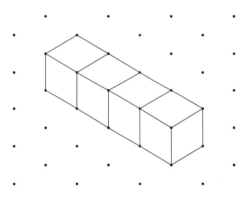

11. Now ask the students to build a different version of a four-room school. Tell the students that each floor in the building must be a rectangle, or array, and each floor must be the same size and shape. Remind the students that a square is a special kind of rectangle.

12. Hold up two buildings that the students built that follow the rule, and have the students explain how they meet the criteria.

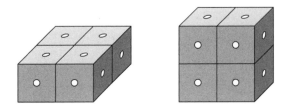

Then hold up any arrangements that do not follow the rule, and have students explain why they do not.

13. Have the students record the two correct configurations on their dot paper. Draw the same arrangements on the dot paper transparency, and have the students revise their drawings if necessary.

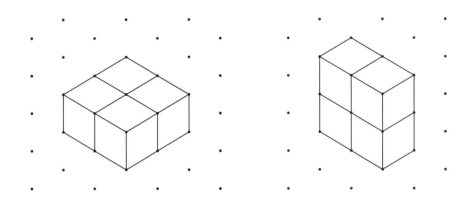

14. Next connect eight Multilink cubes in a column, and ask the students to imagine that it is another version of Wayside School, with eight classrooms. Tell the students that they will work as a group to find different ways a school with eight rooms could look. On the board write the rules that each building must follow:

The building must have 8 rooms.

Each floor must be a rectangle of the same size as the other floors in that building.

Build two sample buildings with eight cubes: one that follows the rules and one that does not.

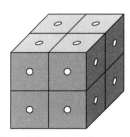

Does follow the rule.

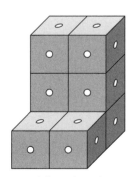

Does *not* follow the rule.

Have the students explain in their own words why the buildings do and do not follow the rules. Remind the students that floors can be squares because a square is a special kind of rectangle.

15. When the students finish making their buildings, select one of each kind of building from those the students made, and place them where all the students can see.

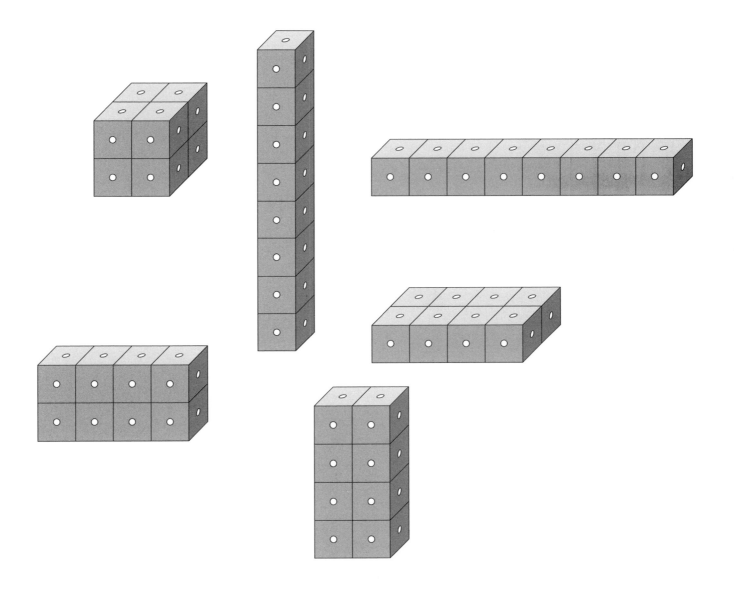

Discuss why you didn't select any students' buildings that didn't fit the criteria.

16. Now show the students another way they will record the buildings they find. Draw this chart on the board:

School with Eight Classrooms	
Number of Floors	**Array of Classrooms on One Floor**

17. Select the building that is four floors tall.

Have the students discuss how many floors it has. In the Number of Floors column, write *4* and under Array of Classrooms on One Floor, write *2 × 1*. Remove a "floor" from the building so the students can see the array that makes up that floor. Remind the students that they are not counting all the cubes, or rooms, on the floor, but are instead describing the sides, or the dimensions, of the floor.

School with Eight Classrooms	
Number of Floors	**Array of Classrooms on One Floor**
4	2 × 1

Now draw that building on a dot paper transparency, and have the students do the same.

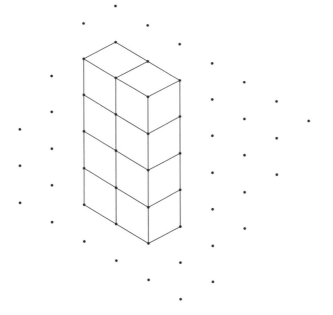

18. Next, choose a different arrangement that the students made—the building that is two floors high with a 4-by-1 array on each floor.

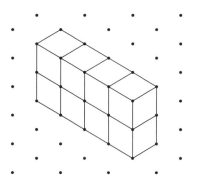

19. Explain that this building would look different from the first one. Ask the students to explain how many floors are in this building, and how they know that. Add this information to the chart. Now remove one of the floors and have the students examine its configuration. Add this information to the chart and draw the building on the transparency.

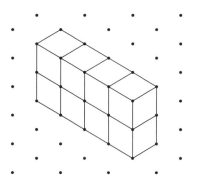

20. Hold up other building arrangements, add their information to the chart, and draw each arrangement on a dot paper transparency. Continue until all possible buildings are recorded:

School with Eight Classrooms	
Number of Floors	**Array of Classrooms on One Floor**
4	2 × 1
2	4 × 1
8	1 × 1
2	2 × 2
1	1 × 8
1	2 × 4

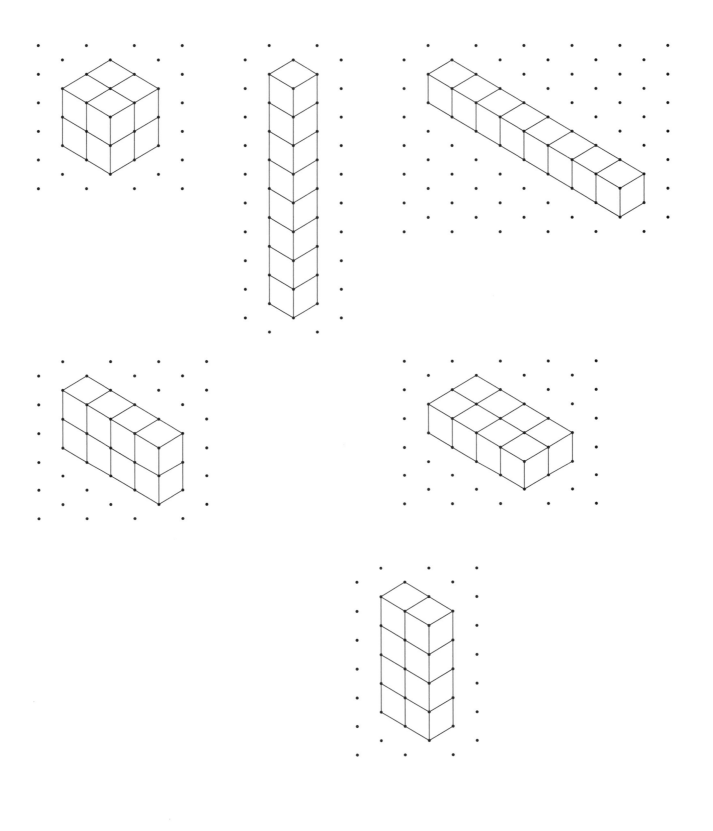

21. Now explain to the students that they are going to investigate all the different ways that Wayside School's thirty classrooms could be arranged. Ask the students how many different buildings they think are possible to make.

22. Draw a new chart on the board:

School with Thirty Classrooms	
Number of Floors	**Array of Classrooms on One Floor**

23. Show the students the tall cube arrangement that you made of the original Wayside School. Have the students look closely at how many floors it has and add that information to the chart. Then have them look at one floor, describe the array of classrooms on that floor, and add that information to the chart. Tell the students that the arrangement will not fit on the dot paper, but that one person in each group will make a chart for the group and record that building on the chart. Rotate the building horizontally and repeat this step for the building with one floor with an array of 30 by 1.

24. Tell the students that they will work in groups to find more arrangements for this Wayside School. Explain that they will record each arrangement they find on dot paper and on a chart. Provide each group with lined paper for the chart.

25. As the students work, circulate around the room. Have students prove that their arrangements follow the rules by referring to their drawings and their charts. Some students may need support in remembering how to record an arrangement on the chart. If so, suggest that they first look closely at the bottom floor, and then record the dimensions of that floor. Then have them find, and record, the number of floors. If students need help in thinking about new arrangements, you may encourage them to use what they know about multiplication. For example, thinking about factors of 30 (1, 2, 3, 5, 6, 10, 15, 30) may help them find additional configurations.

26. To prepare for a group discussion, erase the dot paper transparencies. When the students have found many arrangements, begin the group discussion. First invite students to share how they looked for new configurations. For example, some groups may have worked randomly. Other groups may have built an arrangement and then recorded how it would look when oriented in different ways. Some groups may have thought about multiplication and factors to identify new configurations. Ask the groups how many different configurations they found for Wayside School. Write these numbers on the board.

27. Next ask students to share the arrangements they discovered. For each building, have the student tell you the number of floors and the array on each floor. On a transparency, draw the arrangement as a student describes it, and ask the other groups to verify whether they found that same arrangement. Have the student volunteer add that information to the class chart. Continue in the same manner until you have listed all the arrangements that the class found. Count the total number of arrangements and discuss whether they think they found all the possible arrangements for Wayside School. (See Figures 3–11 and 3–12 on page 144.)

School with Thirty Classrooms	
Number of Floors	**Array of Classrooms on One Floor**
1	1 × 30
30	1 × 1
1	2 × 15
2	1 × 15
15	1 × 2
2	3 × 5
3	5 × 2
5	2 × 3
1	10 × 3
3	1 × 10
10	1 × 3
1	5 × 6
5	6 × 1
6	5 × 1

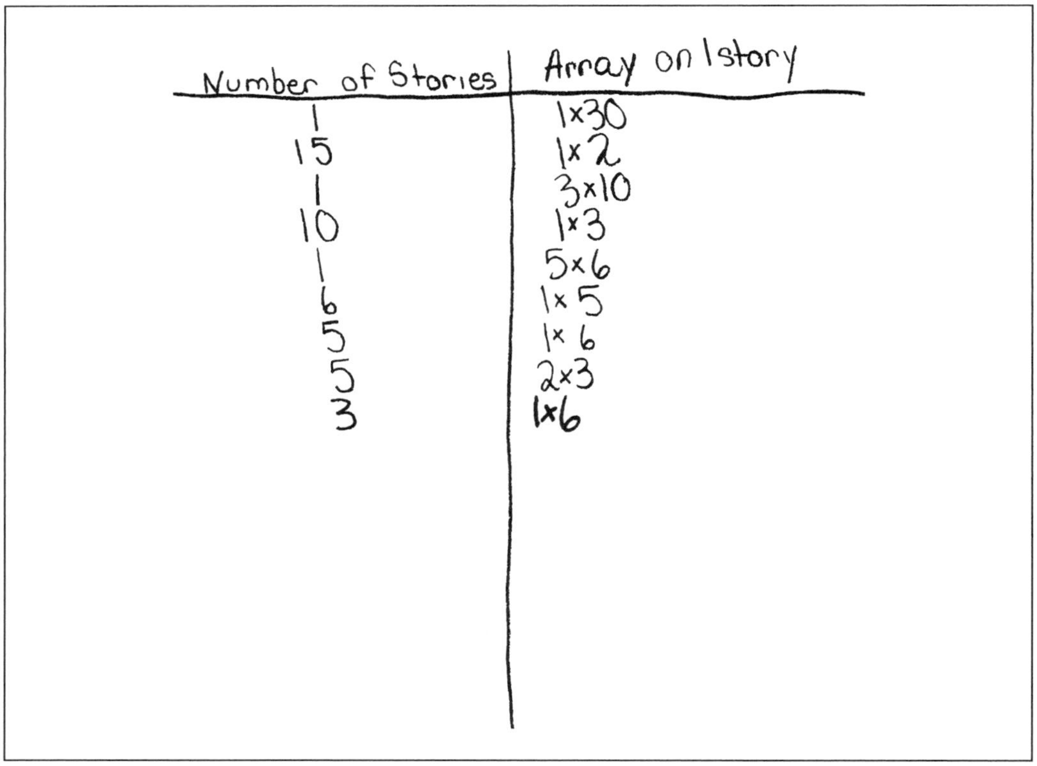

Number of Stories	Array on 1 story
1	1×30
15	1×2
1	3×10
10	1×3
1	5×6
6	1×5
5	1×6
5	2×3
3	1×6

Figure 3–11 *Carlos and Jason found nine different ways that Wayside School could have looked.*

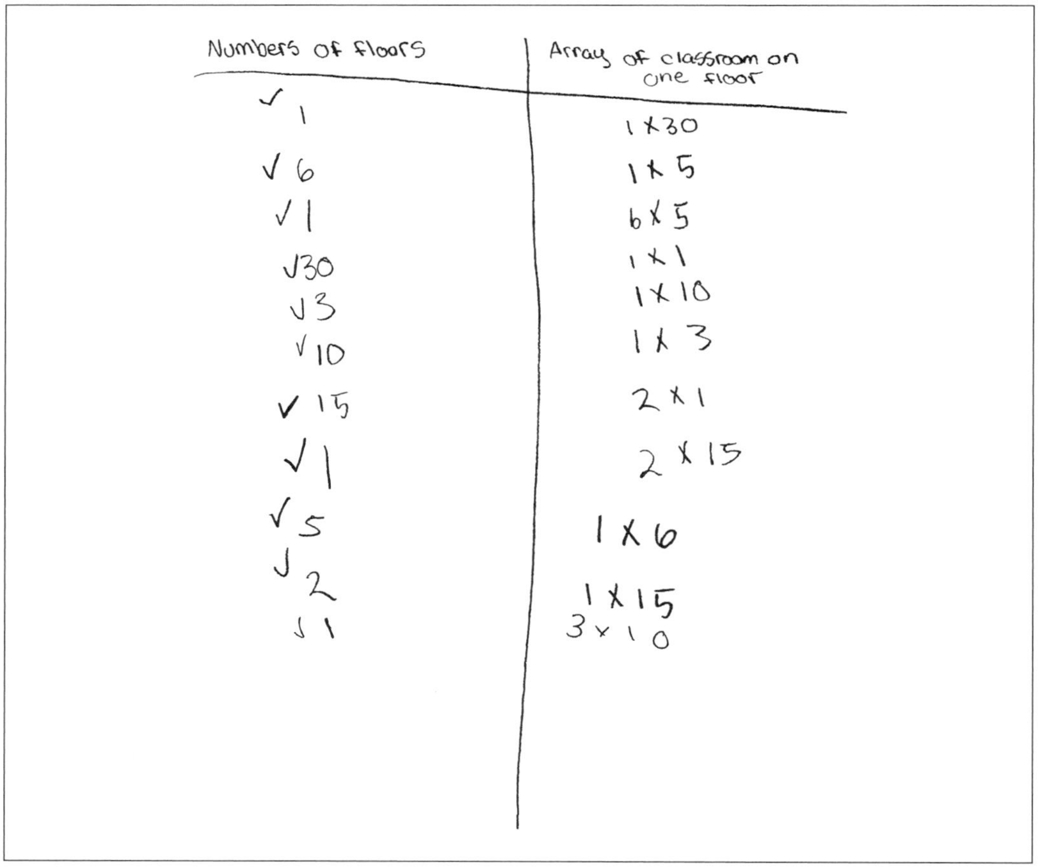

Numbers of floors	Array of classroom on one floor
✓ 1	1×30
✓ 6	1×5
✓ 1	6×5
✓ 30	1×1
✓ 3	1×10
✓ 10	1×3
✓ 15	2×1
✓ 1	2×15
✓ 5	1×6
✓ 2	1×15
✓ 1	3×10

Figure 3–12 *Marnie, Carrie, and Linda found eleven different arrangements for Wayside School.*

Cook-a-Doodle-Doo! Great-Granny's Magnificent Strawberry Shortcake Recipe

....

Overview

In this lesson, students find equivalent measures in Janet Stevens and Susan Stevens Crummel's *Cook-a-Doodle-Doo!* and then use that information to adjust the recipe for strawberry shortcake to make two, three, and eight cakes. The students contribute their findings to a class T-chart and explore the patterns that it shows.

Materials

◈ *Cook-a-Doodle-Doo!* by Janet Stevens and Susan Stevens Crummel (1999)
◈ chart paper, 1–2 sheets
◈ marker

Vocabulary: cup, double, equivalent measures, estimate, grams, half-cups, hour, improper fractions, minutes, mixed numbers, patterns, pints, quarts, seconds, T-chart, tablespoon, teaspoon, triple, unit, volume, whole numbers

Instructions

1. Before class, write on chart paper the recipe on the last page of the book for Great-Granny's Magnificent Strawberry Shortcake.

2. With the students review the book *Cook-a-Doodle-Doo!* For each picture, have the students tell you about the fictional story, and read to them the informational text for that picture. As you find informational text that shares equivalence facts, list that information about equivalent measures on the board, such as:

1 cup = 227 grams

   Note that in the United States we measure dry ingredients in volume using cups, but that most of the world measures them by weight and uses grams. Have the students determine mentally how many grams are in 2 cups, and ask them to share their strategies. For example, some students will say, "Two hundred plus two hundred is four hundred; twenty plus twenty is forty, so that's four hundred forty. And seven plus seven is fourteen, and four hundred forty plus fourteen is four hundred fifty-four grams." Find that information in the book and write it on the board:

2 cups = 454 grams

Continue with the other equivalencies listed in the book:

3 teaspoons = 1 tablespoon = 14 grams

1 stick of butter = $\frac{1}{2}$ cup = 8 tablespoons = 113 grams

1 hour = 60 minutes

1 minute = 60 seconds

Then add the following information:

2 cups = 1 pint

4 cups = 1 quart

3. Now tape the recipe chart to the board. Ask the students read the recipe.

4. Turn to the next-to-last page of the book and reread the paragraph that describes how the animals had to make the strawberry shortcake a second time. Explain to the students that they are going work with a partner to adjust the recipe for the animals. Tell the students that they are going to select one of the following scenarios: What if the animals made two strawberry shortcakes? What if they made three strawberry shortcakes? Or, what if each animal wanted to have his own, and they made eight strawberry shortcakes? How much of each ingredient would they need?

5. On the board write:

    a. *With a partner select a way to adjust the recipe to make two shortcakes, three short-cakes, or eight shortcakes.*

    b. *Figure out how much of each ingredient would you need. Explain your thinking.*

Remind the students to use the equivalency list as a reference. Tell them that recipes rarely use improper fractions, and instead list whole or mixed numbers. Also tell the students that recipes usually display quantities using the largest unit possible, for example, 1 cup rather than 2 half-cups. Provide the students with some examples and discuss the answers:

4 half-cups = ____ cups (2)

$\frac{5}{2}$ teaspoons = ____ teaspoons ($2\frac{1}{2}$)

6 cups = ____ pints (3)

6. As the partners do the task, provide support as needed. Have students explain their thinking to you, even when their answer is correct.

7. When the students finish, explain that they will work in groups to see whether their answers make sense. Tell the students that when their answers differ, they must explain their thinking and then decide whether both answers could be true.

8. Now make three groups of students—those who doubled the recipe, those who tripled the recipe, and those who made eight shortcakes. Have the groups share their answers and discuss whether they agree or disagree. Suggest that each group select a moderator. As students discuss their results, observe how they listen and respond to each other. Do they explain their thinking clearly and logically? Do they ask questions to clarify the thinking of others? Do they accept other logical answers as being possible?

9. When the groups finish, have a class discussion to compare recipe adjustments. Draw a four-column T-chart on the board:

One Recipe	Two Recipes	Three Recipes	Eight Recipes

Add the information that each group agreed upon. The T-chart might look like this:

One Recipe	Two Recipes	Three Recipes	Eight Recipes
2 cups flour	4 c.	6 c.	16 c.
2 tablespoons sugar	4 T.	6 T.	16 T. = 1 c.
1 tablespoon baking powder	2 T.	3 T.	8 T. = $\frac{1}{2}$ c.
$\frac{1}{2}$ teaspoon salt	1 t.	$1\frac{1}{2}$ t.	4 t. = 1 T. + 1 t.
$\frac{1}{2}$ cup butter	1 c.	$1\frac{1}{2}$ c.	4 c.
1 egg	2	3	8
$\frac{2}{3}$ cup milk	$1\frac{1}{3}$ c.	2 c.	$5\frac{1}{3}$ c.
3–4 cups strawberries	6–8 c.	9–12 c.	24–32 c.
1 cup whipping cream	2 c.	3 c.	8 c. = 2 qt.

10. Last, have the class discuss patterns that they see in the T-chart and why those patterns are there. For example, students may notice that many of the whole numbers in each column are multiples of the recipe amounts.

11. Now you may wish to have the class work together to make a strawberry short-cake. If so, determine as a group what would be a reasonable amount to make, mix it, bake it, and enjoy!

Angles

Introduction

Children easily use angles in their world, when opening a door, bending an elbow, throwing a baseball, or opening a carton of milk. However, students often have difficulties understanding angles at school, since angles frequently are taught in an abstract manner.

Children must learn to see angles in a variety of contexts in order to solidify their understanding of what angles are. When presented with a representation of an angle, many children initially have difficulty comprehending what an angle is. For example, children may initially focus on how long the ray is, rather than how far one ray is turned from another.

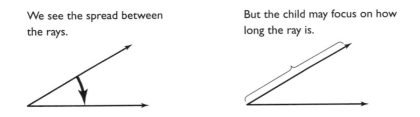

We see the spread between the rays.

But the child may focus on how long the ray is.

When presented with a hexagon during a discussion about angles, children may need to be reminded that they are not looking at the hexagon's area, but instead at the angles that are part of the hexagon.

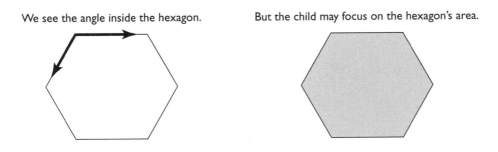

We see the angle inside the hexagon.

But the child may focus on the hexagon's area.

Through a variety of experiences in a variety of contexts, students come to make sense of angles.

In the lessons in this chapter, students learn about angles in a concrete manner that allows them to first see what angles are and then make sense of how angles can be measured. Through these lessons, students discover that angles, two rays that share an end point, are part of the world around them. They find angles in their world, some that turn and some that are stationary. Students describe and classify them according to benchmark angles, such as right angles and straight angles.

Other investigations in this chapter help students learn to see the angles that form polygons and use their knowledge of right angles and logic to identify the measurement of pattern block angles. Students also learn to measure angles, first with nonstandard units—wedges—and then with protractors that they make themselves.

What Is an Angle?

Overview
In this lesson, students put two straws together to create a device that makes angles of different sizes. The students learn that an angle refers to how far apart two rays are spread as they open the straws different amounts to represent angles that equal a quarter turn, a half turn, three-quarters of a turn, and a complete turn. After investigating things in the classroom that open to different angles, the students write their own definitions for *angle*.

Materials
◈ flexible straws, 2 per student and 4 additional straws for the teacher
◈ Writing paper, lined, 1 sheet per student

Vocabulary: angle, complete turn, half turn, quarter turn, ray, three-quarters of a turn, turn

Instructions

1. Before class, create a demonstration angle device with two straws. Cut one straw apart directly below the bendable section and throw away the section that has the flexible piece. Keep the rigid section.

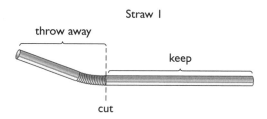

Pick up the other straw. Cut a slit in the part above the bendable section from the end to the part that bends.

Straw 2
Cut a slit in one side.

Slightly compress the slit, there insert it all the way into the long rigid piece from the first straw.

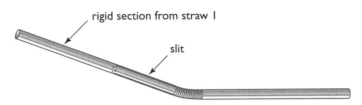

rigid section from straw 1

slit

2. To begin the lesson, show the students the angle device that you created. Tell the students that they will be investigating angles. Begin a vocabulary word chart for the angle lessons by writing *angle* on a piece of chart paper. Tell the students that by the end of this lesson, they will be able to write a definition for *angle* and find things in the class that open to different angles.

3. Explain to the students that the straws represent two rays, or parts of lines, that have the same end point. Show the students the device with the angle closed, so that the straws are right on top of each other. Then open the top straw a quarter turn, halfway, three-quarters of a turn, and then a complete turn. As you make different angles, list the names of the turns that you are making on the board.

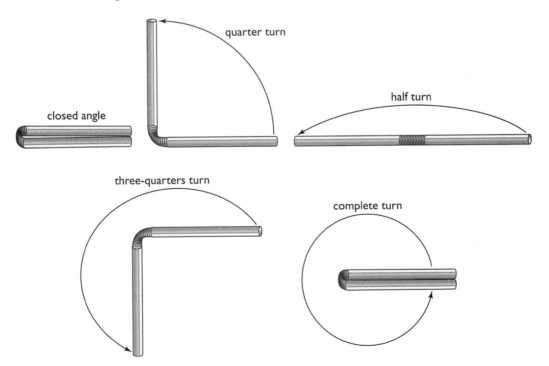

quarter turn

half turn

closed angle

three-quarters turn

complete turn

4. Tell the students that they will make their own angle devices. Provide each student with two straws and a pair of scissors. Have the students do each step as you model the procedures (see Instruction 1) with two straws of your own.

5. When the students finish, allow them some time to use their devices to make angles of their own. Then say the different turns listed on the board and direct the students to model them with their angle devices. Now ask the students to work in pairs in the same way, making angles and describing the kinds of turns that they make.

6. Next tell the students that they are going to look around the room and find things that open up to different angles, such as a door. Explain that they will list each item on a sheet of paper as well as the kinds of turns the item can make. For example, most doors can be closed and make quarter turns and half turns, but not three-quarter turns or complete turns.

7. As the students work, encourage them to use their straws to show the kinds of turns that the items can make. Some items that the students find may include a pair of scissors, a stapler, a paper cutter, and parts of the body such as elbows and mouths. Most pairs of scissors can make quarter turns but not half turns or three-quarter turns.

8. When the students finish, invite partners to share the items they found and the kinds of turns the items can make. Ask other students whether they agree with their classmates' statements. Have a student use the item to demonstrate the kinds of turns it can make.

9. Remind the children that they have been using and making angles all their lives. For example, they know the size of angle they need to open a door so they can walk through it, and they know how far to open the angle of the scissors to insert the sheet of paper they are going to cut. Tell the students that during other lessons on angles they will learn more precise ways to describe angles and what they do.

10. End the lesson by having partners discuss how they would explain to a friend what an angle is. Although you presented the mathematical definition at the beginning of the lesson—two rays that have a common end point—it is important that the students have their own way to explain what angles are. On their sheet of paper, have the students write their definition. When they are finished, have students share what they wrote, and then decide on a class definition for *angle*. Write this on the vocabulary word chart.

11. Keep the straw angle devices for the next lesson, *Body Angles and Simon Says*, and to illustrate what angles are in other lessons.

Body Angles and Simon Says

Overview

In this lesson, students explore different ways they can make acute, right, obtuse, and straight angles with their bodies. They then play Simon says to practice the vocabulary of these words, showing the meaning of each word by using arms, legs, or other body parts to make each kind of angle. The students contribute to a class chart that will serve as a reference for these benchmark angles.

Materials

◈ straw angle devices from *What Is an Angle?* (page 150), 1 per student
◈ sets of 1 of each kind of pattern block, 1 set per student

Vocabulary: angle, narrow, rhombus, vertex, wide

Instructions

1. Distribute the pattern blocks to the students. Ask each student to pick up a blue rhombus pattern block and look at it carefully. Ask the students to describe the shape in as many ways as they can.

2. When a student mentions that the "angles" or "corners" are different, ask her to explain what she means. Use the straw angle device to surround the two kinds of angles and to show the different kinds of angles to the students.

   Have them again describe the two different angles that the rhombus has. The students may say that one angle is wider and the other is narrower.

3. Have the students explain what angles are. On the vocabulary word chart, write any additional explanations that help the students understand angles.

4. Tell the students that an angle is formed when two rays have a common end point. That end point is called a *vertex*. Add this information and a sketch to the chart.

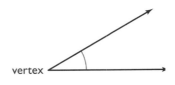

5. Ask the children to see what different kinds of angles they can make using their hands, fingers, and arms.

6. Have them make a special angle: a right angle. Explain that this angle is "just right," that it's an angle that is everywhere around us, such as the corner of papers, of books, of bookshelves, and so on. Write *right angle* on the vocabulary word chart and draw a sketch to illustrate the term.

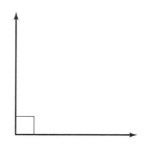

7. Ask the students to use their fingers to make right angles and to use their two hands to make right angles. Explain that mathematicians measure angles in degrees and that a right angle has a measure of 90 degrees. Write *90 degrees* next to the sketch of the right angle.

8. Ask the students to find right angles in the pattern blocks. Tell them to test their choices by holding an angle against the corner of a sheet of paper. Have the class identify the blocks that have right angles.

9. Next discuss the term *acute angle*. Explain that acute angles measure less than 90 degrees. Have the students make acute angles with their fingers, their hands, and their arms. On the word chart write the term, make several sketches, and write *less than 90 degrees*.

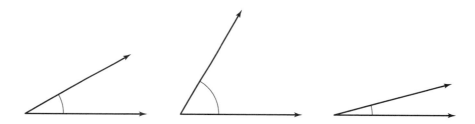

10. In the same way have the students make obtuse angles with their fingers, hands, and arms, and add the term *obtuse angle* to the word chart. Draw several examples of obtuse angles. Tell the students that obtuse angles measure greater than 90 degrees but less than 180 degrees.

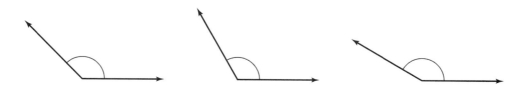

11. Last, introduce the term *straight angle*. Explain that it is an angle that has opened so wide that it is now a straight line and it measures 180 degrees. After you have the students make straight angles with their fingers, hands, and arms, add that term, a sketch, and the measurement to the chart.

12. Now play a game of Simon says to help the students become better acquainted with this new terminology. To play the game, have all the students stand up. Have them do what you say when you make statements such as the following:

"Simon says make a right angle with your fingers."

"Simon says make a straight angle with your arms."

"Simon says make a ninty-degree angle with your fingers."

"Simon says make a one-hundred-eighty-degree angle with your elbow."

"Simon says make an obtuse angle with your legs."

Occasionally make a command without saying, "Simon says." If the words *Simon says* do not precede your command, tell the students that they should not do what you say. Explain if they *do*, however, follow your command and you have not said, "Simon says," they must sit down and are out of the game. The game ends when there is only one person left standing.

◈ Hunt for Angles

Overview

In this lesson students become aware of objects in their environment that are made of different angles as they search for different kinds of angles in the classroom—acute, right, obtuse, and straight. The students divide a sheet of paper into sections and fill each section with sketches of the items they find. In a class discussion, they share their findings and then make a chart describing where different angles can be found.

Materials

◈ chart paper, 1–2 sheets

Vocabulary: acute angle, angle, obtuse angle, right angle, straight angle

Instructions

1. Use the vocabulary word chart to review with the students the different categories of angles they have learned about: acute, right, obtuse, and straight.

2. Have the students fold a sheet of blank paper in half, creating four sections, two on the front of the paper and two on the back. Have the students label each section with one kind of angle, make a sketch, and describe it in degrees.

3. Have the students look for these angles in items in the room. For example, a book leaning back on a shelf might make an obtuse angle. Bookcases are full of right angles. Corners where a wall meets the floor have right angles. Windowpanes have

right angles, as do floor tiles. Two pencils in a pencil can may meet at the bottom and create an acute angle. Each time students find an example of an angle, remind them to sketch the items that created that angle and write what the items are in the appropriate section of their paper.

4. When the students have found many examples of each kind of angle, bring them together for a whole-group discussion. Have students share what they discovered by pointing out an item in the room. For each item, have the class name the angle, describe it in degrees, and then find out if that is how the student categorized the angle.

5. Title a sheet of chart paper *Angles in Our Room*. On the chart, write the angle categories that the students searched for. List the items and the angles they made, and make a small sketch of each item in the corresponding category. Post the completed chart in the room or in the hall as a reminder of the angles that are in the students' environment.

Sorting Angles

Overview
In this lesson students find the angles that make up quadrilaterals and then classify angles in different ways. They draw a variety of quadrilaterals and cut apart the angles. After students sort the angles, they label the categories using their own descriptions. Then they learn the terms *right, acute,* and *obtuse* and use the corner of an index card to sort the angles according to those attributes.

Materials
- 9-by-12-inch white construction paper, 1 sheet per student and 1 for the teacher
- marker
- crayons with no paper covering, 1 per student and 1 for the teacher
- 3-by-5-inch index cards, 1 per student
- 3-inch sticky notes, at least 3 per small group of students
- rulers, 1 per student

Vocabulary: acute angle, angle, end point, horizontally, obtuse angle, quadrilateral, ray, right angle, vertex, vertices

Instructions
1. With the marker, draw a quadrilateral with no right angles on a sheet of construction paper taped to the board. Remind the students that a quadrilateral has four sides, but the sides can be different lengths. Highlight the four corners, or vertices,

by making a dot on each one. Lightly color in the quadrilateral with the side of a crayon. Draw an *x* in its center.

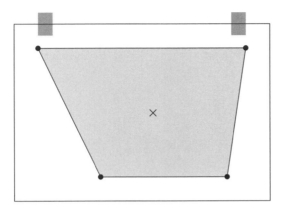

2. Explain that you are going to cut apart the sides of the quadrilateral to show the different angles that compose it. Cut apart the sides from the middle of each side to the *x* and draw arrows on the end of each line.

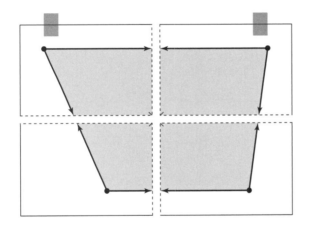

3. Tell the students that an angle is made up of two rays that begin at one end point and continue out forever. Explain that the arrows show how the rays continue out just like light shines out from a flashlight. Tape each angle to the board so that one ray is placed horizontally, so that the students will more easily focus on the angles.

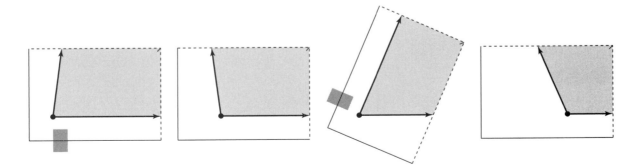

4. Divide the students into small groups and hand out the construction paper, crayons, and scissors. Explain to the students that they will each draw a quadrilateral, but they need to make sure that each quadrilateral in the group is different. Draw several kinds of quadrilaterals on the board as examples.

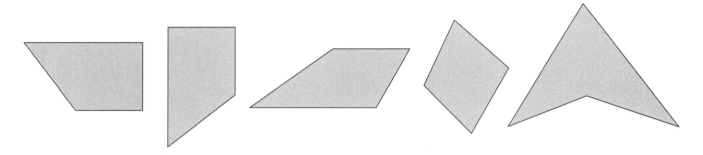

5. Tell the students that they will make their quadrilaterals large on the page. Remind them to lightly color the interior of their quadrilateral with a crayon, put a dot on each vertex, and then cut the angles out, as you just did. Explain that they will keep track of how to cut by making an *x* in the center of the quadrilateral and cutting from the edge of the paper, through the middle of the side, and to the *x* each time. Have the students make an arrow point on the end of each line to show the ray.

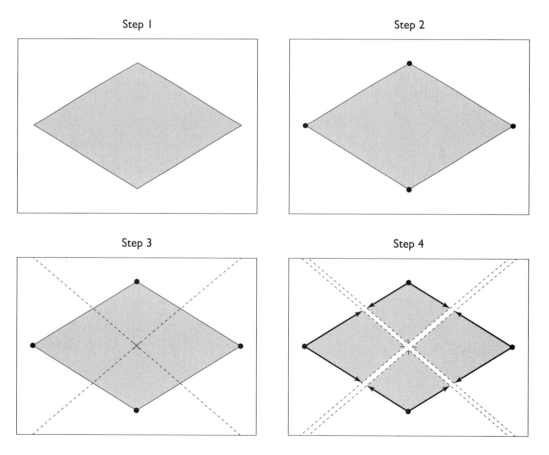

Then tell them to spread their collection of angles out on their desks.

6. Once everyone in their group is ready, direct students to talk about how their angles are the same and different and then sort them into different categories. The students may sort the angles in as many different groups as they wish. Give students a sticky note for each category they made. They will use them to label the categories with words that describe the angles in each category.

7. Have a whole-class discussion about the categories that the groups created. Ask each group to share the name of each category they made. Some groups may use mathematical terminology. Others may use everyday language. As each group shares, write the labels on the board. Discuss how their labels are similar and how they are different.

8. Hand out index cards and remind the students that mathematicians sort angles according to how they compare with a right angle. Explain that a right angle is the angle that they see on the corner of a piece of paper or an index card. Have the students pick up a card and find the right angle. Ask them to use the index card's corner to find the right angles in their pile. Explain that they should line up one line of an angle with one edge of the card. Tell the students that if the other line on the angle is hidden under the corner of the card, or if the other line is visible beyond the edge of the card, it is not a right angle. Have the students write *right angle* on the back of each right angle.

9. Next ask the students to find any angles that have a line hidden behind the card. Tell the students that these are called *acute angles*. Read some of the names that they called this kind of angle. For example, some students may have called these "skinny angles." Have the students write *acute angle* on the back of the angles.

10. Last, ask the students to find any angles that have a side that opens past the edge of the index card. Read some names that they called this kind of angle. For example, some students may have called these "big angles." Explain that these are called *obtuse angles*. Have the students label the back of their remaining angles.

11. Save these sets of angles for use in the next lesson, *Measuring Angles*.

◈ Measuring Angles

Overview

In this lesson students better understand angles by exploring how they can be measured. Students first try to measure a set of angles by using familiar measurement tools such as a ruler. They discover that the length of the ray is not the critical attribute, nor is the linear distance between the rays. Instead they learn that the spread between two rays is the critical attribute. Students then create a nonstandard unit for measuring angles—a wedge—and use it to measure angles.

Materials

- straw angle device from *What Is an Angle?* (page 150)
- rulers, 1 per pair of students
- half-sheets of copier paper
- pan balances, 2
- thermometers, 1 per small group of students
- dry lima beans, about 3 cups
- centimeter cubes, about 10 per pair of students
- *Measuring Angles* worksheets, 1 per pair of students (see Blackline Masters)
- overhead transparency of angles worksheet
- 3-by-5-inch index cards cut in half vertically, 1 half-card per pair of students
- sets of angles from *Sorting Angles* lesson (page 156)

Vocabulary: acute angles, angles, balance, nonstandard unit, obtuse angles, rays, right angles, thermometer, units, vertex, wedge

Instructions

1. Begin by reminding the students about what they know about right angles, acute angles, and obtuse angles. Have the students use their hands to show you examples of these kinds of angles. Have the students describe what an angle is. Focus their attention on how far apart the hands—or rays—are spread.

2. Next show the students an angle from the sets of angles that they made in the *Sorting Angles* lesson. Have the students identify the kind of angle it is. Tell the students that while they have a way to generally compare the angles, they have not yet explored a way to specifically measure the size of the angles.

3. Show the students some tools that they have used to measure during other lessons—cubes, beans, thermometers, pan balances, and rulers. Invite the students to use these or use copier paper to try to find a good way to measure the sizes of different angles. Provide them with the *Measuring Angles* worksheet and access to the measurement tools. Have the students begin their investigations.

4. As they work, watch to see how the students understand angles. Have the students explain why they think some tools work and some tools do not work for measuring angles. Some students may focus on the length of the rays or try to measure the linear distance from one ray to the other. If students choose to not use a specific tool, such as a pan balance or a thermometer, ask them why they aren't using that tool. If they have used, for example, a ruler to measure a ray, ask the students whether that number gives an indication about how wide apart an angle is spread. Encourage them to articulate what an angle is and what attribute of an angle should be measured.

5. After the students have explored different methods, lead a class discussion. Tape an angle onto the board. As the students share a method, have them use the specific tool and explain why it is or is not a good tool for measuring angles. Encourage the other students to add what they think. If students do not bring up the following points, challenge the students' thinking yourself:

- If students measure how long the rays are, for example, with cubes or a ruler, extend the rays farther, and remind the students that the rays continue out infinitely. Tell them that this angle is still the same because the rays are not spread apart any wider. Now show the students some angles that have different measurements because the rays are spread farther apart. Use the angle device to show the students the initial angle.

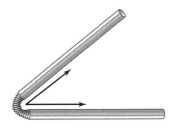

Then spread the device wider, and draw this new angle on the board. Next make the spread narrower than the first angle, and then draw that angle on the board.

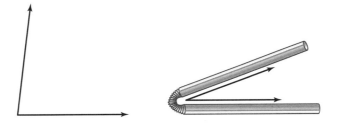

Some students may have difficulty understanding that an angle represents how far one ray is spread, or turned, from another ray. However, through additional experiences with angles in a variety of contexts, students will solidify this understanding.

- If students measure the linear distance between the rays, for example, with cubes or a ruler, use the same tool on the same angle in a different place, to demonstrate that the number changes even though the angle has not changed. Note that this way of measuring angles is not dependable, and that we must only have one number to describe a single angle. Tell the students that if you were designing a house and wanted to tell your builder over the phone what the angle of the roof should be, you would need one number that would help your builder understand what you wanted.

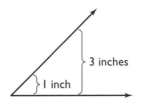

3 inches

1 inch

• If students use beans or cubes to fill in the space between the rays, use chalk to extend the rays. Tell the students that the angle has not changed. Use the straw angle device to show how the angle would look if it *did* change. Note, again, that this way of measuring angles is not dependable and wouldn't help explain to someone far away what the angle looks like.

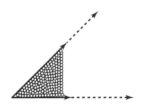

6. Next show the students how to create their own tool for measuring the spread between two rays. Hold up a half of an index card. Make a dot on the right-hand side, about half an inch above the bottom of the card. Draw a line from the left-hand corner to the dot. Cut along the line. Keep the wedge and throw away the rest of the card. Tell the students that they will cut out their own wedge and use it to measure their angles.

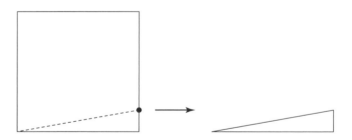

7. Select an angle from the overhead transparency and show the students how to use the wedge, demonstrating as you speak. Tell the students to place the point of the wedge right on the vertex of the angle, lining up the bottom of the wedge with the bottom ray. With an overhead pen lightly draw a line along the top of the wedge. Keeping the point of the wedge on the vertex of the angle, line up the bottom of the wedge with the pen line, and lightly draw another line along the top of the wedge. Continue marking each wedge width until no more wedges fit inside the angle. Count the number of wedges and explain that the angle measures that number of wedges.

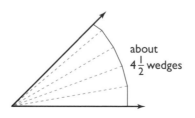

about $4\frac{1}{2}$ wedges

8. Pass out the index cards and scissors. Ask the students to cut their own narrow wedge. Tell them to then select an angle on their worksheet, estimate how many wedges wide it is, and measure it with the wedge. Have the students use their wedge to measure the rest of the angles, recording the measurement of each one. As the students work, support them as necessary. Some students may have initial difficulty placing the point of the wedge on the vertex of the angle. Some may be perplexed about how to use their wedge to measure Angle C, since it is more than 180 degrees.

9. When the students finish, have a class discussion about what they discovered about using a wedge to measure an angle. Have the students share their measurements for Angle A, and if their measurements differ, why that is the case. For example, students may say that their wedges vary somewhat in size. If this comes up, ask the students whether a larger wedge creates a larger measurement or a smaller measurement, and why they think that. It may not be immediately apparent to all students that larger wedges will produce smaller measurements. To identify this inverse relationship, find the class's smallest and largest measurements for Angle B. Write these numbers on the board. Have the students who found these measurements compare their wedges to see which is larger and which is smaller. If the wedges are about the same size, ask the students why the measurements differ. The students may say that it's hard to measure exactly. Do the same with Angle B.

10. Last, discuss how Angle C differs from the other angles and how they measured it. Some students may have measured the smaller angle, while others may have measured the three-quarter turn. Point out the students the symbol used to clarify the angle's turn.

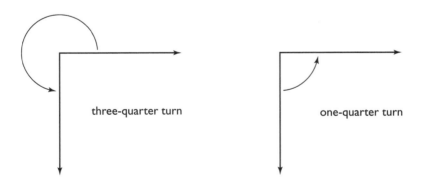

three-quarter turn   one-quarter turn

11. Now invite the students to use their wedges to predict and then measure the angles they made during the *Sorting Angles* lesson.

12. End the lesson by having students explain what an angle is and what it isn't. List their statements on the board under the headings *An angle is . . .* and *An angle is not. . . .* For example, a student may say, "An angle is how far apart two rays are spread," or "An angle is not how long the lines are."

 **Waxed Paper Protractors**

Overview

In this lesson students identify how angles are used in the outside world. Then they create a tool to measure angles—a waxed paper protractor. After they make their protractors, the students use the fact that 360 degrees describes the turn in a complete circle to identify the number of degrees in each wedge of their protractor. Then they learn how to use their protractors to make close estimates of the angles of both concave and convex polygons.

Materials

- ❖ 12-inch waxed paper squares, 1 per student
- ❖ waxed paper protractor (see Instruction 5)
- ❖ *Measuring Polygon Angles* worksheets, 1 per student (see Blackline Masters)
- ❖ overhead transparency of *Measuring Polygon Angles* worksheet
- ❖ overhead transparency of waxed paper protractor (see Blackline Masters)
- ❖ straw angle device from *What Is an Angle?* (page 150)

Vocabulary: angles, central point, concave, convex, degree, divide, estimate, measure, multiplication, protractor, repeated addition, wedge

Instructions

1. Before class, make a waxed paper protractor, following the procedure in Instruction 5.

2. Begin the lesson by discussing, with the students, people who measure angles in the real world. Brainstorm a list of things people who work with angles do and write them on the board. The list may look like this:

Architects

the angle of a roof

the angles at which walls join

the angles walls make as they go straight up

Furniture and Car Designers

the angles of seats

the angles that arms and legs make so that people fit comfortably inside a car

Boat Navigators and Airplane Pilots

the location of the North Star and angles to identify where they are

maps and angles to identify a boat or plane's location

GPS systems, which use angular information from a set of satellites to find locations

Game Players

marbles

pool

City Planners and Surveyors

angles of streets and blocks

information about land dimensions

3. Explain to the students that all these people have standard methods for measuring angles so they can communicate with other people. For example, an architect needs to explain to the builder what angle the roof must be, so their "wedges" must be the same. Tell the students that a protractor is a tool that can measure angles in a standard way.

4. Show the students the waxed paper protractor that you previously made. Then provide each student with a waxed paper square and scissors.

5. As you model how to make a waxed paper protractor, have the students perform each step:

   a. Fold the paper square in half vertically. Crease the fold well.

   b. Keeping the original fold, fold the paper again in half, this time horizontally.

   c. Again fold the paper in half like a triangle, bringing the perpendicular edges together and maintaining the central fold.

   d. Once again fold the paper in half, bringing the outside edges together and maintaining the central point.

   e. Cut off the top edge so the all the edges are even.

   ─ ─ ┼ ─╳─ ─ ─ ─ ─ ─ cut off extra

f. Open the protractor.

6. Ask the students to count the wedges in their protractor. Remind the students that there are 360 degrees in the complete turn in a circle. Use the straw angle device to illustrate a complete rotation. Have them use this information to identify the number of degrees in a straight angle (180). Then ask the students to use this information to identify how many degrees are in each wedge. Have the students share their answers and how they figured them. For example, some students may say, "I divided three hundred sixty by sixteen and got twenty-two and a half." Another student might come to the same answer by dividing 180 by 8, or dividing 90 by 4.

7. On the board draw an angle. Use the waxed paper protractor to show the students how to center the protractor on the angle's vertex and line up one ray with a line on the protractor. Then show them how to count the wedges that are within the angle. Ask the students to figure out how that information can help them find the angle. For example, students may use repeated addition ($22\frac{1}{2}° + 22\frac{1}{2}° = 45°$) or multiplication ($2 \times 22\frac{1}{2}° = 45°$) to identify the angle. As a group, decide how to estimate parts of wedges and convert that information into degrees. Add that number to the previous number ($45° +$ about $11° = 56°$). (**Note:** If you have a chalkboard that makes chalk lines that aren't visible through the waxed paper protractor, you will need to draw the angle on paper with a black marker and tape it to the board.)

8. Distribute the *Measuring Polygon Angles* worksheets. Ask the students to find concave polygons that have at least one angle larger than 180 degrees. Have the students work in pairs to estimate and then measure each angle, using their waxed paper protractors.

9. As students work, observe their different strategies and provide them with support as necessary. You may find that some students initially have difficulty lining up the protractor correctly, especially when measuring convex angles.

10. When the students finish, begin a group discussion. First have them share what was easy or what was hard about using the protractor. For example, some students may say that it was hard to hold it down, or it was hard to remember which angle on the polygon they were trying to measure. Students may also identify particular polygons that were difficult to measure. Next ask the students what they did to

make the task easier. For example, some students may have made a with the measurement of each wedge:

Wedges	Angles
1	$22\frac{1}{2}°$
2	$45°$
3	$67\frac{1}{2}°$
4	$90°$
5	$112\frac{1}{2}°$
6	$135°$
7	$157\frac{1}{2}°$
8	$180°$
9	$202\frac{1}{2}°$
10	$225°$
11	$247\frac{1}{2}°$
12	$270°$
13	$292\frac{1}{2}°$
14	$315°$
15	$337\frac{1}{2}°$
16	$360°$

Record this on chart paper. Ask the students to identify the patterns that they see in the numbers and consider why they are there.

11. Place the transparency of the worksheet on the overhead. Begin a class discussion about the students' results and ask them to share the measurements that they identified. Have the students discuss any differences in their answers, using the transparency of the waxed paper protractor to illustrate students' thinking. Students may state that differences are due to estimations, slight differences in protractors, or measurement errors.

12. Save the protractors and the T-chart to use with *Measuring with Plastic Protractors* (page 174).

 **Combining Angles**

Overview
In this lesson students draw a variety of triangles and color the angles in different colors. Then, after tearing off the angles, the students arrange them together so that each vertex is touching, to see what occurs when all the angles in a triangle are combined.

They discuss whether the outcome is always the same and why. Another day students investigate quadrilaterals in the same way.

Materials
◈ crayons, 1 black and at least 3 other colors per pair of students
◈ rulers, 1 per pair of students
◈ chart paper, 1 sheet

Vocabulary: angle, degrees, quadrilateral, rotate, straight angle, triangle, vertex, vertices

Instructions
Day 1

1. Distribute the materials. Explain to the students that they are going to investigate what happens when angles are added together, just as numbers can be added together. Tell them that today they are going to find out what happens when they combine all the angles in a triangle.

2. Ask each pair of students to draw three very large triangles on one sheet of paper using a black crayon. Tell them to make their lines dark and to try to make the three triangles look as different as possible.

3. Now, tell them that they are to explore what happens when they combine the angles in their triangle. Cut out a triangle as an example. Color the angles, using a different-colored crayon for each. Remind the students to color the angle at least an inch from the vertex, leaving some of the original paper color visible in the middle of the triangle. Tear off each angle. Emphasize that they must tear off the angles rather than cut them, so they will be able to tell where the vertex is.

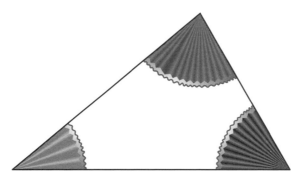

4. Show the students how they will combine the angles. Make a small dot on a sheet of blank paper. Explain to the students that each angle vertex must touch that point, and that the angles must be rotated until their sides touch each other. Glue

two angles together onto the blank paper as an example. Wonder aloud how the new angle will look when all three angles are combined.

5. Tell the students that after they investigate each of their three triangles, they are to compare all three outcomes and write about what they discovered.

6. When the students finish, have them share their discoveries. Most students will note that when they combined the three angles of a triangle, the new angle was a straight angle, or 180 degrees. Wonder aloud whether that will always happen. If the students are not convinced, invite them to make new triangles to see whether they can produce a different outcome.

7. As the children watch, explain that you are going to cut out a very large triangle from a sheet of chart paper. Color and tear off the angles. Ask the students to predict what new angle will be made when you combine these angles. The very large size of this new triangle will challenge the students to consider whether their previous outcome will still occur.

8. Put the angles together, making a straight angle once again.

9. Last, wonder aloud why the same thing happens for all triangles, even though the triangles have different-size angles, and even though the triangles were different sizes. Have partners discuss this question and then share their explanations with the group. Encourage the students to respond to others' theories. For example, one student might say that a triangle has three equal angles, an idea with which other students may disagree. Other students may say that when one angle gets larger, the other angles have to get smaller, so the total is the same.

Day 2

1. Do the same lesson with quadrilaterals. Draw a variety of quadrilaterals on the board as examples.

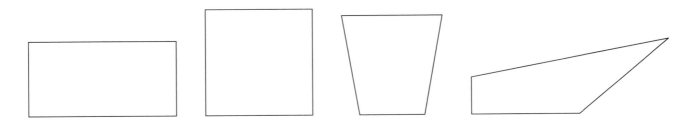

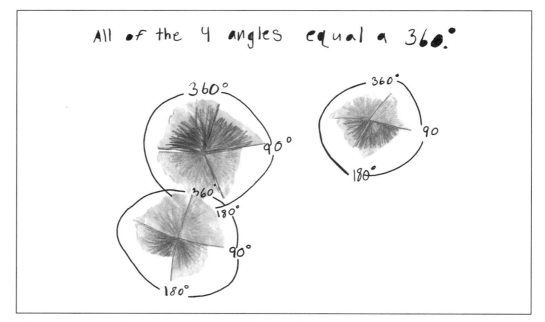

All of the 4 angles equal a 360°

Figure 4–1 *Elena discovered that the angles in each of her quadrilaterals totaled 360 degrees.*

2. Investigate the angles in the same way. The students will find that when the four angles are combined, they make a circular rotation of 360 degrees (see Figure 4–1). When you gather the students for a discussion, use a concave quadrilateral to test their theories.

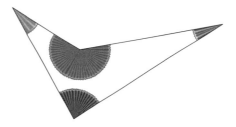

The students will discover that even this unusual quadrilateral has angles that total 360 degrees. Again invite a discussion about whether this will always happen and, if the students are sure that this will be the case, why this happens. As the students discuss their theories with each other, encourage them to compare this outcome with that of the triangle investigation and consider why the different totals occurred. Some students may wonder about pentagons and hexagons. Encourage this investigation, as there is an interesting pattern that students will discover—each polygon's total angles increase by 180 degrees. Students will enjoy pondering why this happens.

Number of Sides	Total Degrees
3	180
4	360
5	540
6	720

Pattern Block Angles

Overview

In this lesson students develop their understandings of angles by solving a problem: *What are the measurements of each of the angles in each of the pattern blocks?* Students find equivalent angles and use what they have learned about the measurement of benchmark angles, such as right angles, straight angles, and full circle rotations, to deduce the measurement of each angle in their set of pattern blocks.

Materials

- ◈ straw angle device from *What Is an Angle?* (page 150)
- ◈ set of overhead pattern blocks
- ◈ sets of pattern blocks containing at least 4 hexagons, 8 trapezoids, 8 triangles, 8 squares, 8 blue rhombi, and 16 tan rhombi, 1 set per small group of students

Vocabulary: angle, circle, degrees, hexagon, horizontal, infinity, point, ray, rhombus, right angle, square, straight angle, three-quarter angle, trapezoid, triangle, vertex

Instructions

1. Before beginning the investigation you may want to review with the students what angles are. On the board make a dot, and tell the students that this represents a point called the *vertex* of the angle. Then draw a horizontal ray out from the vertex, telling the students to imagine a flashlight that sends out a ray of light forever in that direction. Tell the students that they can imagine that ray continues through the wall, outside the school, and on into infinity. Explain that the arrow on the end shows that the line is infinitely long. Now draw a diagonal ray from the same point. Explain that this might represent another ray of light that goes out from the same point forever. Finally, point out that the angle is the spread between the rays.

2. You may also wish to review the measurements of the benchmark angles: right angles (90 degrees), straight angles (180 degrees), the three-quarter-turn angles (270 degrees), and the full turn or circles (360 degrees).

3. Now introduce the investigation. Tell the students that they are going to work in groups to find the measurement of each angle in the sets of pattern blocks you have put together. Remind the students how to see the angles in the pattern blocks. On the overhead, place a hexagon. Use the straw angle device to show the students one of the angles, and then remove the straws. With an overhead marker trace the two adjacent sides of the block that create that angle.

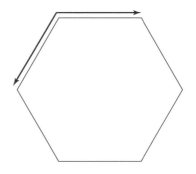

Remove the block so the students can clearly see those two sides. Draw a point where the lines come together and tell the students it is the vertex of that angle. Draw arrows on the ends of the lines and remind the students that those lines extend out infinitely. To check how the students see the angles, have them each select a hexagon and figure out how many angles the hexagon has. If students have difficulty seeing all six angles, hold the straw angle device against each of the six angles of the hexagon.

4. Next place a blue rhombus on the overhead and ask the students how many angles it has, and whether all the angles are the same size. Tell the students that they will determine how many degrees each of those angles measures.

5. Draw that rhombus on the overhead. Tell the students that they will need to record their thinking by tracing each pattern block that they investigate. Draw partial circles inside each angle, explaining that this is a symbol we use to indicate the angle that is being discussed.

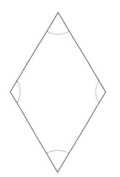

Tell the students that they will figure out the number of degrees in each angle, write that number next to the angle, and then explain in writing how they figured it out.

6. Tell the students that they can figure out each angle in all the pattern blocks by using what they know about one angle to figure out a new angle, and by using information about benchmark angles. Review the measurements of benchmark angles—right angles measure 90 degrees, straight angles measure 180 degrees, and full circles measure 360 degrees. Distribute the sets of pattern blocks and have the students begin the investigation.

7. As the students work, observe them to see how they approach the task. Some students may forget that they are investigating angles, and revert to area investigations that they have previously done with pattern blocks. If so, remind them that they are investigating the angles, and use the straw angle device to reorient them. You may need to trace two sides of the block on their paper, adding the vertex point and the rays' arrows, to help them remember how to see the angles. Depending on your students' level of experience, they may easily use what they know about angles to figure out what they don't know.

8. If many of your students simply estimate the angles, remind them that there are ways to find the exact measurement of each angle. Allow the students time to work through the challenges this problem presents. However, you may need to provide some students with additional support. Possible support includes the following:

   • Show the students the square. Suggest that they use the square to figure out the measure of the acute angles in the tan rhombus. (Three of the acute angles equal the square corner, so since ninty divided by three is thirty, each acute angle is 30 degrees).

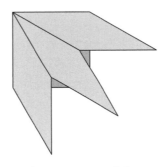

   Once the students identify the measure of this angle, they often are able to use that information to find the measures of the other angles. For example, they see that two of those angles equal the angles in the triangle, and since $30 + 30 = 60$, the angles in the triangle measure 60 degrees.

   • Make a rotation of the same kind of pattern block around a point. The students can use what they know about the number of degrees in a circle to figure out the angle of each block (360 degrees divided by 6 blocks equals 60 degrees).

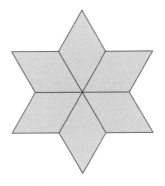

9. When the students are finished, begin a discussion. Have a group of students draw on the board the diagram of a pattern block they investigated, and explain how

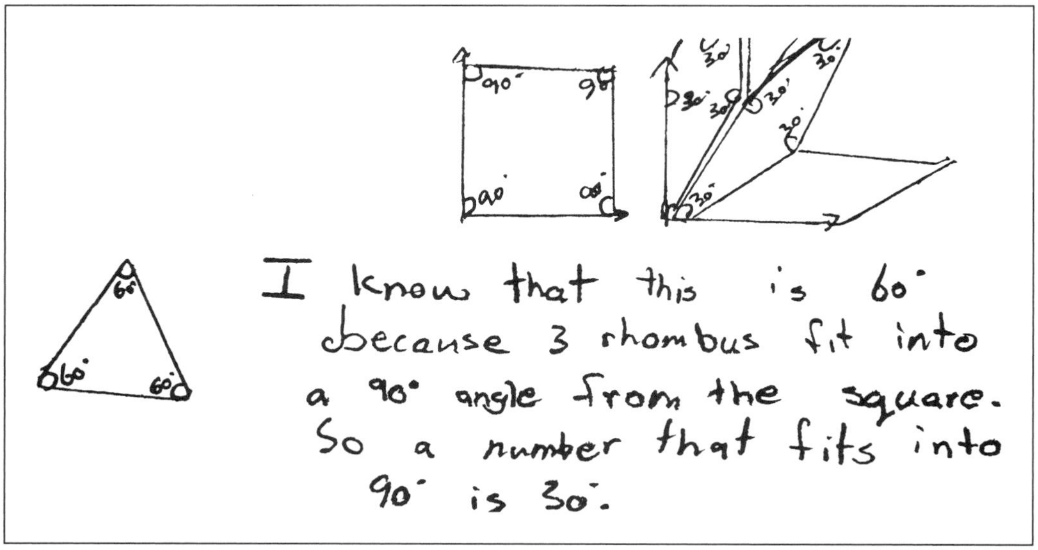

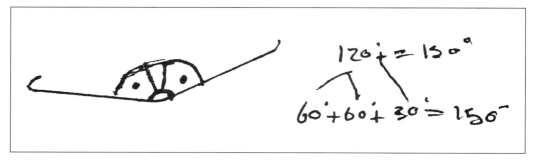

Figure 4–2 *Hannah knew that the square's right angle measures 90 degrees. Since three of the tan rhombus's narrow angles equal 90 degrees, they must each measure 30 degrees. And two of them equal an angle in the triangle, so the triangle's angle must equal 60 degrees.*

Figure 4–3 *Hannah found that the hexagon's angles measured 150 degrees. When she combined two 60 degree angles and the 30 degree angle from the tan rhombus, she discovered it was equivalent to the angles of a hexagon.*

they figured out the measure of each angle. (See Figures 4–2 and 4–3.) Have the other students listen to the presentation and explain those students' thinking in their own words. Then have the listeners consider how their information compares with what the others said. Encourage the students in the class to discuss with each other the differences they found, make logical arguments about what they think, and come to an agreement on their own.

◈ Measuring with Plastic Protractors

Overview

In this lesson, students develop their understanding of angles by making an angle estimator, a tool that lets them make an angle that widens and narrows. The students create angles with their estimators and then learn how to use a traditional protractor to measure angles.

Materials

◈ angle estimator pattern (see Blackline Masters)

◈ cardstock in two contrasting colors, 1 sheet of each color per student and 1 each for the teacher

◈ protractors from *Waxed Paper Protractors* lesson (page 164), 1 per pair of students

◈ T-chart from *Waxed Paper Protractors* lesson (page 167)

◈ plastic protractors, 1 per student (**Note:** Circular protractors are easier for students to use than half-circle protractors.)

Vocabulary: angle, circle, degree, protractor, right angle, rotate, straight angle, unit, vertex

Instructions

1. Before class, duplicate the angle estimator pattern on each piece of cardstock. Also, make an angle estimator for yourself. Cut out a circle of each color card-stock and cut a slit along the line in each circle. Open up each slit and interlock them together so they rotate, making an angle that widens and narrows.

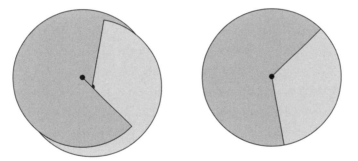

2. Begin the lesson by showing the students your angle estimator and how to rotate the top circle to widen and narrow the different-colored angle. Pass a cardstock circle of each color and a pair of scissors to each student. Have them cut out the circles and cut the slits to the center of each circle. Show the students how to open up the slits and interlock the circles together so the circles rotate, making an angle that widens and narrows.

3. Ask the students to make sure that their angle estimators show angles of the same color. Then have the students make the narrowest angle that they can. Then have them make the widest angle that they can. Ask the students to find the ver-tex, or center point, of their angles.

4. Use the angle estimators to have the students review how benchmark angles (right angles, straight angles, three-quarter turns, and complete turns or circles) look. Remind the students of the number of degrees that each of these benchmark angles measures. Play Simon says (see Instruction 12 on page 155) with the students making benchmark angles with the angle estimators.

5. Next, show the students a plastic protractor. Explain to the students that a protractor measures angles in the same way the waxed paper protractor measured angles, but this protractor is much more precise. Provide each student with a protractor. Allow the students time to look closely at the protractor and to see if they can figure out how to create benchmark angles with their estimator and measure them with their protractor.

6. Have students share what they noticed about the protractor and how they think it can be used to measure an angle. During the discussion, have the students identify the patterns in the numbers on the protractor's edge, the value of each space between the shorter lines (one unit called a degree), the value of the spaces between the longer lines, and how the numbers on some protractors grow larger from left to right and from right to left.

7. Demonstrate for the students how the protractor measures angles. Gather the students closely around you. Open your angle estimator to about 45 degrees and tape it to the board. Show the students the center hole of the protractor, and explain that the hole must cover the vertex of the angle. Then show the students the 0 line that must line up with one ray of the angle. Next have the students read the multiples of ten that grow larger from the 0: 10, 20, 30, 40, and so on. Then have the students count the value of each remaining space: 41, 42, 43, 44, 45 degrees. When students first learn to use a protractor, it helps to have them begin at the 0 point and then count by tens and then ones so they focus on how the angle spreads. If your protractors are the half-circle variety, show students how to use the protractor to measure angles larger than 180 degrees.

8. Provide each pair of students with a waxed paper protractor. Have them work together to use the plastic protractor to measure the degrees in each wedge. Encourage students to help each other, and support those who need help. Have the students compare their measurements to the T-chart from the *Waxed Paper Protractors* lesson.

9. Now retrieve the waxed paper protractors and show the students how to practice using the plastic protractors with their angle estimators. Demonstrate several angles. Be sure to include an angle larger than 180 degrees, especially if the protractors are half-circles, and help students understand how to measure these larger angles.

10. Invite the students to work in pairs to practice making angles, estimating how many degrees they are, and then using the protractor to measure them. Check to see that the students are using their protractors correctly. Tell the students that they will use this skill in a game during a future lesson.

11. Save the angle estimators for the next lesson, *The Target Angle Game*.

The Target Angle Game

Overview

In this lesson, students use their angle estimators from the previous lesson (*Measuring with Plastic Protractors*) to play a game. The students roll dice to identify a target angle. Then they use their angle estimator to make an angle they think has that measurement. Next they use a protractor to find out the actual measurement of that angle. Last they figure out how far off their estimate is from the actual measurement to determine their points. The students end the game by adding their points to find the winner—the person with the fewest points.

Materials

- angle estimators from *Measuring with Plastic Protractors* lesson, 1 per student
- regular dot dice, 2 per pair of students
- sticky circles, 3 per pair of dice
- plastic protractors, 1 per pair of students
- *Target Angle* recording sheets, 1 per student (see Blackline Masters)

Vocabulary: angle, difference, estimate, hundreds place, landmark angle, protractor, tens place, vertex

Instructions

1. Prior to the lesson, prepare the dice. Leave one die in each set as it is. On the other die cover the 4, 5, and 6 with sticky circles, available in office supply stores. On one sticky circle, draw one dot, on another face, draw two dots, and leave the third face blank. (Alternatively, use blank wooden cubes. On two faces, draw one dot; on two other faces, draw two dots. Draw three dots on the fifth face, and leave the last face blank.)

2. Begin by handing out the angle estimators and telling the students that they will use their angle estimators from a previous lesson to play a game. Explain to the students that they will need to use what they know about benchmark angles to play the game. Remind the students that benchmarks are like landmarks: "In a city, a tall building can be a landmark. In the country, a nearby mountain can be a landmark. It helps you keep track of where you are. Landmark numbers, such as one hundred and one thousand, also help you keep track of where you are when you use strategies for computation. In the same way, benchmark angles will help you keep track and make estimates when you are working with angles."

3. Review the names and measures of right angles, straight angles, three-quarter-turn angles, and full turns, or circles.

4. Give the students an opportunity to use their angle estimators to make land-mark angles. Then ask the students to make angles such as 100 degrees, 210 degrees, and 340 degrees. Remind the students that they may find it help-ful to make the closest benchmark angle first, and then make the angle larger or smaller according to whether the target angle is larger or smaller than the benchmark angle.

5. Gather the students in a circle on the rug to demonstrate how to play the game. Show the students the materials that they will use: a regular dot die, a modified dot die, a protractor, an angle estimator, and a recording sheet. Explain to the students that this is a partner game in which they should try to get as few points as possible. In this game they estimate angles as closely as possible and on each turn they get points for how far off the estimate is.

6. Demonstrate the game with a student volunteer. Have the students read the label on the first column of the recording sheet, Target Angle. Show the students the two dice, which you will roll to find out the size of the angle that you're going to try to show. Explain that the die with sticky circles tells the hun-dreds place. Roll the die and write that number in the hundreds place. Explain to the students that if the blank face comes up, they will leave the hundreds place blank.

7. Next explain to the students that the other die is the tens place. Roll it and write that number in the tens place. Now have the students read the number of degrees in the target angle, the angle that you are going to try to make.

8. Have the students read the label on the next column, Estimate. Hold up your angle estimator so that the angle is very narrow. Remind the students about the color of the angle that you are making. Slowly begin to widen the angle. Ask the students to hold up a hand when they think they see the target angle.

9. When a majority of the students' hands are up, stop widening the angle.

10. Now use a protractor to measure the angle, explaining the process as you perform each step. Tell the students that they must first place the protractor on the angle so that the words are readable. (When a protractor is placed upside down, the words will appear backward.) Tell the students that the second step is to place the hole of the protractor on the angle's vertex. Next explain the third step: aligning the protractor's 0 line with one ray of the angle. The fourth step is to identify the width of the angle by counting up from zero by tens and then by ones. (If you are using a half-circle protractor, you may wish to have the students measure angles larger than 180 degrees by measuring the other angle and

subtracting the number from 360. Ask the students to explain why that tells the angle measurement of the first color.)

11. Write the measurement of the angle on your recording sheet in the Estimate column.

12. Next, have the students read the label of the final column, Difference (Points). Have the students mentally figure the difference between the target angle and your estimate. Then write that figure in the last space.

13. Have your partner repeat the entire process—rolling a target angle, estimating its size, measuring with a protractor, and writing the information on his or her own recording sheet. Then explain that after five rounds, each player totals his or her score. Explain that the player with the fewest points wins that game.

14. Provide partners with a set of dice, a protractor, and two recording sheets.

15. As the students play, watch to see how they use the protractor. You may have to help students first think about which color paper shows their angle, so they know what part of the circle they are focusing on. Students may also need help lining up the protractor correctly. Still other students will need help using benchmark angles to make good estimates for the target angle.

16. After students play several games, bring them together for a discussion. Ask them to explain how they estimated their angles. Many students will describe strategies based on finding a benchmark angle. For example, if a student is trying to show an angle of 110 degrees, the student might say, "I know it's more than ninety degrees, so I make a right angle. Then I think of where one hundred eighty would be, and I know it has to be a lot closer to ninety." Over time, students develop a sense of the size of the 10-degree increments, and their estimates become more exact. (See Figure 4–4.)

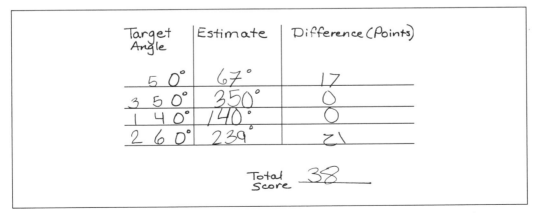

Figure 4–4 *Amanda's angle estimates matched or were very close to her target angles.*

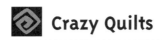 **Crazy Quilts**

Overview

In this lesson, students draw and then color crazy quilt patches made of straight lines. Then the students estimate the angles they created and measure them with protractors. Last, the students color their patches, which are then combined to make a class quilt.

Materials

- ❖ rulers, 1 per student
- ❖ plastic protractors, 1 per student
- ❖ crayons or colored pencils, 1 set per small group of students
- ❖ black or other dark-colored paper, about 3 feet wide and as long as needed to provide a backdrop for students' crazy quilt patches
- ❖ optional: fine-line black markers, 1 per student

Vocabulary: angles, estimate, lines, measure, polygon, protractor, random

Instructions

1. Begin by telling the students that they are going to work together to make a class quilt. Lay several sheets of blank $8\frac{1}{2}$-by-11-inch paper side by side to show the students the paper "quilt patches" that they will put together to make a class crazy quilt. Explain to the students that crazy quilt patches look a bit crazy because the lines point randomly in different directions.

2. Demonstrate what the students will do. With a ruler, draw four to six straight lines on a sheet of paper, angling the lines in different directions. Tell the students that they, too, will draw four to six lines on their papers, making the lines go from one edge of the paper to another. Encourage the students to all make different, unique designs.

3. Explain that once they have made all their lines, the students will estimate and then measure as many angles in their patch as possible. To do this, tell them that next to each angle they will make a curved line to identify the angle that they are measuring and write E and their estimate. Explain that lastly, they will measure each angle with a protractor and write M and the number of degrees that it actually measures.

4. Tell the students that they will color the polygons created by the lines they've drawn, making those that touch different colors. Explain that they need to color lightly so that the measurements can be seen through the color. (See Figure 4–5.)

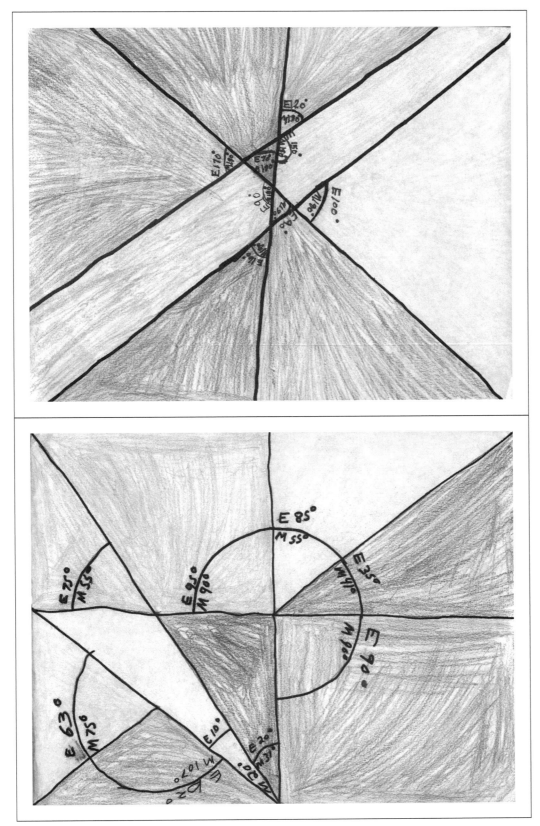

Figure 4–5 *The crazy quilt lesson provided students with an engaging opportunity to create, estimate, and measure angles.*

5. Hand out the materials and have the students get to work. When the students finish, ask them to explain in writing how to make a good estimate.

6. Optionally, invite the students to use a marker to darken their lines and make their measurements more visible.

7. Gather the students in a circle and have them place the patches on the floor. Ask the students how the patches can be arranged to create a rectangular array. Explore the different rectangular arrangements that are possible and decide as a group on the arrangement that the students prefer. You may find that students need to make more patches to complete an array.

8. Glue the patches onto the black or dark-colored paper, leaving strips of black between each patch.

CHAPTER 5

Weight

Introduction

When measuring weight, students can no longer trust what they see. While students can use their eyes to compare length, area, and volume, the size of an object does not necessarily correlate to its weight; small objects can weigh more than large objects. What does help students compare and estimate weights is how an object feels when it's held—its heft.

Technically, weight measures the pull of gravity on an object, while mass measures the amount of matter, or "stuff," that makes up an object. While identical items may have different weights on different planets because of differences in gravity, those of us who live on Earth experience mass and weight in nearly the same way. So this chapter addresses both weight and mass, with U.S. customary units used for weight and metric units used for mass.

In these lessons, students have opportunities to experience how benchmark weights feel. In order to develop and retain a sense of these weights, students find things in their world with weights of 1 pound and 5 pounds and masses of 1 gram and 1 kilogram.

Students learn to use and interpret scales and other measurement devices while investigating weight in a variety of contexts. They put together packages of books for an imaginary birthday present and find combinations of fruit for an imaginary 3-pound fruit salad. Students decide whether it's better to buy apple juice for a party in a plastic jug or juice boxes, after considering a variety of factors such as the mass of the trash that each generates. Students collect food for a food drive, each day estimating and weighing the donations and finding how far they are from their goal. Throughout these lessons, students think, reason, solve problems, and communicate about their growing understandings of measurement.

What Do You Know? What Can You Discover?

Overview

In this introductory lesson, students discuss their prior knowledge about weight, what *heavy* and *light* mean, and why and how people weigh things in the world. Then groups of students explore a single scale to find out what they can discover about it. During a class discussion, students compare differences in scales: how they work, number patterns that appear on them, different maximum weights they show, and different units that they measure.

Materials

❖ various scales, such as food scales, postal scales, spring scales, balance scales, and bathroom scales, 1 per small group of students
❖ 36-by-40-inch chart paper, 1 sheet per small group of students
❖ markers, 1 per small group of students

Vocabulary: column, compare, grams, heavy, light, multiples, ounces, pounds, scale, units, zero

Instructions

1. Begin the lesson by telling the students that each person brings different background experiences with him or her, and that a group has a "collective intelligence." Explain that they will work in groups to find out what they know about weight. Ask the groups to think of things that are heavy and things that are light and list them on a sheet of paper. Make sure that the students, especially English language learners, differentiate between a light weight and the light we turn on to see better.

2. After the discussion, invite the groups to share what they said. As they share, ask them to explain how they know an item is heavy or light, and list this information on the board. For example, the list might look like this:

Heavy Things	**Light Things**
elephants	a balloon
trucks	cell phones
a twelve-pack of soda	a plastic grocery bag

3. Have students share their disagreements so that they realize *heavy* and *light* are relative terms. For example, a brick may be heavy to a three-year-old but light to a weightlifter. Encourage this kind of discussion, as it helps students consider the complexities of the concept of weight. The students may also decide that an item like a brick needs an additional column such as Medium-Weight Things, or that an item like a dream would need a column such as Things That Don't Have Weight. If these ideas come up, adapt the chart on the board accordingly.

4. Have the students discuss whether small things are always light and large things are always heavy. If students believe this to be true, keep this in mind during other investigations, and include small items that are heavier than larger items.

5. Now turn the discussion to situations where people want to know the weight of something and how they find it out. For example, some students may suggest that customers at a grocery store might want to choose the largest piece of meat, so they will read the packaging to find out its weight in pounds. Other students may say that doctors track children's weight to see whether they are growing normally and do so by having the children stand on a scale. Have several students share their thoughts, and ask the other students whether they have encountered similar situations.

6. On the board write *A purse and a book in our classroom* and *Your dog and the dog of your friend in Mexico* side by side. Ask groups of students to think of a plan for how they would compare the weights in each of these two different situations. Have several students share what they would do. As they share, list beneath each phrase what they say. For example, for the first situation, the students might consider comparing the items directly, saying, "Hold them in different hands and see how they feel." Introduce the term *heft* as a way to describe what we do to feel which item is heavier. In the second situation it is not possible to directly compare, so they might say, "Have your friend weigh his dog on a scale and tell you how many pounds he weighs. Then weigh your dog and compare both numbers." Again encourage discussion about complexities, such as that a tall skinny dog might not be heavier than a shorter fat dog, and that in Mexico a dog would be weighed using metric units such as kilograms rather than pounds and ounces.

7. Explain that often we can't directly compare the weights of things by hefting with our hands, so instead, people use scales and standard units of weight, such as pounds or ounces. Show the students the scales that you have available. Talk about the rules for how the scales should be used so that they do not break.

8. Now introduce the task to the students. Tell them that they will work in groups to discover whatever they can about a scale of their choice. Explain that after the group selects the scale it is interested in, the students will take turns looking carefully at the scale. Tell them that they are to try to figure out how the scale works, what numbers it has, what patterns they see in the numbers, what words are on their scale, and anything else they notice. On the board write:

What Can You Discover About Your Scale?
- *How does it work?*
- *How do you use it to weigh things?*
- *What numbers and words does it have?*
- *What patterns do you see?*
- *What do the lines and spaces represent?*
- *What else can you discover?*

Provide each group with chart paper and a marker to record its discoveries.

9. As the students work, observe what they understand about the scales and what they do not yet understand. Encourage them to find patterns in the numbers on the scale as well as patterns in the lines. Support them as they figure out how to interpret abbreviations or decide on the meaning of the lines and spaces.

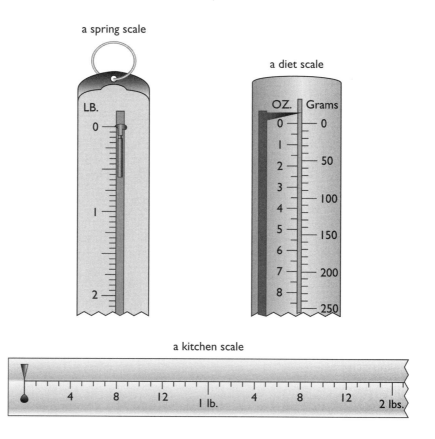

Consider your observations as you plan the discussion. For example, if many students do not see the need to ensure that the scale shows 0 when nothing is on it, make sure to address this in the whole-class discussion.

10. After the groups have listed their discoveries, have a group share one of its findings with the class. For example, a group might say that its scale has *lbs.* and *oz.* on it, and that means pounds and ounces. On the board, write *Words* followed by *pounds (lbs.)*, *ounces (oz.)*, and words that other groups have found on their scales such as *grams (g)* and *kilograms (kg)*. Discuss abbreviations and what they represent. Write *Units* next to Words and explain that pounds, ounces, grams, and kilograms are units that are used to compare the weights of objects.

11. Have another group share something else it noticed, write it on the board, and again have the other groups share how their scale shows that same thing. Continue until you have listed all the discoveries made by the class.

At the end of the discussion the board might look like this:

Numbers:
50, 100, 150, 200, 250 . . . (multiples of 50)
5, 10, 15, 20, 25, 30 . . . (multiples of 5)

The biggest weight it can measure is:
5 pounds, 32 ounces, 300 pounds

Each line shows:
2 more pounds
4 more ounces

How it works:
When you push on it more, the arrow points to a bigger number.

To weigh something, you make sure the arrow points to 0 before you put the thing on it and see where the arrow points then. That's how much it weighs.

If the arrow points in between lines, it shows fractions of that unit.

The scale reminds me of the thermometer scale and the scale for measuring liquids.

12. Explain to the children that during other investigations into weight they will continue discovering and rediscovering these ideas. Tell them that they will come to understand even better how scales work, what these units of measure mean, and how to measure weight.

 ## Put in Order—Mass

Overview

In this lesson, students investigate the mass of common classroom objects by placing them in order from lightest to heaviest. They first predict by hefting the objects and then check their predictions by using balance scales. Lastly, using gram weights and their balances, students find the actual mass of each item.

Materials

- sets of 7 common classroom items similar in mass (see Instruction 1), 1 per small group of students
- balance scales, 1 per small group of students
- 3-inch square sticky notes, 2 per small group of students
- gram weights including 1 gram, 5 grams, 10 grams, and 20 grams (see Instruction 1), 5 to 10 of each weight
- large food storage bags, 2 per small group of students
- *Put in Order—Mass* recording sheet, 1 per student (see Blackline Masters)

Vocabulary: balance scale, grams, heaviest, heft, lightest, mass, measure, outcome, predict, transitivity, unit, weight

Instructions

1. Before class, prepare two bags for each group—one filled with the items to be ordered by mass and the other filled with gram weights. In one bag, put items that are somewhat similar in mass, for example, a pair of children's scissors, a clothespin, a box of crayons, a pad of sticky notes, a number cube, a domino, and an empty pencil can. Be sure that the sets you create are identical.

   In the other bag, put at least one of each kind of gram weight. The total number of grams must be more than the heaviest item. If you do not have gram weights, you can use items about a gram in mass such as small paper clips or wooden 1-centimeter cubes, or you can place the equivalent mass of sand in snack-size bags, labeling each bag with its mass.

2. Hand out the sticky notes and recording sheets. Begin the lesson by showing the students a bag with a set of classroom items. Explain that in small groups, they will explore the weight, or mass, of each item in the bag. Tell them that they will decide how to order the items from lightest to heaviest. Have one student from each group label one sticky note *Lightest* and another sticky note *Heaviest*. Tell the students to place the labels at opposite ends of their work space.

3. Next, give each group a set of items. Invite them to predict the order of the items, discussing it until they come to an agreement. Tell the groups that they are to place the items in a line on the work space, from lightest to heaviest, and then record their prediction on the recording sheet. Remind the students that a prediction is an educated guess. It may turn out to be correct, but it may not, and that's OK.

4. When all the groups have recorded their predictions, lead a class discussion. Have volunteers show their ordered items and explain how they made their decisions. Many students may have hefted the items. Explain that when hefting, we use our bodies as a natural scale, comparing how the items feel. Ask the students whether they switched hands to see whether their nondominant hand gave them the same information and why this might be useful.

5. List each group's prediction on the board. Discuss how the groups agreed and how they disagreed, and what produced that disagreement. As students share, reword their sentences using the term *mass*. For example, if a student says, "I think that the clothespin was lighter than the scissors," you might say, "So you think the mass of the clothespin is less than the mass of the scissors." On the first

group's list, make a star next to the items for which there was most disagreement between the groups. For example one, class list showed the following:

Group 1	Group 2	Group 3	Group 4	Group 5
clothespin	clothespin	clothespin	clothespin	clothespin
*scissors	cube	domino	scissors	scissors
*domino	sticky notes	sticky notes	sticky notes	sticky notes
*sticky notes	domino	cube	domino	domino
*cube	scissors	scissors	cube	cube
pencil can	pencil can	pencil can	pencil can	crayons
crayons	crayons	crayons	crayons	pencil can

6. Next provide each group with a balance scale. Allow the students a few minutes to explore the balance scale before using it with their items. Then stop the students and have them describe how the scale works and how to make sure the balance is centered.

   Explain that a balance scale is used to measure the mass of an item—the amount of matter or stuff it contains.

7. Now have the groups plan how they can check their predictions by using only the balance scale and the seven items that they were given. Tell the students to check their predictions about the items' mass and write the new order on their recording sheet. As the students work, you may see them compare two objects at a time and determine the order in a logical manner. Other students may work in a more random manner.

8. Discuss how each group used the scales. Then discuss what each group found out, what surprised the students, and what they were sure of. Modify each group's list on the board, and again star the items that produced the most disagreement. Ask the groups to come up with an explanation for discrepancies. For example, they may have discovered that placing a large item so it is not centered on the pan affected their results.

9. Ask the students how they know that the lightest object is lighter than the heaviest item, if they did not directly compare the two items. Encourage the students to articulate the logic of *transitivity*: if the scissors weigh more than the clothespin, and each of the other items weighs more than the scissors, then the crayons weigh more than the clothespin.

10. Next tell the students that they will again check their predictions, this time by finding the actual mass of the objects using a standard unit of measure called a gram. Provide each group with a set of gram weights. Ask the students to find the

mass of each item in grams and record this information in the third section of their recording sheet. While students find the total gram weights that balance an object, observe them to see the computational strategies they use.

11. When the students are finished, discuss the item that most of the groups thought was the lightest. On the board, write *Class Outcome*, and list each item along with the number of grams that each group identified. Discuss and resolve any large discrepancies between the groups' information. Write the number of grams the class agrees upon, or if some disagreement still exists, write the range of results for example, *6–8 grams*. Remind the class that measurement is never exact.

12. Number the items from 1 to 7, from lightest to heaviest. Have the groups compare the class outcome with their original predictions.

Fruit Salad

Overview

In this lesson students develop a sense of U.S. customary units of weight by choosing 3 pounds of fruit for an imaginary fruit salad. Given a scale and a collection of fruit, students weigh one piece of fruit at a time and then use this information to select a combination that would weigh about 3 pounds. The students describe their fruit salad in words, pictures, and equations and then have a whole-class discussion about their decisions.

Materials

◈ collections of different fruit, such as 1 apple, 1 orange, 1 grapefruit, 1 strawberry, and a small bag of 6 grapes, 1 set per small group

◈ food scales or other scales that can weigh the largest fruit available, 1 per small group

Vocabulary: benchmark, discrepancy, equations, estimate, ounce, pound, reasonable, round, scale, ton, weigh, zero

Instructions

1. Begin the lesson by discussing with the students the times they've gone to the grocery store and either watched someone weigh produce or weighed produce by themselves. Ask the students what they weighed and the procedure they used to weigh it. Then ask them what units they used to weigh the produce—ounces, pounds, or tons.

2. Ask students what items they associate with each unit of measure. On the board label three columns *Ounces*, *Pounds*, and *Tons*. Beneath each heading,

list the students' benchmarks for that unit. For example, students might say that a small ball weighs about an ounce, a box of dry spaghetti weighs about a pound, and a small car weighs about a ton. Discuss why tons would not be a reasonable unit to use to weigh produce and what things might be reasonably measured with tons.

3. Next have students share how the units relate to each other. On the board write what the students say, or tell the students the information that they need to know:

16 ounces = 1 pound

2,000 pounds = 1 ton

4. Explain to the students that they are going to imagine that they need to make a fruit salad. Ask them which units they would probably use to weigh an apple or a strawberry. Tell the students that their fruit salad must have about 3 pounds of fruit. Discuss what *about* means. Have the students identify some weights that they think are about 3 pounds and weights that are not about 3 pounds. Students may say that 3 pounds, 2 ounces is close to 3 pounds, but 3 pounds, 5 ounces is not. Make sure the students understand that they can have a little more than 3 pounds or a little less than 3 pounds. Also note that the fruit may not weigh an exact number of ounces, and they may either use fractions or round the weight to the closest ounce, that is, if an apple weighs about $8\frac{1}{2}$ ounces, they may just call it 9 ounces.

5. Show the students the collection of fruit and the scale that their group will use during the investigation. Tell the students that they will use this collection to decide what fruit they will put in their fruit salad. Explain that they can weigh only one piece of fruit at a time, and they must estimate its weight before they weigh it. Remind them that they need about 3 pounds of fruit altogether, and once they weigh each piece separately, they can decide what fruit will go into their salad. Tell the students that even though they have only one of each kind of fruit in their collection, they can decide to buy as many of that kind of fruit as they want. For example, although they have only one apple, they can imagine that they will buy three apples for their salad.

6. On the board write the task:
   a. *You need about 3 pounds of fruit for a fruit salad. Even though you only have one sample of each kind of fruit, the salad you plan may have several of the same kind of fruit. What might you put in your salad?*
   b. *Weigh only one piece of fruit at a time. Before you weigh each piece, estimate what its weight will be.*

c. On your paper write what you will buy and how you know that you have about 3 pounds of fruit. Include pictures, words, and equations in your explanation.

d. What other fruit salads could you make that also use 3 pounds of fruit?

7. Pass out the materials. As the students work, observe to see whether they remember how to use a scale. For example, a group may have a scale that does not point to 0 when empty and therefore produces weight measurements that are too large. If so, help the group become aware of the discrepancy, perhaps by pointing out that a different group found that its apple weighed significantly less. Have the groups trade apples to see if the discrepancy still exists. Suggest that they examine their empty scales. In doing this, the groups should realize that one scale points to 0 when empty and the other scale points to a different number. Discuss with the students how this difference impacts the results and how to adjust the scale to 0 when empty.

8. As the students work, make sure they predict the fruit's weight before weighing it. Each time, ask them why that prediction makes sense to them. For example, one student might say that the apple weighed 8 ounces and the orange feels heavier, so she predicts that the orange will weigh 12 ounces. Encourage the students to find as many different ways to make a 3-pound fruit salad as possible. If a student's fruit salad varies significantly from 3 pounds, encourage him to find a way to make it closer. Some students may not know that they need 48 ounces. If this is the case, you may encourage them to make a T-chart that shows this relationship:

Pounds	Ounces
1	16
2	32
3	48

9. When everyone is finished, have a whole-class discussion about the fruit salads the children created. As one student shares a combination of fruit, encourage the others to verify that it weighs close to 3 pounds. Then have the student share the equation that represents this combination of fruit. For example, a student who included three apples, two oranges, and four strawberries might write:

$$(3 \times 8) + (2 \times 10) + (4 \times 1) = 48 \ ounces$$

Another student might describe the same salad this way:

$$8 + 8 + 8 = 24$$
$$10 + 10 = 20$$
$$24 + 20 + 4 = 48 \ ounces$$

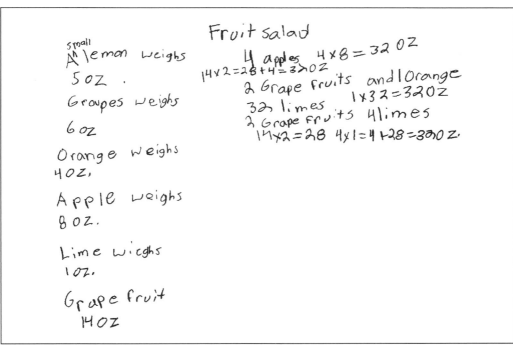

Figure 5–1 *Jonathan made several versions of a 2-pound fruit salad.*

Have other students share their fruit salads and the equations they used to describe them. (See Figure 5–1.)

 I See Something

Overview

To begin this lesson the students share what they already know about ounces and pounds. Then, in small groups, they play *I See Something*. Pairs of students look around the room to identify an item that they think weighs between a certain range, for example, $\frac{1}{2}$ pound and 1 pound. They weigh it and decide whether it is too light, too heavy, or within the target weight range.

Materials

◈ scales that measure the range of weights you want students to explore, 1 per small group

◈ classroom items such as books, scissors, markers, masking tape, and balls of yarn

◈ nonclassroom items, both light and heavy, such as pinecones, tools, rocks, cups, and cans of food

Vocabulary: fluid ounces, ounces, pounds, prediction, range, scale, T-chart, units, weigh

Instructions

1. Begin the lesson by showing the students a scale that measures the units you plan to address. In this description, the students will explore ounces and pounds. Tell the students that they will play a game using these units.

2. Ask the students to talk in pairs about what they know about pounds, and then invite them to share with the class. List what they say on the board. For example, the list might look like this:

    What We Know About Pounds
    - A student might weigh 60 pounds.
    - You can write *pounds* as *lbs*.
    - The abbreviation comes from the Latin word *libra*, which means balance or scales.
    - *Pound* can mean "hit with a hammer."
    - You can eat pound cake.
    - The weights my mom lifts are 5 pounds each.
    - There are 16 ounces in a pound.

3. Acknowledge other meanings of the word *pound*, especially for students who are just learning English. Identify those words as everyday meanings and distinguish them from mathematical meanings. If students refer to fluid ounces, such as saying a soda has 8 ounces in it, remind them that fluid ounces are units we use to measure liquids. Tell them that the game they will play explores weight, so the units they will use are simply called *ounces*.

4. Next have the students use what they know about the number of ounces in a pound to identify the number of ounces in different weights. Ask pairs of students to figure how many ounces are in half a pound. On the board write:

    $$\tfrac{1}{2} \text{ pound} = \underline{\hspace{2cm}} \text{ ounces}$$

    If students need support, ask them what they know about halves (they must be the same size). On the board write:

    $$1 \text{ pound (16 ounces)} = \underline{\hspace{1.5cm}} + \underline{\hspace{1.5cm}} \text{ ounces}$$

    Remind them that in order to find the number of ounces in half a pound, the numbers must be the same. With this hint, most students will realize that half a pound is 8 ounces. Write 8 in the blanks.

5. Now discuss other relationships between pounds and ounces that relate to what the children said. For example, ask: "How many ounces are in the five pounds that Annie's mom lifts?" Again have pairs consider that question. If students have difficulty thinking about it, have them consider a smaller number of pounds, such as 2. Have students share their answers and how they arrived at those answers.

6. Introduce the students to a tool—a T-chart—that may help them think about how units of weight compare with each other. On the board write the following, helping the students interpret each part as you write:

Pounds	Ounces
1	16
2	32
3	48
4	64
5	80

7. Next introduce the game *I See Something*. Tell students that in this game they and a partner will identify something in the classroom that they can see that they predict weighs an amount within a target range, such as between $\frac{1}{2}$ pound and 1 pound. Explain that when everyone is ready, each pair of students will retrieve the object or combination of objects they've identified, weigh it to find out if it falls within the target range, and list it on a class chart. On the board make a chart like this:

$<\frac{1}{2}$ Pound	$\frac{1}{2}$ Pound to 1 Pound	>1 Pound

8. Now begin a sample game. Have partners stay seated and look around the room to find something that might weigh between $\frac{1}{2}$ pound and 1 pound. Remind the students that it can be one item or a combination of items. On a sheet of paper have the students write the target range, *$\frac{1}{2}$ pound to 1 pound*, and the item(s) whose weight they think is within that range.

9. Choose a pair of students to retrieve the item they've selected and weigh it. Have them refer to the T-chart if necessary to determine how $\frac{1}{2}$ pound would look on the scale (8 ounces). Have the students determine if their choice falls within the target range and record it in the correct column. Play again. Tell the students that they can keep their last prediction or make a new prediction. Encourage the students to use the information on the chart to help them make their decision. When everyone is ready, select another pair of students to weigh their item and post the information. Continue the game until you have several items that fall within the target range.

10. Now place a scale at each work space and invite groups to play the game themselves. As groups continue playing, you may wish to have them explore a new range that can be measured on their scale, such as between $\frac{1}{4}$ pound and $\frac{1}{2}$ pound or between 2 pounds and $2\frac{1}{2}$ pounds. Have the students adjust the T-chart and continue playing the game, recording their findings on a sheet of paper.

11. End the lesson by returning to the original list that the students generated, "What We Know About Pounds." Add new information that the students have discovered from playing *I See Something*.

Stuff a Bag

Overview

In this lesson, students practice reading scales and develop a sense of benchmark weights. Groups of students fill plastic grocery bags with classroom items that they estimate will weigh a total of 10 pounds, 5 pounds, 1 pound, or $\frac{1}{2}$ pound. Each group weighs its bag and then adjusts its weight by adding or removing items. The students try to weigh their bags as few times as possible, and when they finish, they contribute their data to a class tally chart. The class examines the data and draws conclusions about it.

Materials

◈ spring scales that measure up to 10 pounds, 1 per small group of students, or a bathroom scale, 1 for the class to share

◈ plastic grocery bags, 2 to 4 per small group of students

◈ 3-inch paper squares, 2 to 4 per small group of students

◈ overhead transparency with the numbers 1 through 20 written in a column on the left side

Vocabulary: benchmark, data, equal, fact, heft, inference, ounce, pound, predict, scale, sense of weight, summary statements, units

Instructions

1. Begin by explaining to the students that in order to understand units of weight, people need to have a sense of what that weight feels like. Ask them how they know if something is heavy or light, and have them explain what those sensations feel like. For example when students talk about holding heavy things, they might say that their arm hurts or it starts to shake or that they have to push up. When describing what light things feel like, students might say that it's easy to hold them or you don't have to work hard to hold them in your hand.

2. Tell the students that they are going to have an experience that will help them develop a sense of specific weights. Explain that they will find things that weigh $\frac{1}{2}$ pound, 1 pound, 5 pounds, or 10 pounds and that as they find things that weigh those amounts, they will try to remember how it feels to heft those items. Tell them that memories of how those key weights feel will be the benchmarks they will use when they need to estimate weights of new things.

3. Explain to the students that they will work in small groups to stuff a grocery bag with items from the classroom until the bag weighs a benchmark weight. Write these weights on the board: *10 pounds, 5 pounds, 1 pound, and $\frac{1}{2}$ pound.* Tell the students that they will use a spring scale (or bathroom scale) to weigh their bag, and then add or take out items until their bag weighs the benchmark weight they've chosen. Explain that everyone in the group must have a chance to heft the bag each time the group changes what is inside the bag, and they must agree on the items to be added or removed. Tell them that each time the group weighs the bag, a group member must make a tally mark on a sheet of paper, and their goal is to weigh the bag as few times as possible. (**Note:** If students use a bathroom scale it may not register small weights, so they may have to weigh themselves with and without the filled bag and find the difference.)

4. Let the students know whether any areas in the classroom are off-limits to them as they collect things. Also tell the students that after their bag weighs the target amount, they will write the weight on a paper square and place the square inside the bag.

5. On the board, write these instructions:
    a. *As a group, choose a target weight.*
    b. *Find items in the room that together make the bag equal the target weight.*
    c. *Each time that you weigh your bag, make a tally mark on your paper.*
    d. *When you reach the target weight, one member of the group writes the weight on a label and places it in the bag. Another member of the group makes a tally on the overhead transparency by the number of times the group weighed the bag.*
    e. *Select another bag and a new target weight.*

6. Distribute the materials. As the students work, observe how they interpret the lines and spaces on the scale. Some students may need help in interpreting the scale on their measurement device. If any scale needs to be read in ounces, see whether they know that 16 ounces equals 1 pound. If they don't, see whether they can deduce this by looking at the scale. If not, tell them and explain how the scale shows this. Also observe the students to see how they interpret the information from the scale. For example, if they are trying to create a bag that weighs 5 pounds and the scale reads 3 pounds, do they check to see how 3 pounds feels and select an item that is slightly more than that weight? Or do they randomly choose any object?

7. After the groups have filled at least two bags and recorded their data on the chart, gather them for a discussion. Have a student select a "mystery bag." Ask the student to close his or her eyes, heft the bag, and predict whether it weighs 10 pounds, 5 pounds, 1 pound, or $\frac{1}{2}$ pound, explaining why. Then invite the student to look inside at the contents and the label to see what the bag actually weighs. Repeat with several other students.

8. Have the students examine the tally chart on the overhead to see what the data tell them. After each student makes a statement, see if the class agrees. If so, write the statement on the overhead. Discuss whether the statement is fact or an inference. For example, it may be a fact that four bags had to be weighed six times, or it may be a fact that most of the bags had to be weighed from seven to nine times. But it would be an inference to say that the half-pound bags had to be weighed fewer times than the other bags. It would be an inference to say that it is harder to find things that weigh heavier amounts. Discuss how data could be gathered to change an inference to a fact.

Mailing a Birthday Package

Overview

In this lesson, students select favorite books that they pretend to mail to a friend for a birthday gift. The total weight of the books that the students choose must be close to, but not more than, 5 pounds. The students weigh each book individually, figure the total weight of the package, and list this information on a packing slip.

Materials

- books from the classroom or school library, about 8 per pair of students
- spring scales, or food scales that can weigh the books, 1 per pair of students
- chart paper, 1 sheet
- plastic grocery bags, 1 per pair of students
- 5-pound bag of flour
- 1-pound package of pasta

Vocabulary: benchmark, convert, heft, ounces, pounds

Instructions

1. Before class, prepare a sample packing slip on the chart paper, like this:

Packing Slip	
Book 1: *Martians I Have Known*	6 oz.
Book 2: *Little-Known Facts About Fleas*	12 oz.
Book 3: *Dogs and Cats*	5 oz.
Total Weight:	_____

(**Note:** While this lesson is described using standard English units [ounces and pounds], it can also be done using metric units [grams and kilograms].)

2. To begin the lesson, explain to the children that they are going to imagine mailing a birthday package to a friend who lives far away. Tell students that the package will contain a set of books that they think the friend would enjoy. Explain that they will choose a set of books that weighs close to, but not more than, 5 pounds.

3. Show the students the package of flour and tell them that it weighs 5 pounds. Heft it in front of the students. Tell the students that they will heft it as well to see how 5 pounds feels, so that when they hear "five pounds" they can imagine how that weight feels. On the board, write *flour: 5 pounds (5 lbs.)*. Pass the package of flour around the class so the students can heft the package for themselves. Tell the students that the package will be available throughout the lesson for them to refer to.

4. Do the same with the package of pasta. Show the students the label and have a student read the weight. Tell the students that it weighs 1 pound, heft it, and remind the students that they will also heft that package to gain a benchmark for how 1 pound feels. On the board write *pasta: 1 pound (1 lb.)*. Pass the package around the class so the students can heft the package for themselves. Tell the students that this package will be available throughout the lesson for them to refer to.

5. On the board, draw an enlarged copy of the scale increments on the measuring devices that they will use. Ask the students to identify the units that the numbers represent (ounces and pounds). Have the students find the line that is marked 1 pound. On the board, write *16 ounces = 1 pound (16 oz. = 1 lb.)*. If any students speak Spanish, note that *lb.* comes from a Latin word similar to the Spanish word *libra,* which means 1 pound.

6. Ask the students to work in pairs to read the numbers on the enlarged scale and identify the amounts that the lines represent. Some scales have lines that represent whole numbers and others have lines that represent fractions of ounces. Have students share what they think and why until the class is in agreement about how to read the scale. Provide the students with practice by pointing to different lines and having the students interpret the value of the lines.

7. Explain to the students that packages often contain a packing slip. On the board, tape the chart paper that contains the sample packing slip. Ask the students to work in pairs to figure out the total weight of the books on the chart. Have the students share what they think. On the board write equations to

represent the different strategies students used to solve the problem. For example, some students may total the ounces and then divide the total by sixteen, since there are sixteen ounces in a pound. Others may add 6 ounces and 12 ounces and find 18 ounces and then convert that amount to 1 pound, 2 ounces. Still others may find a group of sixteen, call it a pound, and then look at the leftovers as ounces.

8. Tell the students that when they divided or grouped the weight of the books by sixteen, they "converted," or changed, the unit of measure from ounces to pounds, and they will need to do the same during this activity.

9. Write the instructions on the board:
   a. *Choose a set of books you think your friend would like, and place them in a plastic bag. The books must weigh close to, but not more than, 5 pounds. Use the flour and pasta packages to help you estimate.*
   b. *Weigh your books one at a time. As you weigh each book, list its title and weight on the sheet of paper that will be your packing slip.*
   c. *Find the total weight of the books in your bag by adding the amounts together. Add or remove books to make the total weight as close as possible to, but not over, 5 pounds. Edit your packing slip and write the final total weight.*

10. Distribute the scales, bags, and paper. As the students work, observe how they read their scales. If they have difficulty interpreting the lines, ask them to read the numbers that they see. Next ask them what each space represents, and then what numbers would be on the lines that do not have numbers. Tell them to try reading the numbers and the lines that way to see if their idea makes sense. For example, a scale might have the numbers 0, 4, 8, and so on, with adjacent numbers having four spaces between them. This means each line would be represented by a whole number and the space between any two consecutive lines would represent 1 ounce.

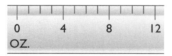

Another scale might have the numbers 0, 1, 2, and so on, with consecutive numbers having four spaces between them. In this case, each line would be represented by a fraction and the space between any two consecutive lines would equal a quarter ounce.

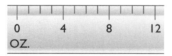

Also observe how students figure the number of pounds and ounces their books total and how they adjust their bag of books if they have gone over 5 pounds.

11. As students finish choosing items and filling out their packing slips, have pairs of students exchange packages and take on the role of workers at the shipping company. Have them check the slips for accuracy, and return those with errors to the packers for revisions.

12. When everyone has finished, begin a class discussion. Invite a pair of students to share the weight of each book on their packing slip. On the board, write the weight of each book, for example:

9 ounces

8 ounces

8 ounces

12 ounces

4 ounces

10 ounces

11 ounces

12 ounces

Have the class work in pairs to identify the total number of pounds and ounces. They may do this mentally or they may need to record on paper to keep track of their thinking.

13. Ask a student to share how she computed the total. As the student describes her thinking, write equations on the board so the others can understand that student's strategy. For example, a student might say, "I see that eight ounces and eight ounces makes sixteen ounces, and so does twelve and four, so that's two pounds. Then nine and ten makes another pound with three ounces left over, so that makes three pounds and three ounces in all. Then three and eleven and twelve makes twenty-six ounces, and that's another pound and ten ounces, so in all that makes four pounds, ten ounces." You might record her thinking this way:

8 oz. + 8 oz. = 16 oz. (1 lb.)

12 oz. + 4 oz. = 16 oz. (lb.)   *2 lbs. total*

9 oz. + 10 oz. = 19 oz. (1 lb., 3 oz.)   *3 lbs., 3 oz. total*

3 oz. + 11 oz. + 12 oz. = 26 oz. (1 lb., 10 oz.)   *4 lbs., 10 oz. total*

Then ask the pair of students who created the packing list whether they computed their total in the same way. If not, record their thinking on the board. Next have another pair of students share a different packing list in the same way. (See Figures 5–2 and 5–3.)

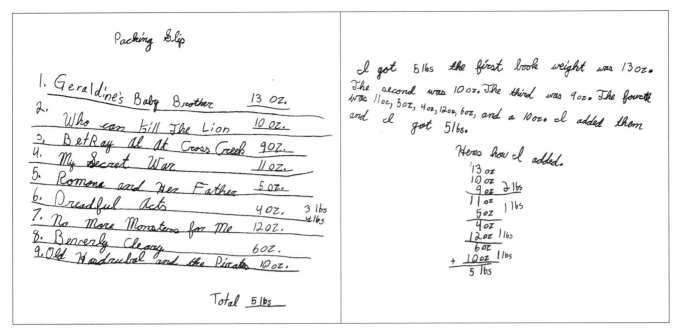

Figure 5–2 *Amanda and Oscar added groups of sixteen to find 5 pounds.*

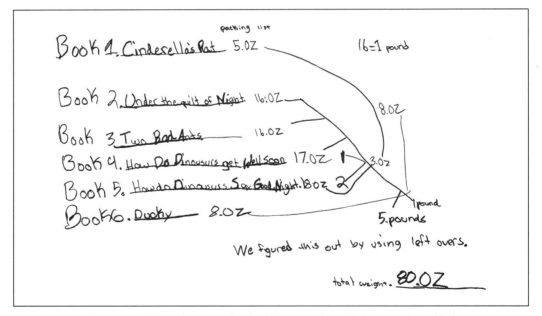

Figure 5–3 *Brian and Kevin kept track of whole pounds and then combined leftover ounces to create an additional pound.*

The Fewest Weights

Overview

In this lesson, students solve a problem that requires conversion between units. They examine pictures of specific weights and figure out what is the fewest number of these weights that together equal 5 pounds (Schuster and Anderson 2005, 136).

Then the students explore other combinations of weights that also equal 5 pounds.

Materials

◈ *Weights* worksheets, 1 per student (see Blackline Masters)

Vocabulary: grams, heavy, kilograms, measure, metric, ounces, pounds, units, U.S. customary, weight

Instructions

1. Tell the students that they are going to solve a problem about weight. Ask them what units we use when we measure how heavy things are. List what the students say on the board, separating the units according to whether they are U.S. customary units or metric units. Label the units accordingly:

   U.S. customary units: tons, pounds, ounces

   Metric units: grams, kilograms

2. Next tell the students that they will do an investigation involving U.S. customary units, specifically pounds and ounces. Ask the students to explain how ounces and pounds relate to each other. Record what they say on the board. For example, students may say the following:

   It takes 16 ounces to make 1 pound.

   Sixteen ounces equals 1 pound.

   One ounce is $\frac{1}{16}$ of 1 pound.

   Ask the students how they would use abbreviations to write the same sentences, and alter the previous sentences so they read:

   It takes 16 oz. to make 1 lb.

   Sixteen oz. equals 1 lb.

   One oz. is $\frac{1}{16}$ of 1 lb.

3. Introduce the investigation to the students. Explain that they will be given a picture of a set of weights and that their task is to figure out the fewest number of weights that will make a total of 5 pounds. Distribute the worksheets. Tell students that they may use only the weights drawn on the page; they may not use any additional weights. With the students, read the names of each weight. For example, read 2.5 ounces as "two and a half ounces" as well as "two and five-tenths ounces." Make sure that the students understand the decimal notation.

4. Explain to the students that they must write an explanation of how they solved the problem, using words and equations to convince the reader that their solution

makes sense. Tell the students that after they find one way to solve the problem, they are to find other combinations of weights and prove that each combination equals 5 pounds.

5. As the students work, offer support as necessary. For example, a student may look for ways to make 5 ounces instead of 5 pounds. Refer this student to the relationships listed on the board, and remind him or her that the task is to look for ways to make 5 pounds. Other students may misinterpret 2.5 ounces as 2.5 pounds. Still others may find combinations of 10 ounces (such as 2.5 oz. + 7.5 oz.) and interpret each group of 10 as 1 pound. You may find it helpful to suggest to students that they use a T-chart to find out how many ounces are in 5 pounds:

Pounds	Ounces
1	16
2	32
3	48
4	64
5	80

6. When students have solved the problem in more than one way, have several students share what they discovered. Select students who managed the numbers in different ways. For example, some students may randomly combine consecutive weights to make a total of 80 ounces:

Weights I Used	*Weight I Have So Far*
$2.5 + 2.5 = 5$ *oz.*	
$2.5 + 2.5 = 5$ *oz.*	10 *oz.*
$5 + 5 = 10$ *oz.*	$10 + 10 = 20$ *oz.*
$10 + 10 + 10 = 30$ *oz.*	$30 + 20 = 50$ *oz.*
$7.5 + 7.5 = 15$ *oz.*	$50 + 15 = 65$ *oz.*
$7.5 + 7.5 = 15$ *oz.*	$65 + 15 = 80$ *oz.*

Other students may use the strategy of finding combinations of 10 ounces and then add them to make 80 ounces:

$$2.5 + 7.5 = 10 \text{ oz.}$$
$$5 \times (2.5 + 7.5) = 50 \text{ oz.}$$
$$10 + 10 + 10 = 30 \text{ oz.}$$
$$50 + 30 = 80 \text{ oz.}$$

Students may also represent their answers in various ways. Some may record on the recording sheet, while others may keep track by writing equations. (See Figures 5–4 and 5–5.)

We had to find out 2 ways to make
5 Lbs. I think it was kind of hard
because you had point.5 stuff "scales".
I did 2 ways to make 5 lbs. The
part that I had the most trouble
is when I added. I thought each
10 ozs. was a pound so I had to start
all over.

Figure 5–4 *David thought that 10 ounces was a pound, so he had to start over.*

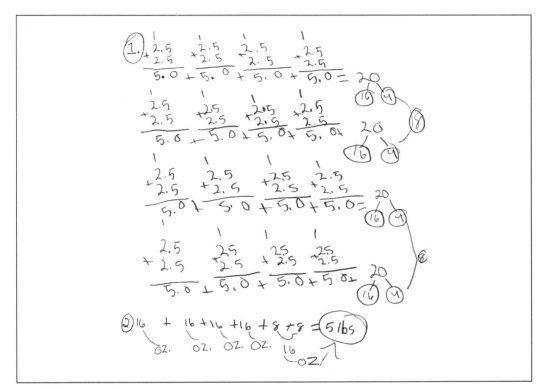

Figure 5–5 *Samantha found groups of 20 ounces, which she decomposed into 16 ounces (1 pound) and 4 ounces. Then she combined four groups of 4 ounces to get another pound.*

7. Discuss which solution uses the fewest weights and whether the students think there are any other combinations of weights no one has shared yet.

How Much Is a Kilogram?

Overview

This lesson helps students develop benchmarks for a kilogram. Students weigh light items on a bathroom scale by first weighing themselves, then weighing themselves holding the item, and lastly subtracting the first amount from the second. The students select items, or groups of items, in the classroom that they believe weigh about a kilogram. After determining the weight of their selection, the students place the it on a table to create a classroom kilogram museum.

Materials

◈ bathroom scale that measures kilograms (**Note:** Discount stores often sell digital scales that measure weight in kilograms as well as pounds. Simply flip the switch to change the unit. If you cannot find this type of scale, use a balance scale by placing one or more items on one side that you know weigh a kilogram, or 2.2 pounds.)

◈ chart paper, 1 sheet

◈ table sectioned into three areas with masking tape

◈ 8-by-12-inch construction paper, 3 pieces

Vocabulary: decimal, estimate, kilogram, open number line, range, tenths

Instructions

1. Create a kilogram museum. Label each section of the table with a piece of construction paper folded so it stands up. The labels should read "About a Kilogram," "More than a Kilogram," and "Less than a Kilogram." Also, prior to the lesson, ask a relatively short student and a relatively tall student whether they would be willing to be weighed in front of the class, using kilograms. It may be best to not choose the shortest and the tallest students, as they may be sensitive about their height or weight.

2. Begin the lesson by telling the students that they will be learning about a unit of weight called a *kilogram*, and they will make a classroom museum of items that weigh about a kilogram, less than a kilogram, and more than a kilogram.

3. Show the students the bathroom scale that measures kilograms. Ask the shorter student to stand on the scale. On the board, write the student's weight, including the decimal, such as *28.5 kilograms*. Discuss the meaning of the decimal. Remind the students that it is a fractional amount recorded in tenths. In this case the 5 stands for five-tenths of a kilogram.

4. Next have the taller student stand up. Ask the others to estimate that student's weight in kilograms. Write these estimates on the board, including the unit kilograms after each one. Label these weights *Estimates*.

5. Have that student stand on the scale. On the board write the student's weight and again interpret the decimal. Label this amount *Weight*.

6. Now tell the students that they are going to find objects in the classroom that weigh about a kilogram. Have the students discuss a range of weights that *about* would refer to. For example, they may decide that objects that weigh anywhere

from .8 kilograms to 1.2 kilograms would qualify. (Many digital scales record kilogram in multiples of .2 kilograms.)

7. Explain to the students that the bathroom scale will not register the weight of the object alone, since it is very light. Therefore they will have to weigh the objects in a different manner. As an example, ask a volunteer to find an object in the room that weighs about a kilogram. Have the shorter (or taller) student hold the object and then stand on the scale. Write the weight on the board, for example, *46.2 kilograms*. Have the students discuss how they can find out what the object alone weighs, without putting the object on the scale by itself. The students will likely realize that they need to know what the student alone weighs, and that they can subtract the weight of the student alone, and see how close that difference is to 1 kilogram. So if the student alone weighed 45.6 kilograms, they could subtract that amount from 46.2. You might want to show this difference by using an open number line.

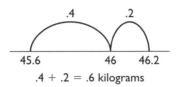

.4 + .2 = .6 kilograms

Another strategy the students may identify is to begin by weighing the student, then adding a kilogram to that weight. So if the student weighs 45.6 kilograms, they would add 1 kilogram and get 46.6 kilograms. Then the student would weigh himself holding the object and compare the weight shown on the scale to 46.6 kilograms.

8. As a group, decide whether the object is about a kilogram, more than a kilogram, or less than a kilogram. Then show the students the table with three areas sectioned off, each labeled with one of those choices. Place the item in the appropriate space.

9. Since you have only one scale, you will need to have the students take turns using it. Engage the students in an independent activity while pairs of students take turns weighing themselves with and without the item they've chosen. Before pairs choose an item, allow them to visit the kilogram museum to get information that will help them with their selection.

10. When all the students have contributed items to the museum, invite them to sit around the table. Discuss what they see and whether any items don't seem to be in the correct place. If this is the case, reweigh the item and change its placement if necessary. Ask the students to make a mental note of an item that they want to remember as a benchmark for 1 kilogram. Tell the students that when they hear "kilogram," they should think of that item. On chart paper, write *Kilogram* at the top and list the benchmark items that the students want to remember.

 **Metric Hunt**

Overview

In this lesson students develop a sense of grams and kilograms by filling bags with items that they estimate weigh 1 gram, 10 grams, 100 grams, and 1,000 grams (1 kilogram). They weigh and then adjust their bags. During a class discussion, they make a bulletin board display of these bags. Then they consider the relationship among these benchmark metric units and how easily conversions among them can be made.

Materials

- balance scales, 1 per small group of students
- metric weights, with at least a 1-gram weight, a 10-gram weight, and weights that total 100 grams, 1 set per small group of students
- item or items that weigh about a kilogram, such as two cans of fruit, 1 per small group of students
- sandwich bags, 3 per small group of students
- gallon-size bags, 2 per small group of students
- sticky notes, 4 per small group of students
- items of varying weights from the classroom, such as paper clips, pencils, crayons, rulers, erasers, wooden cubes, student scissors, books, packages of index cards, and so on, that can fit in the bags and be part of a bulletin board display
- items of varying weights from home, such as cans of food, metal washers, pieces of foam, packing peanuts, buttons, floppy disks, CDs, and so on, that can fit in the bags and be part of a display
- pushpins for the bulletin board, about 40
- 3-by-11-inch paper labels, 5 (see Instruction 1)

Vocabulary: benchmarks, centimeters, convert, decimeters, gram, kilogram, liters, mass, meters, metric units, milliliters, millimeters, multiples, ounce, place value, pound, U.S. customary units, weigh

Instructions

1. Before class, create the bulletin board labels and title. Write *1 gram, 10 grams, 100 grams*, and *1,000 grams/1 kilogram* on four labels. On the fifth label write the title *Metric Units of Mass*. Pin the labels onto the bulletin board.

2. To begin the lesson, explain to the students that in the United States we use U.S. customary units of weight such as pounds and ounces, and we have many fewer chances to understand what metric measures of mass feel like, even though metric units of mass are used throughout most of the world. Tell the students that they are

going to create their own personal benchmarks for these important units and use them to create a bulletin board display.

3. With the students, read the metric units on the board. Invite the students to share what they know about those units and ideas they have about what items are of those same masses.

4. Tell students that they will work in groups to pick a target weight from the board and select items that they think together weigh about that amount. They will fill a bag with the items and then weigh it. Explain that if the bag is not close enough to the target weight, they are to repeat the process with new sets of items until they find a set close to the target weight. Once they find a set of items that is the right weight, they should write the target weight on a sticky note, place it in the bag, and then select a new target weight and repeat the process.

5. Give each group a scale, a set of weights, some bags, and some sticky notes. When most of the groups have completed the activity, begin a group discussion. First discuss whether any weight took more tries than the others. Have students share why that might have happened. Next invite groups to tell what items weigh 1 gram. Pin those bags to the bulletin board and have students share what they notice about the items. For example, some of the items may be large (a piece of foam) and some may be small (an eraser). Note that size doesn't determine weight. Have the same discussions with all the weights as they are posted on the board. The bags with kilograms will be too heavy to pin, so place them on a nearby shelf or table along with the label.

6. Now discuss the relationships between the units. Select a bag in the 1-gram category. Ask the students how many of those bags would weigh 1 kilogram. Have the student visualize what one thousand of those bags would look like. Do this with several items. Then have the students explain in their own words the relationship between grams and kilograms. (**Note:** It would take one thousand of that item to equal a kilogram.) Discuss how many 10 gram bags equal a kilogram and how many 100 gram bags equal a kilogram. (**Note:** It takes one hundred 10-gram weights to equal a kilogram, and it takes ten 100-gram weights to equal a kilogram.)

7. Last, select a bag that has one item that weighs 1 gram. Ask the students how many of that item would weigh 10 grams or 100 grams or 1 kilogram. They will think it's a trick question because, of course, it would take ten or one hundred or one thousand of that item. Use this moment to reinforce how the metric system functions. Tell students that whether it's mass, length, or volume, the metric system is designed so that the various units are multiples of ten, exactly like our numerical place-value system. Explain to the students that this simple pattern is what makes the metric system easy to use. Compare this procedure with the procedure used to

correct units in the U.S. customary system. Have them convert 1,325 ounces into pounds and ounces. Since 16 ounces equal 1 pound, you must divide 1,325 by 16, not an easy task to do mentally. Similarly, length is measured in the metric system using millimeters, centimeters, decimeters, and meters, all units that are multiples of ten. Likewise, volume is measured in the metric system using milliliters and liters, again using the familiar place-value pattern of multiples of ten.

8. Keep the "metric units of mass" display up to use as a reference in future lessons, such as the next lesson, *Apple Juice Container Debate*.

◈ Apple Juice Container Debate

Overview
In this lesson, students investigate how juice is packaged: in juice boxes and in larger plastic bottles. They first choose the container they would prefer to buy for a party. Then, after comparing the containers in terms of cost, volume, convenience, and the amount of trash that is produced, the students reconsider their choice and write a convincing argument for their position.

Materials
- ◈ 1.89-liter (64-ounce) plastic container of apple juice
- ◈ ten-pack of juice boxes, totaling 2 liters
- ◈ gram scale, such as one that measures portions of food
- ◈ punch bowls or pitchers, 2
- ◈ plastic grocery bags, 2
- ◈ 8-ounce paper cups, 1 per student

Vocabulary: decimals, difference, estimate, grams, liters, mass, volume, weight

Instructions

1. Show the students the large plastic container of apple juice and the ten-pack of juice boxes. Initiate a discussion about which kind of apple juice would they buy if they were having a party. As students bring up attributes of one container, examine how the other container compares. For example, if a student reads "100 percent juice" on the label of the ten-pack, read the label on the plastic container to see whether it is also 100 percent juice. As the discussion continues, list the criteria that the students would consider as they decided which apple juice they would buy. The list may contain the following ideas:
   - 100% juice
   - vitamin C
   - cost

- recyclable container (**Note:** plastic containers are often recyclable, but juice boxes are not.)
- convenience
- volume

2. When the students mention volume, make sure that all the students understand what *volume* refers to. Then have the group determine how the volume of the large plastic container compares with the volume of all the apple juice boxes combined. Some students may initially think that the juice boxes have more juice because there are ten of them. Have the students figure out whether the difference in volumes is significant or insignificant. (The plastic bottle is only .19 liter less than the juice boxes, so the two volumes are nearly the same.) Examine the cost of each, and determine which container is more cost-effective.

3. Next, introduce the idea of how much is thrown away when the juice is used up. Ask the students to predict which container produces more trash. Add *amount of trash produced* to the previous list. Ask the students to estimate in grams how much of each kind of container is to be thrown away after the juice is gone. To help them estimate, have the students refer to the "Metric Units of Mass" bulletin board from the *Metric Hunt* lesson (page 208). Remind the students that when we find the number of grams, we are finding the mass or weight of the packaging.

4. Open one juice box at a time, and have volunteers empty each juice box into a punch bowl or pitcher. Then place the juice boxes in the plastic grocery bag, tying the bag tightly so the package is snug and will sit compactly on the portion scale. Have a student read the number of grams, and write that amount on the board: *Weight of juice boxes: 110 grams.*

5. Next empty the juice from the plastic container into the remaining punch bowl or pitcher. Find the weight of the plastic container. Have a student read the number of grams on the scale, and write that amount on the board: *Weight of plastic container: 20 grams.* Have the students find the difference between the amounts, and write the difference on the board. Have students share their strategies for finding the difference. Some might subtract the smaller amount from the larger, and others might think of how much they would need to add to the smaller amount to get the larger amount.

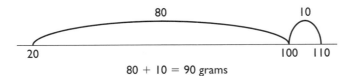

80 + 10 = 90 grams

6. Now have the students consider the impact of choosing juice boxes instead of large bottles of juice over time. Ask the students how many parties they might have in a year. On the board, write the number of parties that they agree would be reasonable. Ask the students to figure the weight of what they would throw away if they always purchased the plastic container or if they always purchased the juice boxes. Have the students find the difference between those amounts, and write the difference on the board. Again have students share their strategies for finding the difference.

7. Return to the original question: "Which would you purchase if you were having a party?" Review the information on the board. Have the students not only write what they think but also make a persuasive argument for their choice using the data they've collected. Note that there is not a right or a wrong answer. Some students may believe the convenience is an important factor. Others may point out that more trash would be generated if paper cups were used with the plastic container. If students say this, invite them to weigh a cup and identify how this would impact the weight of the trash that was generated. What is important is that the students justify their thinking and use the data that they generated during the investigation to support their position. (See Figures 5–6 and 5–7.)

8. Have several students read their paragraphs to the class. After each student shares, ask the others to respond to the student's position. After the discussion, pour the juice into individual cups for the students to drink. After the students have drunk the juice, tie the cups up in a plastic grocery bag. After the students estimate the weight of the cups, use the scale to find their weight. As a group, consider how this information might impact the students' thinking.

> Juice Boxes vs. Large container
> I think you should buy the Large container because you can recycle and it costs less. The Juice Boxes will not recycle and it costs more. For a party the container would not be wasted fast. The Juice boxes weigh 110 grams the container weighs 20 grams. If you buy 4 containers and 2 Juice boxes the container will cost $4.00 and the juice box will cost $8.00 plus tax.

Figure 5–6 *Veronica advocated buying the large container of juice, based on cost, amount of trash generated, and the fact that the plastic container can be recycled.*

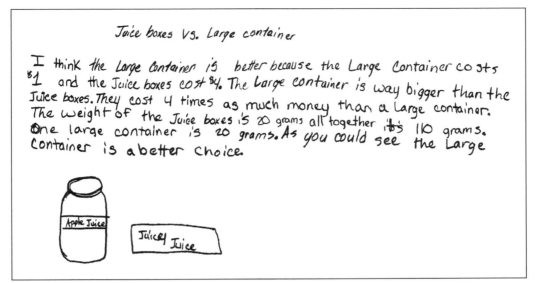

Juice boxes vs. Large container

I think the Large Container is better because the Large Container costs $1 and the Juice boxes cost $4. The Large container is way bigger than the Juice boxes. They cost 4 times as much money than a Large container. The weight of the Juice boxes is 20 grams all together it's 110 grams. One large container is 20 grams. As you could see the Large Container is a better choice.

Figure 5–7 *Jaime believed the large container was a better choice, due to cost and the amount of trash that juice boxes create.*

 A Food Drive

Overview

In this series of activities, students develop their abilities to estimate and measure weight while conducting a food drive. The students create a display to keep track of the weight of incoming contributions. Each day they calculate how many pounds of food they brought that day, how much they have collected so far, and how many more pounds they need to collect to meet their goal.

Materials

◈ several large cardboard boxes to hold the food drive donations
◈ plastic grocery bags, enough to hold the food drive donations
◈ 3-inch-by-8-foot piece of adding machine tape
◈ spring scales that measure ounces and pounds, 1 per small group of students (**Note:** A bathroom scale can be used, but it may not register small numbers of pounds. If this is the case, students will have to weigh themselves with and without the food, and find the difference.)
◈ 24-by-36 inch chart paper, 1 sheet
◈ red crayon
◈ string, 1 foot for each filled plastic bag
◈ 3-inch paper squares, with a small hole punched into one corner, 1 for each filled plastic bag
◈ black marker

Vocabulary: add on, calibrated, convert, convincing argument, estimate, fractions, guess and check, half, horizontally, multiply, numerical reasoning, open number line, ounces, pounds, reasonable, round, scale, skip-count, spring scale, strategy, weight

Instructions

1. To begin the investigation, identify with the students a community organization that would benefit from a food drive. Decide how the students will obtain these donations and from whom. To be safe, you may want to limit donations to those obtained from family and friends. Have the students decide how to publicize the food drive so that they will acquire as many donations as possible. Begin the drive.

2. The next day, have the students place their initial donations in the large box. Explain that each day the class will measure the weight of the food that has been donated. Show the students a spring scale and explain that it measures pounds and ounces. Draw a copy of the spring scale on the board and highlight a line. Ask the groups to determine what weight that line represents and have them explain their thinking. Practice this with several other lines, including lines that represent fractions of pounds or ounces.

spring scale

3. Explain to the class that one way to motivate people is to have a goal and keep track of how close they are to that goal. Tell the students that they will decide on a reasonable goal for their food drive by measuring the weight of several food items collected that day.

4. Provide each group of students with a few donated food items, a plastic grocery bag, and a spring scale. Invite the students to heft the items to make an estimate and then weigh the items. Write this weight on the board. Have the students use

that information to determine what they think would be a reasonable goal for the food drive. Tell the students that they need to make a convincing argument for why that number of pounds would represent a reasonable goal. Encourage them to make estimates based on numerical reasoning. For example, they may count how many students are likely to donate and multiply that number by the bag's weight, or they may determine the portion of the bag's weight that they feel one person is likely to donate. As the students work, check to see that they understand how to read their scales.

5. When everyone is ready, have a class discussion to select a reasonable class goal that is a multiple of ten. As each group presents, invite the other groups to respond to its thinking. Finally, have the class decide on a reasonable goal. If several groups' thinking makes sense, the students may choose to select the average amount.

6. Next have the students create a display on a wall in a central area where the school can watch how the food drive progresses. Ask two students to stretch out the adding machine tape horizontally. Explain to the children that each day they will color portions of the paper red to show how close they are to their goal. When the goal is met, the entire paper will be colored. Label one end of the paper *0* and the other end with goal number.

7. Fold the paper in half. Ask the class to mentally figure half of the goal weight. Have students share their answers and how they figured them. With a marker, draw the halfway line and label it with that number.

8. Have the class help determine how to fold and label smaller sections so that each line is a multiple of ten or a multiple of five. Ask groups of students to think of a plan. For example, they may say, "Fold each of those sections in half, and figure half of the half number, and use that information to find how many pounds three-fourths is." Other groups may suggest a guess-and-check strategy. As a class decide on a strategy, and complete the lines and numbers on the display scale.

9. Have the students label the display scale and attach it vertically to the wall. Ask a student to label the chart paper *Number of Pounds to Our Goal*.

10. Next find out how many pounds of food the students brought that day. First, decide how to deal with fractions of pounds. If your students are new to weight concepts, you may decide to round up if the weight equals a half a pound or more and round down if the weight is less than half a pound. You may, however, want your students to consider exact fractions or to convert from ounces to pounds. Discuss with the students how you want them to approach fractions of pounds.

11. Pass out to each group the rest of the donated food and additional plastic bags. Have the students fill the bags with the food items. For each bag, have the students heft to predict its weight, perhaps by hefting that bag, and then hefting the bag for which they know the weight (see Instruction 4). Then have them use a scale to determine the actual weight. Have the students use string to tie each bag closed. Then have them write the weight on a paper square, list that weight on the board, and then tie the paper square to the bag. Last, have each group figure the total weight of all their bags. Observe the strategies that students use.

12. Now have the groups take turns recording the weight in their bags on the adding machine tape. Have them lightly color in the section that represents the amount they bagged. (You may wish to have the students place a sheet of scrap paper behind the adding machine tape to protect the wall from the crayon.)

13. While each group is coloring its section, have the other students determine how many more pounds they need to meet their goal. Ask the students to share their strategies. Some students may use the traditional procedure to subtract the total that day from the goal: 180 − 22, for example. Other students may add on:

$$22 + 8 = 30$$
$$30 + 70 = 100$$
$$100 + 80 = 180$$
$$8 + 70 + 80 = 158$$

Other students may use an open number line in a manner such as this:

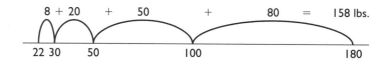

14. When all the groups have recorded, determine the pounds needed to reach the school goal. Have a student record this information on the chart paper.

15. Tell the students that on the first day, every group bagged, estimated, weighed, and recorded, but on subsequent days, only one group will do this. On the board, list what one group of students will do each day of the food drive:

a. *Place the donated food into bags.*

b. *Estimate the weight of each bag by hefting it and comparing it with a labeled bag.*

c. *Weigh the bag.*

d. *Tie it and label it.*

e. *With crayon, mark the new amount on the display.*

f. *Figure out how far the class is from the goal.*

g. *On the chart paper, list how many more pounds are still needed.*

16. When the food drive is over, take the food to the organization the class chose. Many organizations weigh the food and provide a receipt with the total weight. If so, share this receipt with the class. Have them compare the weight on the receipt with the information on their display. If the weights are different, determine why this might be. For example, the scales may be calibrated differently. Additionally, the organization weighed all the items at once, while the class weighed each bag individually, rounding up or down each time, impacting the total.

Heavy and Light Animals

Overview

Students listen to David Taylor's *Heavy and Light Animal Book,* a book that visually compares animal weights with the weight of an eight-year-old child. From a list of animals, they select one to investigate. They estimate and then figure out how many babies or eight-year-olds or adults that, on average, equal the weight of their animal. The students explain in writing how they figured out this relationship and represent it usually by drawing a balance scale with the animal on one side and the number of people that equal the animal's weight on the other side.

Materials

◈ *The Heavy and Light Animal Book,* by David Taylor (1996)

Vocabulary: average, balance scale, conversion, convert, estimate, ounces, pounds, tons

Instructions

1. Read *The Heavy and Light Animal Book* to the students. As you begin reading the book, closely examine the "Weight Box" page, where the weights of the animals are compared with the average weight of an eight-year-old child. Discuss the possible advantages and disadvantages of animals being very light or very heavy.

2. The book's introduction tells how standard English measurements relate to one another—that there are 16 ounces in a pound and 2,000 pounds in a ton. Help the students relate to these units by reminding them that a tennis ball weighs about 2 ounces and an average car weighs about $1\frac{1}{2}$ tons.

3. As you continue to read the book, help the students get a sense of the different measurements that are discussed.

4. Tell the students that they are going to explore how the weights of different animals compare with the average weights of different-age people. On the board write *newborn baby* and have the students make estimates about its average weight. Throughout this discussion, remind the students that there is a lot of variation, but you're talking about the average, or what a typical newborn would weigh. Tell the students that the average weight of a newborn baby is about 7 pounds (Martin et al. 2006), and write that information on the board.

5. Write *eight-year-old child* on the board, along with the information found in the book—*55 pounds*.

6. Next write *grown man*. Have the students predict the average weight; then write *about 190 pounds* (CDC National Center for Health Statistics 2004).

7. Repeat the process for *grown woman* and write *about 160 pounds* (CDC National Center for Health Statistics 2004).

8. Return to the page that describes the kori bustard. Remind the students that the kori bustard can weigh up to 40 pounds, about the weight of a terrier dog. Ask the students to estimate, and then figure out, about how many newborn babies would equal the bird's weight. Have the students share what they think and why. Show the students' thinking on the board. For example, a student might multiply and say, "I know that one seven is seven, two sevens are fourteen, three sevens are twenty-one, four sevens are twenty-eight, five sevens are thirty-five, and six sevens are forty-two. Forty-two is closer to forty than thirty-five is, so about six newborns are about the same weight as a kori bustard." For this explanation, you would write:

$$1 \times 7 = 7$$
$$2 \times 7 = 14$$
$$3 \times 7 = 21$$
$$4 \times 7 = 28$$
$$5 \times 7 = 35$$
$$6 \times 7 = 42$$

9. Explain that one way to show the comparison visually is by sketching a balance scale and drawing six newborns on one side and one kori bustard on the other side. Do a simple sketch as an example.

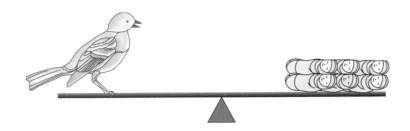

Tell the students that you are illustrating a mathematical relationship so the drawing doesn't have to be perfect—a simple sketch is fine.

10. On the board draw a line under the average human weights. Tell the students that you are going make a list of animals and the number of pounds they weigh, which they will use to make human comparisons of their own. Write a list of animals and their weights, some from the book, and others from other sources. For example:

sea otter: 99 pounds

anaconda: 441 pounds

red kangaroo: 200 pounds

Siberian tiger: 660 pounds

gorilla: 450 pounds

giant clam: 750 pounds

ostrich: 340 pounds

11. Discuss how to convert information that is presented in tons, such as the hippopotamus, which can weigh 3 tons, and the polar bear, which can weigh 1 ton. If necessary, remind the students that a ton is 2,000 pounds, and have them mentally convert the animal weights to pounds. Add the following information to the list on the board:

hippopotamus: 6,000 pounds

polar bear: 2,000 pounds

12. Tell the students that they will choose an animal to investigate and a human age to compare it with. Explain that they will first make an estimate and then calculate using any operation that makes sense to them. Following this, they should make a sketch of a balance to show the relationship that they discovered.

13. As students finish their work, have them share their papers with each other to see if their partner's conclusion makes sense and to marvel at the comparisons that they discovered.

14. When everyone is ready, have several students share their work with the class. Write their calculations on the board, so other students can see the operations and strategies that were used. Note that some students added or multiplied, while others divided. (See Figure 5–8.)

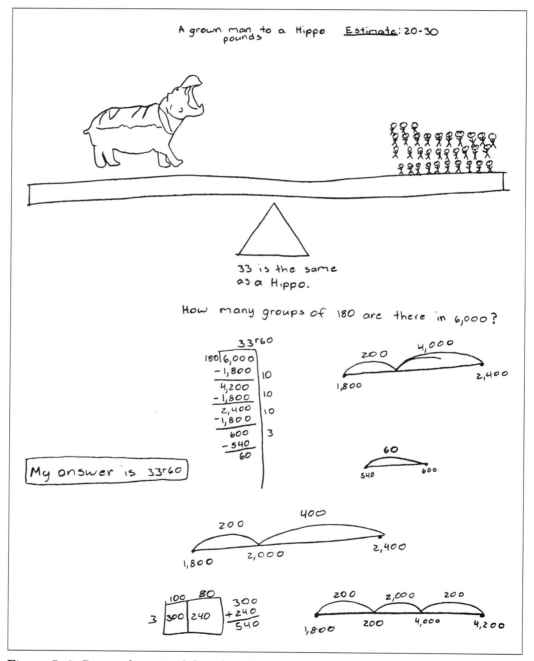

Figure 5–8 *Roman determined that about thirty-three grown men weigh the same as a hippo. When dividing using the partial quotient method, he checked his subtraction using an open number line.*

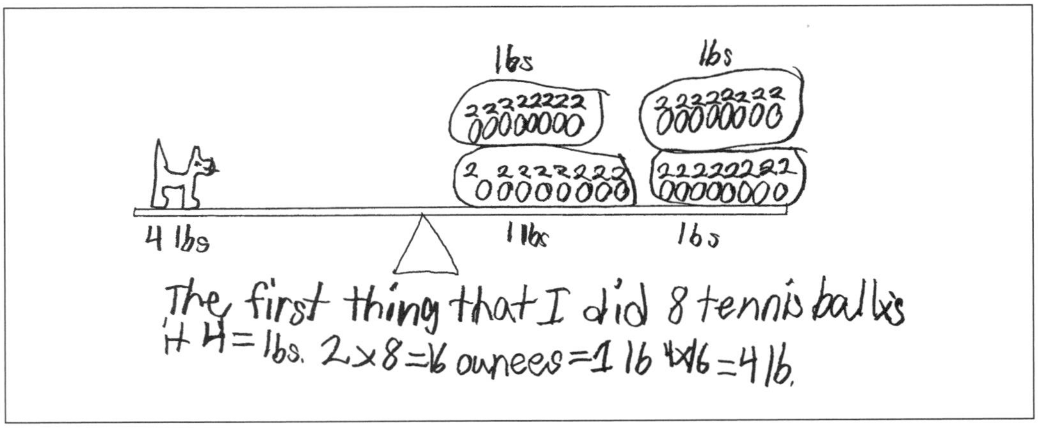
lbs
lbs
4 lbs
1 lbs
lbs
The first thing that I did 8 tennis balls
+ 4 = lbs. 2x8=16 ounces=1 lb 4x16=4 lb.

Figure 5–9 *Courtney compared the weight of a Chihuahua with thirty-two tennis balls.*

15. Offer this same investigation to students another day. Invite them to gather data about other animals or investigate a different animal on the list, and compare the animal with a different-age human.

Extension

- Add animals that are lightweight to the list, such as Kitti's hog-nosed bat (.1 ounce), the Goliath beetle (3 ounces), a Chihuahua (4 pounds), and a mouse deer (7 pounds). Invite the students to compare the weights of animals from the new and old lists not only with people but also with a tennis ball (2 ounces), a car ($1\frac{1}{2}$ tons), and a school bus (12 tons). (See Figure 5–9.)

Time

Introduction

"Hurry up!"

"When will we get there?"

"How long until vacation comes?"

Time significantly impacts our students and their lives, and they come to school with an abundance of personal experiences with time. And yet time is difficult for them, and for us, to quantify: time speeds by quickly when we are happily engaged in something we love and drags on slowly when we sit in the dentist's chair. Tools for representing the passage of time, such as clocks, calendars, and time lines, help frame how we understand time in our culture, and so the lessons in this chapter help students build on and extend their understandings of these tools. Throughout these investigations, students develop benchmarks for units of time, such as seconds, minutes, hours, days, months, and years.

In these lessons, students explore time in a variety of contexts and investigate their world in terms of time. They examine tools we use to keep track of time, by exploring patterns on clock faces and calendars. Students do "minute experiments" to find out how many times they can perform an action in a minute, an hour, a day, or a year. Students investigate elapsed time by using a movie schedule to figure out when movies will end and planning a schedule for seeing the most movies possible in one day. They make time lines for a special day, investigate how much time they spend watching television. Students also explore how time zones change across the world by determining what time they would need to call a friend in a far-away country.

◈ Classroom Decisions

Overview

Opportunities to make decisions about time abound in the classroom. In this type of lesson, teachers include students in making real-life decisions, providing students with chances to recall time equivalencies, to estimate duration, and to compare and add units of time.

Materials

◈ chart paper, 1–2 sheets
◈ standard size calendar

Vocabulary: April, August, day, December, February, Friday, hour, January, July, June, March, May, minute, Monday, month, November, October, Saturday, September, Sunday, Thursday, Tuesday, Wednesday, Year

Instructions

1. Begin a class chart with units of time for the students to refer to when opportunities to explore time occur naturally in the classroom. Label the chart *Units of Time*. Ask the students to help you fill in the following information, and provide them with information about units of time that they do not have:

   _60_ seconds in a minute

   _60_ minutes in an hour

   _24_ hours in a day

   _7_ days in a week

   _12_ months in a year

2. Have your class keep track of the passing days on a regular calendar by crossing off each day that passes. This will provide a classroom reference that students can use to recall the days of the week and months in the year when the need arises. It will also encourage students to ask and answer their own questions about time, such as "What day will my birthday be on?" and "How long is it until summer vacation?"

3. As you teach, be aware of opportunities to include students in timing decisions that you might typically make yourself. When such an opportunity arises, tell the students about the decision that must be made. Here are some examples:

   • Do we have time to share the results of our geometry investigation before lunch, or should we wait and do it after lunch?
   • How many students can read their stories aloud before we go home, if each story takes about 3 minutes to read?
   • How many weeks do we have until our field trip to the science museum?
   • If the final draft of your Arizona report must be completed by Friday, when do you plan to have the first draft finished? When do you plan to have a peer review? When do you plan to conference with me about it?
   • If our graduation party is May 23, what things do we need to accomplish to plan for the party, and by when do we need to do these things?

4. Ask the students what they need to know in order to answer a question such as those in the previous list. For example, they might need to know how many more

minutes it is until lunch or perhaps how many minutes are in an hour. Remind students to refer to the "Units of Time" chart when necessary, and add any additional equivalencies that will help them determine the answer.

5. Have groups of students discuss what a reasonable answer would be and why they think that answer makes sense. Encourage students to come to an agreement about what a reasonable duration of a particular activity might be. For example, one student might think that it would take about 15 minutes to hear the next chapter in the class read-aloud, but another student might think it would take a half hour. Encourage the students to choose a time upon which they can all agree.

6. Have the students share their thinking, come to a consensus about the decision, and then carry out the decision. Later, have the students reflect about whether they had to modify their decision or whether it worked as it was.

◈ Minute Experiments

Overview
Students explore how long a minute is by doing experiments. They predict, and then find out, how many times they can repeat an action in a minute, such as make a star, bounce a ball, or say, "Rumpelstiltskin." The students compare their results with their predictions, determining how much they over- or underestimated. Lastly, they use the results of their experiment to figure out how many times they could do that action in a longer period of time, such as an hour, a day, a week, and/or a year.

Materials
◈ classroom clock with a minute hand that the entire class can see, or watches with a minute hand or timers, 1 per pair of students
◈ materials needed for specific experiments, such as balls to bounce, 1 per student

Vocabulary: day, estimate, hour, minute, overestimate, underestimate, week, year

Instructions

1. Tell the students that they are going to do an experiment to see if they can estimate how long a minute is. Explain that they will close their eyes, you will say, "Go," and you will begin to time a minute. Explain that each of them will put up a thumb when he or she thinks a minute has passed.

2. Now ask the students to put their heads down so they can't see anyone or the clock, and do the experiment. At the end of a minute, say, "Stop."

3. Afterward, discuss how easy or hard the experiment was, and whether they underestimated or overestimated. Have the students share strategies that they used to estimate a minute. For example, some students may have counted to sixty and other students may just have sensed how long a minute feels.

4. Discuss different things that people can do over and over, list them on the board, and have the students predict how many of them they can do in a minute. For example:

In a Minute We Can:

bounce a ball 20 times

make a star 70 times

say, "Rumpelstiltskin," 37 times

snap our fingers 50 times

sing "Happy Birthday" 10 times

do 42 jumping jacks

write our name 25 times

5. Ask the students to pair up, discuss the experiments, and select one that they would like to do. Have the students record what they will do and predict how many times they can do it in one minute.

6. Discuss how partners can help each other. For example, one student might do jumping jacks and count them while the other student keeps an eye on the clock, starting and stopping the experiment. In some instances tallies might be helpful. For example, one student might say, "Rumpelstiltskin," over and over, making a tally mark each time, while the other student watches the clock, starting and stopping the experiment.

7. Have partners perform the experiment and record how many times they actually did the task. Have the students figure out, and record, how far off their prediction was from the actual outcome, and whether they overestimated or underestimated.

8. Have partners share with the class what they discovered, whether they underestimated or overestimated, and how far off their estimates were.

9. Invite the students to use their data to figure out how many of the same task they could do in an hour, in a day, in a week, and/or in a year. To do this, students will need knowledge of time equivalencies, such as there are 60 minutes in an hour, 24 hours in a day, 7 days in a week, and 52 weeks in a year. If necessary, list this

information on the board as a reference. Ask the students to record on paper what they figured out and how they figured. Then have several students share their thinking with the class.

◈ Time Lines of a Wonderful Day

Overview

In this lesson, students make a time line that represents the things they would like to do on a wonderful day, such as at home on a summer day or a day at Disneyland or a day exploring the jungle. Students decide what activities they will do and how long they will do each one and record their day on a time line. In this way, students develop understanding of duration, and they use units on a scale to represent the linear way that we experience time.

Materials

◈ time line paper, 1 per student, plus a few extra (see Blackline Masters)
◈ crayons, 1 box per student
◈ demonstration clock

Vocabulary: A.M., half, hour, minute, P.M., quarter, time line

Instructions

1. Explain to the students that today they will plan the most wonderful day they can imagine—a day when they can do anything they want anywhere they want! Tell the students that they will create a time line to describe all the things they would like to do at any place that has a lot of different things to do. Begin by having the students brainstorm some places where they would like to be, for example, at home, at Disneyland, at Sea World, in the jungle, or on Mars. On the board list the places the students suggest. As the students add to the list, have them tell some different things they might want to do at those places.

2. Tell the students that they will decide in what order to do those activities and how long to do them. Explain that the time line will help them represent their day. Show the students the time line paper that they will use.

3. Make a sample time line as the students watch. Cut apart the three time line sections and glue the tabs under each succeeding piece so that you create a blank time line. Explain that the longer vertical lines will represent the hours they will be awake that day.

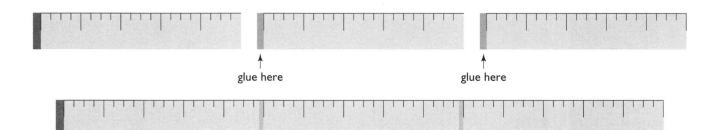

4. Discuss what a reasonable time would be to wake up and to go to bed. On your sample time line, beneath the long vertical lines, write the whole hours that will make up your day. For example, if you decide to wake at 7:30 A.M. and go to bed at 9:00 P.M., the vertical lines will represent the hours 7:00 A.M., 8:00 A.M., 9:00 A.M., and so on until 9:00 P.M. Tell the students that they may need to cut an additional section so that their time line will be long enough.

5. Ask the students to write the hours on their own time lines. Their time lines will only vary slightly, depending on when they wake up and when they go to bed. When the students finish, have them read the hours aloud. Hold up a demonstration clock and, as the students read each hour, move the hands of the clock to show how an analog clock would look. Pause when the students say each hour so they have a chance to make that visual connection.

6. Next have the students examine the spaces between each hour and predict how many minutes each of those sections must represent. As the students share what they think, note that there are four equal pieces between hours, and these must be fourths of an hour, or quarter hours. Use the demonstration clock to show how a quarter hour looks and to verify the correct answer: 15 minutes. Write *15 minutes* on the board. Next ask the students to tell how many minutes are in two quarter-hours, and then three quarter-hours. After verifying the answer on the clock, write on the board *30 minutes* and *45 minutes*.

7. Show the students how they will use the time line to represent their day. Tell the students that you would like a peaceful day at your house all by yourself. At the bottom of your time line, write A *Peaceful Day at Home*.

8. Tell the students that the time lines will show activities that last 15 minutes, 30 minutes, 45 minutes, 1 hour, 1 hour and 15 minutes, 1 hour and 30 minutes, and so on. But explain that the amounts of time must be reasonable. For example, you wouldn't be likely to eat breakfast for two hours.

9. As the students watch, decide how you will spend this wonderful day at home, recording each activity in order. Be sure to include things such as eating meals, and include activities that last different amounts of time, such as an hour and a half or 1 hour and 45 minutes. Record how long the first activity will last by using a crayon to color in the top part of the time line. Record the second activity with a contrasting color and label it as well. Continue filling in parts of your day until you feel that the students understand their task.

	Read in bed	Eat breakfast	Bake cookies	Eat a leisurely	Read my book	Work out
10:00 A.M.	11:00 A.M. in bed	12:00 P.M.	1:00 P.M. lunch with	2:00 P.M.	3:00 P.M.	4:00 P.M.
Wake up			Mr. Confer			

Watch Oprah	Dress for	Eat at LeRondezvous with		Go to a movie		
4:00 P.M. Winfrey	5:00 P.M. going	6:00 P.M. friends 7:00 P.M.	8:00 P.M.	9:00 P.M.	10:00 P.M.	
	out				Go to sleep	

My Peaceful Day at Home

10. Give each student time line paper, crayons, scissors, and a glue stick. As the students create their time lines, engage them in discussions about their choices. While they are working, have students explain why they think their choices are reasonable.

11. When students finish, have several of them share their time lines with the class. Have them explain why they chose the order they did and why they think the amounts of time they chose make sense. (See Figures 6–1 and 6–2.)

12. Post student's a time line on the board. Have the student who made the time line select a favorite activity and tell the times he began and ended that activity.

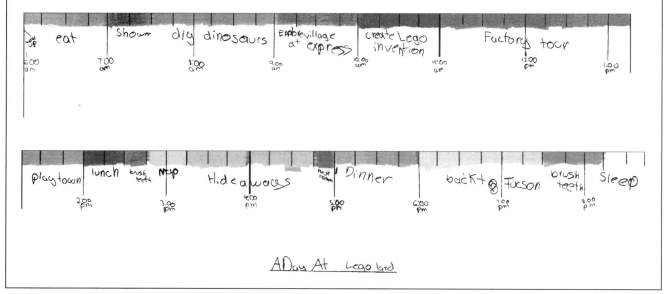

Figure 6–1 *Jonathan's day at Legoland included digging for dinosaurs for one-and-a-half hours and creating a Lego invention for one hour.*

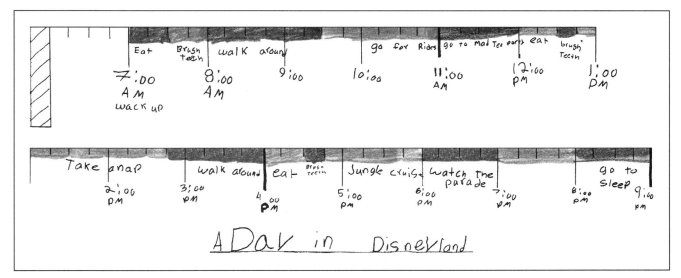

Figure 6–2 *Courtney went on the Disneyland Jungle Cruise for an hour and fifteen minutes.*

Write the name of the activity, the start time, and the end time on the board. Provide students with blank paper. Ask partners to figure out how long the student did that activity and how they know that. Have several students explain their thinking. Show the students' thinking using the time line.

Then show the same thing using the demonstration clock and an open time line. For example, an activity that began at 9:45 A.M. and ended at 11:00 A.M. could be shown on the student's time line and the open time line in the following ways:

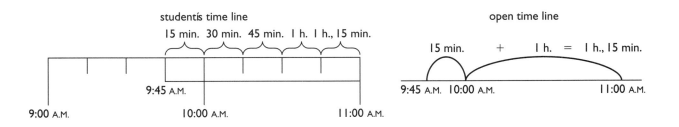

To provide students with additional practice thinking about elapsed time, repeat this process with other students' time lines.

Variations

During a social studies unit on a foreign country, have the students make a time line about a day in the life of someone from that culture. Or during a science unit, have the students make a related time line. For example, when studying oceanography, the students could make a time line about a day in the life of a scuba diver, or when discussing gravity, they could make a time line of a day without gravitational pull. Students can record a biography of a historical figure on a time line with years rather than minutes.

 **Time to Go Home**

Overview

Students are frequently interested in how much time must pass until the bell rings to go home after school. This lesson capitalizes on their interest, providing students with several opportunities to repeatedly try out different strategies to answer this question. This activity provides students with opportunities to use models such as a T-chart and open time line to keep track of duration and elapsed time.

Materials

◈ large Judy clock or other analog demonstration clock with moveable hands

Vocabulary: A.M., estimate, half, hour, minute, open time line, P.M., quarter, T-chart, three-quarters

Instructions

1. Begin this lesson in the morning, and return to it periodically during the day. Have the students read the classroom clock and then talk to a partner to come to an agreement on the present time. Ask a student to share what the current time is, and write it on the board, with the label *Current time*. Include the abbreviation A.M. Remind the students that this indicates the hours prior to noon. Then ask the students to estimate in hours how much time must pass until it is time to go home. Remind the students that an estimate means *about* how much time, and would include the number of hours and perhaps a friendly fraction such as a quarter hour, a half hour, or three-quarters of an hour. Write *Estimates* on the board, along with several of their estimates.

2. Tell the students that they will work in pairs to find out how many hours and minutes must pass from that time until it's time to go home. Ask the students what time the dismissal bell rings, and have a student write that time, with the abbreviation P.M., on the board with the label *Dismissal time*. Remind the students that P.M. indicates the hours after noon.

3. Explain to the students that they are to solve the problem and record their thinking. Tell the students that someone reading their paper must be able to understand the steps that they took to figure out the answer without having to ask them. Remind the students about various models they might use to solve the problem, such as pictures of clocks, a T-chart, or an open time line.

4. As the students work, observe the strategies they use to solve the problem and how they keep track of any partial answers they get. When they finish, encourage the

students to compare their answer with their estimate, to make sure that the answer makes sense.

5. Bring the students together for a class discussion. Have students who have different models or ways to think about time share their work. As students share their thinking, make sure that the class understands how that student subdivided the time and how the student kept track of the time that elapsed for each segment. For example, to represent the time that must pass from 8:43 A.M. to 2:35 P.M., a student might count forward in complete hours, from 8:43 to 9:43, to 10:43, 11:43, 12:43, and 1:43. Then she might go to 2:00, then to 2:30, then 2:35. The open time line might look like this:

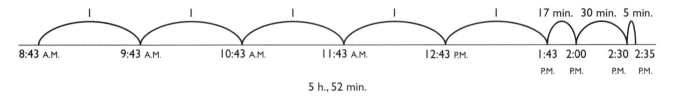

Have the class compare the student's answer with the class estimates. Tell the class that it is important to compare their answers with their estimates to make sure their answers are reasonable.

6. Next use the demonstration clock to show the each student's thinking. Show the class how a T-chart can show the same information and help keep track of each division of time and the cumulative elapsed time.

Time	Elapsed Time	
9:43 A.M.	1 h.	
10:43 A.M.	1 h.	
11:43 A.M.	1 h.	5 h.
12:43 P.M.	1 h.	
1:43 P.M.	1 h.	
2:00 P.M.	17 min.	
2:30 P.M.	30 min.	52 min.
2:35 P.M.	5 min.	

7. Another way a student might think about the time is to count forward to even hours, such as from 8:43 to 9:00, then to 12:00, then 2:00, and then 2:35. The open time line would then look like this:

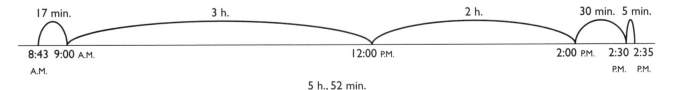

Show this strategy on the demonstration clock and how a T-chart can help keep track of this same method.

Time	Elapsed Time
9:00 A.M.	17 min.
12:00 P.M.	3 h.
2:00 P.M.	2 h.
2:30 P.M.	30 min.
2:35 P.M.	5 min.

5 h.

52 min.

8. Return to this lesson several times during the day, to see how much less time must pass until dismissal time. Repeated experiences allow students to use their previous strategies more efficiently and to try out new models or strategies that they've seen other students use.

TV Time!

Overview

How much television do children watch? In this lesson, students investigate this question by gathering data, and then they draw conclusions about their television viewing habits.

Materials

◈ *This Book Is About Time*, by Marilyn Burns (1978)
◈ chart paper, at least 2 sheets
◈ cubes, enough so that each student has the same number of counters as hours he watches television in a week, about 30 per student
◈ *TV Time!* recording sheets, 1 per student (see Blackline Masters)

Vocabulary: average, data, hours, minutes, typical

Instructions

1. Read parts of *This Book Is About Time* to the class. As you read, invite students to react to some of the statements.

2. In small groups, have the students discuss their beliefs about whether or not children watch too much television. Ask them to predict a typical amount of time a student their age watches television each day. Explain that "a typical amount of time" means the time that is common for students to watch television on a regular day. Discuss how this might be different on weekends or school days.

3. In a class discussion, have groups share their beliefs and predictions. As each group shares, write the group's prediction on chart paper. Title the paper *Television Time Predictions*.

4. Distribute the *TV Time!* recording sheets to the students. Explain that for the next week, they will keep track of the amount of time they spend watching television.

5. When the week is over, have students bring their recording sheets to school. In small groups, have them compare their data, looking for similarities and differences.

6. On the board, write the following questions:
   - *How much television did you watch each day?*
   - *How much television did you watch during the entire week?*
   - *What do you think about the amount of television you watched?*

7. Have the students use their own data to calculate the answers.

8. Discuss the total hours that they watched television. Compare their data to their predictions. Find the shortest amount of time anyone watched TV and the longest time. Have the students discuss their reactions to their data and whether they were surprised. (See Figures 6–3 and 6–4.)

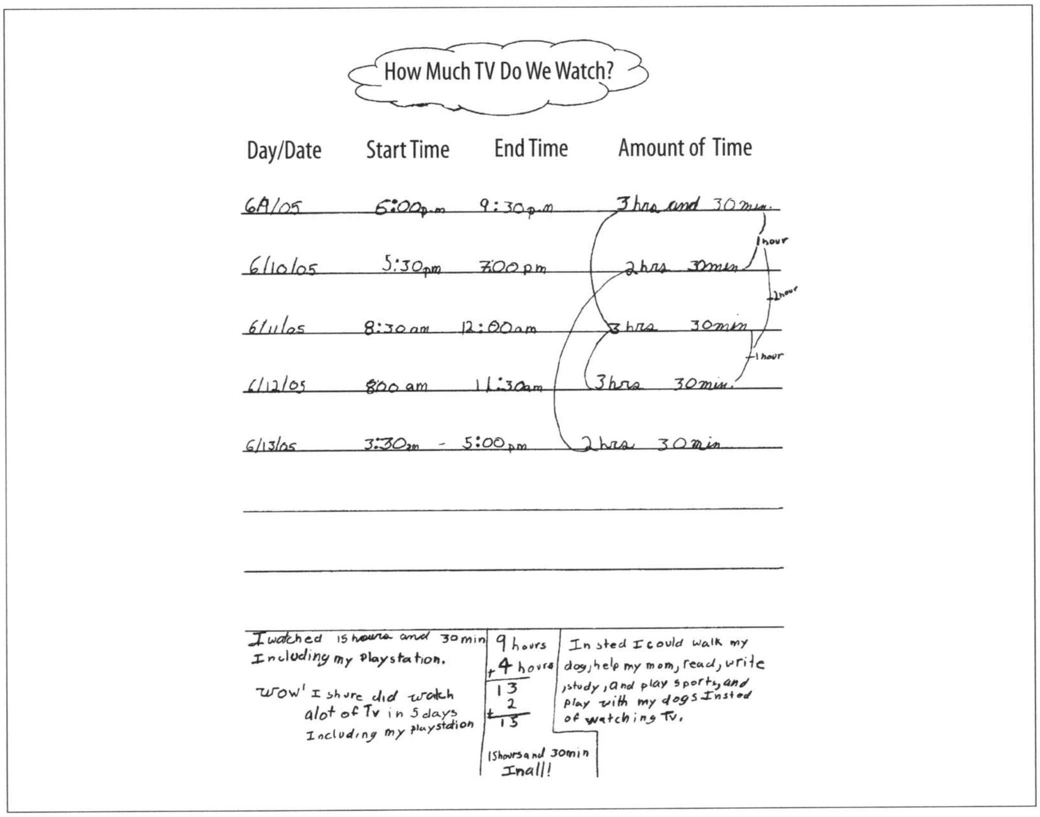

Figure 6–3 *Catalina had some difficulty interpreting elapsed time, but she used effective strategies for adding the total amount of time she watched television.*

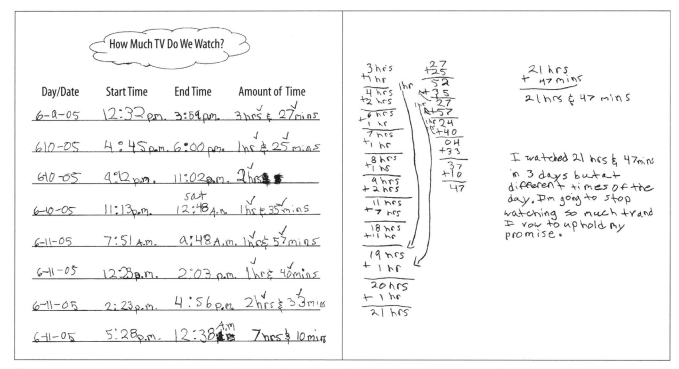

Figure 6–4 *Arnulfo added minutes and mentally subtracted out sixties to make hours. He was surprised to find that he watched 21 hours and 47 minutes of television in only three days.*

9. Discuss how to find what is a typical, or average, amount of time for the entire class. Suggest that each student get a cube for each full hour that he or she watched television that week.

10. Have the students in each group "even out" how many cubes each has, by giving each other cubes until everyone in the group has as close to the same number as possible.

11. Then, have pairs of groups gather together to even out their cubes, so that each person has as close to the same number as possible.

12. On the board, write the number of cubes that each student has. Ask if any students need to give other students a cube so that everyone in the room will have as close to the same number as possible. If so, have those students make the exchanges.

13. Explain that the number of cubes that most students have at this point can be considered the average. Write this number on the board. Explain that this process of evening out is a mathematical way to determine what is typical. Compare this information with the class predictions listed on the "Television Time Predictions" chart.

14. On the board, write:

- *Does this amount of time surprise you?*
- *In your opinion is this amount of TV OK?*
- *If not, what would be a more reasonable amount?*

15. Have the groups discuss these questions. Then have a class discussion about their conclusions. Encourage students to respond to their classmates' opinions and beliefs.

16. Ask the students to consider what people outside of school would like to have their data and conclusions. The students may suggest their parents, the school board, or a television station. Have the students select one of these people or places to communicate their findings to. For example, they might want to write a letter to their family or send a letter to a television station. Or perhaps they might share this information with their city recreation program directors in order to encourage more programs that provide alternative activities to television watching.

Let's Go to the Movies!

Overview

In this lesson, students work with elapsed time as they make a schedule for an imaginary day at the movies. From a list of movies with beginning and running times, students select a movie that is shorter than an hour and a half and calculate when it will end. After students share strategies with this simple problem, they figure out a schedule for seeing as many movies as possible for the entire day. During a class discussion, students share their strategies for both finding the ending times of their movie choices and how they fit in as many movies as possible.

Materials

❖ *Let's Go to the Movies!* worksheet, 1 per student (see Blackline Masters)

Vocabulary: elapsed time, equations, hours, minutes, open time line, schedule

Instructions

1. Begin by explaining to the students that they are going to plan an imaginary day at the movies. Provide the students with the *Let's Go to the Movies!* sheet, showing the imaginary movies from which they may choose. Tell the students that real movie schedules have this organization: the name of the movie, its running time, and the times the movie begins. Invite the students to read the movie choices and think about which movies sound interesting to them.

2. Next tell the students that they are going to imagine that one Saturday their mom tells them that they can go see any movie they want, but since they have many chores to do, they can only see a movie that lasts less than an hour and a half. Ask them which movies they can see and how they know those movies are less than an hour and a half. On the board list this information:

$$1 \ hour = 60 \ minutes$$

$$1\tfrac{1}{2} \ hours = 90 \ minutes$$

3. Now ask the students to look at the movie *Cartoon Capers*. Ask them to examine the different times the movie begins, and then look at the 2:20 start time and the running time of the movie—85 minutes. Have students work in partners to figure out what time that showing of *Cartoon Capers* ends.

4. When the students finish, have several of them share what they did. As each student shares, record on the board how he or she identified the ending time. This will provide the students with possible models for keeping track of their thinking when doing problems with elapsed time. For example, a student might use an open time line to solve the problem:

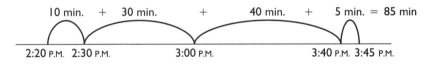

Ask the student to explain to the others how the numbers at the bottom helped her keep track of the time, and the numbers at the top helped her keep track of how many minutes had passed.

You may find that some students subtract from the running time to keep track of how many minutes passed. For example, the student might write:

$$85 - 10 = 75$$

$$75 - 30 = 45$$

$$45 - 40 = 5$$

$$5 - 5 = 0$$

Another student might write equations to solve the problem. For example, the student might write:

$$85 \ minutes = 60 \ min. + 25 \ min.$$

$$2{:}20 + 1 \ hour = 3{:}20$$

$$3{:}20 + 25 \ minutes = 3{:}45$$

5. Do several other examples together by selecting a movie and a start time, and having the students determine the time that show would end.

6. Now introduce the students to a new investigation. Tell them that their imaginary day is a very special day: they get to spend all day at the movies. And since the movies are all free, they can see as many as they want. On the board write:

> *Work with a partner to choose the movies you will see that day. Try to see as many as possible. For each movie, list its name and its running time. Then write the beginning time that you choose and the time the movie ends. Show how you figured out the ending time.*

7. As the students work, support them and adapt the lesson as needed. For example, some students may be less proficient at modeling elapsed time, so you may have them explore beginning and ending times for a single movie or a pair of movies. Encourage more proficient students to fit the most movies possible in a single day.

8. When the students finish, have a whole-class discussion. Invite a pair of students to share a movie they selected and the starting time that they chose. As those students put their work on the board, have the other students in the class predict the ending time of that movie. Next have the pair explain its strategy and its answer. Invite the listeners to ask questions. If there is a disagreement about the correct ending time, use an open time line to show how the time elapsed during each step. This kind of visual representation often helps students keep track of partial answers.

9. Invite another pair of students to share in the same way. After several pairs of students have shared their work, have a discussion about how many movies fit into their day and how they were able to fit that many. Ask students to share their strategies. For example, many students look for the earliest showing of a movie and begin with that one. Then, after they find the ending time of that movie, they find the movie with a beginning time that is closest to the ending time of the previous movie. (See Figures 6–5, 6–6, and 6–7.)

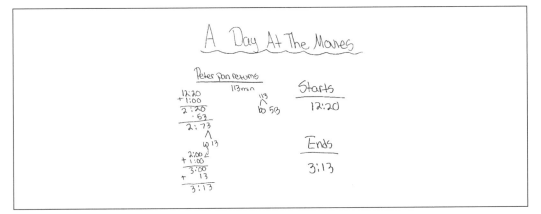

Figure 6–5 *Sarita decomposed 113 minutes into 60 minutes and 53 minutes. When she added that amount she came to 2 hours and 73 minutes, so she decomposed 73 into 60 minutes and 13 minutes.*

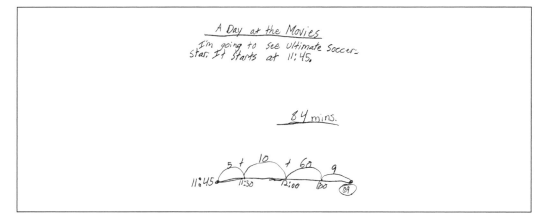

Figure 6–6 *Uyen used an open time line to figure out when the soccer movie ended.*

Figure 6–7 *Nura calculated how much time she spent waiting for movies to start.*

The Last Day of School

Overview

One of the best ways for students to consider the concept of duration, or elapsed time, is to connect it to their real lives. In this activity, the students figure out how long it is until one of the most significant days of the year, the last day of school. The students first explore real calendars. Then they use the calendars to solve the problem or use more abstract representations such as an open time line. As the students work, they become more familiar with the consecutive month names, the numbers of days in each month, and they develop flexible strategies for computation.

Materials

◈ calendars for the current year, 1 per pair of students

Vocabulary: calendar, month, open time line, year

Instructions

1. Pass out a calendar for the current year to each pair of students. Provide the students with some time to explore their calendars, finding months and dates that are

important to them, such as their birthdays. Ask the students to share what they discovered about the calendars. As they talk, highlight information that will be helpful for all the students to recognize, for example, how many days are in a week, how many days are in specific months, consecutive names of the months, and so on. List this information on the board.

2. Explain to the students that they will figure out how many days must pass until the last day of school. Ask the students what else they need to know in order to solve a problem like that. List what they say on the board. They may mention things such as the current date or the date of the last day of school.

3. Ask the students what the current date is, and write it on the board. Then, if the students don't know it, tell the students the date of the last day of school and write it on the board as well.

4. Now invite the students to solve the problem with a partner. Explain that although they may work together, they are to individually record what they're thinking in words, numbers, and pictures, as well as the solution.

5. As the students work, encourage them to make their writing so explicit that a reader can understand what each calculation represents without asking them.

6. To begin a whole-class discussion, ask several students how many days they think must pass until the last day of school and to explain how they figured it out. As each student shares, make sure the others understand the student's model and thinking. For example, some students might list the days left in the current month and add on the remaining months one at a time. Other students might multiply the months that have the same number of days, and then combine those numbers, adding on the remaining days in the current month. If students do not use an open time line, demonstrate how that tool can be helpful to keep track of time in a consecutive manner.

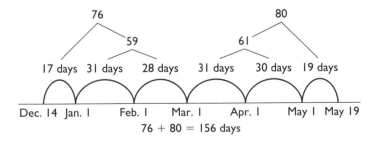

7. Repeat this lesson periodically, as the last day of school gets closer and closer.

 **How Old Are You?**

Overview

In this lesson, students hear the lovely story *On the Day You Were Born*, by Debra Frasier. They then use a calendar and a time line to explore how many months old a two-year-old is, and finally how old they are in months. This large number frequently surprises and impresses them.

Materials

◈ calendars (old or new), 1 per small group of students

◈ *On the Day You Were Born*, by Debra Frasier (1991)

Vocabulary: months, time line, years

Instructions

1. Read the book *On the Day You Were Born* to the students. Enjoy the book's message about how special each newborn is, and discuss the different ways that families welcome babies into the world.

2. Ask several students to share their birthday, including the year they were born. Pass out a calendar to each pair of students. Give them some time to explore how their calendar is organized and notice its particular features. Then have the students share some things they discovered. Make sure they mention how many months are in a year. Have them find their birthdays on the calendar.

3. Have the students figure out how many months old a two-year-old is who was born on December 31, 2002, if the current date is March 31, 2005. On the board draw a time line to represent this situation.

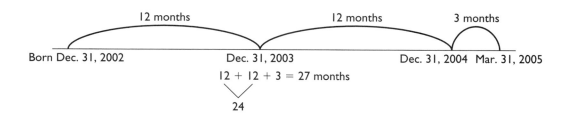

Make sure that the students understand that they need to count each month after the child turned two, by listing *January, February, March* on the board. Have the students share what they think and why they think that.

4. Next explain to the students that they are going to investigate how old they are, not in years but in months. Ask them to record not only their answer but also how

they figured it out. Suggest that the time line might be a helpful model, but encourage the students to use anything that makes sense to them. Discuss how they might deal with parts of months. For example, they might use fractions of months for remaining days. Or they might round up or down: if there is more than a half month, they might count a whole month, but if there is less than a half month, they might not include those days.

5. As students finish, have them exchange papers and see if their partner's results make sense. Invite two students to show their work on the board.

6. When the class is finished, gather the students for a whole-group discussion. Ask a student to share her age and how she figured it out. Have the class ask questions about the student's work. Do the same with another student's work.

7. Explain to the students that they can now tell people that they are, for example, 142. When people say it's not true, the students can explain that yes, it's true. They are 142 *months* old!

Extension

◈ Follow the same procedure but have the students figure out how many days old they are. (See Figure 6–8.)

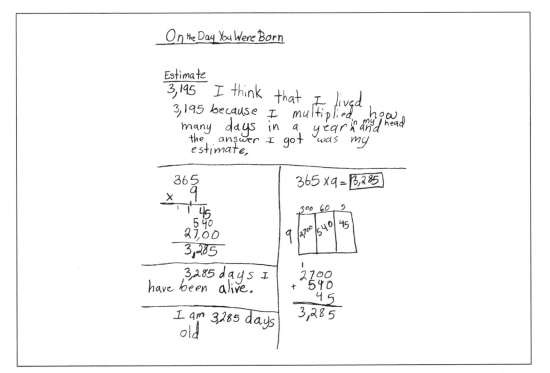

Figure 6–8 *Lara determined that she is 3,285 days old by multiplying using partial products and an open array. She did not add on the number of days that she had lived beyond her ninth birthday.*

 **Calendar Patterns**

Overview

This lesson provides students with an opportunity to become acquainted with characteristics of calendars. As students search for and describe all the patterns that they can find on calendars, they become acquainted with how calendars are organized and how units of time relate to each other.

Materials

- ◈ calendars from any year, 1 per pair of students
- ◈ chart paper, 1–2 sheets

Vocabulary: calendar, date, day, diagonal, month, multiples, patterns, vertical

Instructions

1. Provide each pair of students with a calendar. Give the students a few minutes to become acquainted with their calendars. They will most likely want to find their birthdays and other days that are special to them in some way. As the students do this, make sure they know how to determine what day a date falls on.

2. Label a sheet of chart paper with the title *Calendar Patterns*. Explain to the students that they will investigate patterns in the calendar. Tell them to find as many different patterns as they can. Suggest to the students that they search for patterns in the words as well as in the numbers. Ask the students to make notes of the patterns that they find so they can share what they discover during a class discussion.

3. After the students have made a list of patterns, begin the discussion by having students take turns sharing a pattern. Write each pattern on the chart, and then have the other students find that same pattern on their calendar. Ask the students to verify whether that same pattern occurs each month.

4. Students usually identify the pattern of the days of the week. On the chart list each day along with its abbreviation. Students may also call the names of the months a pattern, since they happen in the same order year after year. List the months along with their abbreviations.

5. Students will find a variety of number patterns. A student might find the diagonal number pattern 6, 12, 18, 24. Write those numbers on the chart. Ask the students the mathematical name for that pattern. Write *multiples of six* next to the numbers. Ask the students whether that same pattern appears each month. As the students compare how this pattern appears in different months, they will find variations, with some months having 6 and 12 in one diagonal line and 18, 24, and 30 in

another diagonal line. Ask the students if they can explain why that happens in some months but not in others. (A month that has 6 in the first row will have 6, 12, 18, 24, and 30 in the same diagonal line.)

6. Students may find other diagonal patterns such as numbers that increase by six each time, starting with a number other than six, or numbers that increase by eight each time. Likewise, students may find vertical patterns such as multiples of seven or numbers in other columns that increase by seven each time. Discuss these patterns and the students' theories about what makes those patterns occur.

7. Another number pattern that students usually find is that of even numbers. Ask the students whether the final date in each month is even or odd. Students may find that some months have the thirtieth day and/or the thirty-first day written in an unusual way. If so, have them consider why that happens. (These are months with first days that begin late in the week, which would require an additional row of dates.) Make a vertical list of the final date of each month and ask the students if there is a pattern. Underline the months that end with 31:

<u>January 31</u>   <u>July 31</u>

February 28   <u>August 31</u>

<u>March 31</u>   September 30

April 30   <u>October 31</u>

<u>May 31</u>   November 30

June 30   <u>December 31</u>

Read the pattern as "long month, short month, long month, short month . . ." and identify where the pattern breaks down. Share with the children a way to help them remember which months are long and which are short. Have the students hold up their fists together and label each knuckle as a long month and each space between each knuckle as a short month.

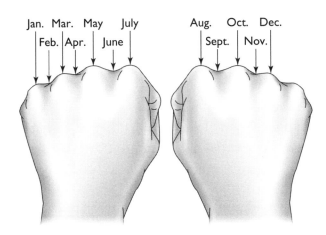

8. Discuss any other patterns that the students find.

 **Patterns on the Clock Face**

Overview

In this lesson, students explore the different patterns they see on a clock face, both in how the hands move on a demonstration clock and in the numbers written and implied by the lines between numbers. Then students work in pairs to find all the different ways the minute hand can move evenly in multiples as it passes from 1:00 to 2:00. As they do this investigation, students gain a better understanding of how to read an analog clock and facility with recording time.

Materials

◈ demonstration analog clock

◈ *Patterns on the Clock Face* recording sheets, copied on both sides of the paper, 5 per student (see Blackline Masters)

◈ transparencies of *Patterns on the Clock Face* recording sheet, 1–2

◈ rulers, 1 per student

Vocabulary: clock, hour, hour hand, minute, minute hand, multiple, pattern

Instructions

1. Show the students the demonstration clock. Turn the hands on the clock. Ask the students what patterns occur over and over. They may say things such as "The hour hand makes a circle over and over" or "The minute hand moves from the 1 to 2 to 3 . . ." or "Whenever the minute hand points to the six, the hour hand is halfway between two numbers."

2. Next place the hour hand at 1:00, turn the minute hand, and have the students consider the number patterns in the minutes on the clock. For example, a student may note that the minute hand can show multiples of five, as it goes from 5 to 10 to 15 to 20, and so on, up to 60, which is implied when the clock shows 2:00. Have the students count by twos as you move the minute hand from 1:00 to 2:00. Note that, again, the minute hand ended evenly on 60 minutes (2:00).

3. Next have the students look at multiples of 9 on the clock: 9, 18, 27, 36, 45, and 54. Note that the minute hand won't end on 60, that there are leftover minutes. Explain to the students that you can't go from 1:00 to exactly 2:00 when counting by nines.

4. Tell the students their task: they are to work with a partner to find all the different numbers of minutes that can evenly go from 1:00 to 2:00, with no leftover minutes. Explain that these numbers have 60 as a multiple. Write multiple on the board.

5. Show the students the transparency of the clock face recording sheet. Explain that each time they find a number that works, they are to draw all the places that the minute hand will point. Do an example for counting by fives.

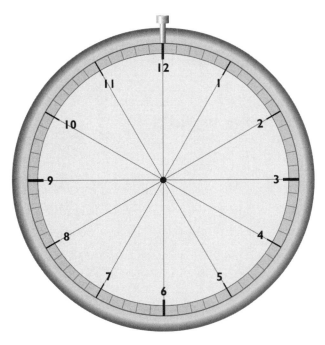

1:05, 1:10, 1:15, 1:20, 1:25, 1:30, 1:35, 1:40, 1:45, 1:50, 1:55, 2:00

After you draw the short lines, continue drawing the lines all the way to the center dot. Explain to the students that they will do the same so a reader can more easily see the pattern. Also tell the students to write all the times on the lines beneath the clock face: 1:05, 1:10, 1:15, 1:20, 1:25, and so on.

6. Ask the students to quickly predict whether they will find more than two numbers that work, or more than five, or more than ten. Pass out two clock face recording sheets to each student, and place the remaining papers in a pile in a central area where the students can help themselves.

7. Now have the partners begin the investigation, finding all the different numbers whose multiples include 60. Observe the students as they work. Some will count on by each trial number, while others may use their knowledge of multiplication, and still others may think about what numbers sixty can be evenly divided by. Also observe the students' facility with reading time on a clock face and writing time in the standard manner.

8. After the students have found many patterns, have a pair of students share one pattern that works. As they share, show that pattern on the demonstration clock and list the number and its multiples on the board. Then have the students share the strategy they used to find that number pattern. For example, some students may have looked for factors of 60 or factors of a number they already found that work. If a student mentions factors, write that term on the board and remind the students that factors are two whole numbers that can be multiplied to get a third number. Next have a different pair share a different pattern of multiples. Continue sharing until all the different ways are listed on the board: 1, 2, 3, 4, 5, 6, 10, 12, 15, 20, and 30. If the students mention that 60 should be on the list, decide as a group whether 60 meets the criteria for the task, since the minute hand did not move at all.

Somewhere in the World

Overview

Stacey Schuett's poetic book *Somewhere in the World Right Now* helps children recognize what people might be doing in different places around the world during a single moment. In this lesson, the children select a place on the other side of the world where a friend might live. They find that place on a world map and then figure out what time that friend would need to call to wish them a happy birthday during their birthday party.

Materials

◈ *Somewhere in the World Right Now,* by Stacey Schuett (1995)
◈ world time zones charts, 1 per pair of students (see Blackline Masters)
◈ world map

Vocabulary: A.M., analog, digital, hemisphere, north, P.M., time zone

Instructions

1. Show the students the cover of *Somewhere in the World Right Now*. Discuss what the book might be about. Point out clues, such as the clock and the maps and city names that are in the background.

2. Examine the picture of the world map with the students. Ask them what they notice. Discuss different features of the page, such as the analog clocks across the top, which increase one hour at a time, the digital times across the bottom, the continent names, names of different countries and cities, and the different colors on the map.

3. Read the story to the class. Enjoy the language, the rhythm of the words, the pictures, and the ideas that the book expresses.

4. Return to the section titled "A Note to the Reader." Examine the picture of the globe that shows how the earth has light and dark places at the same time. Discuss

why the original method of measuring time, from when the sun was highest overhead at noon, would cause nearby places to have slightly different times. Talk about the scheduling confusions that the advent of rapid train travel caused, and how in 1884 an international meeting was convened to agree upon a standard time system.

5. Now show the students the time zone map at the end of the book. Examine the twenty-four time zones, and note how the lines curve to keep similar political and geographical areas in the same time zone.

6. Pass out a world time zones chart to each pair of students. Give them a few minutes to examine the chart and share what they notice.

7. Tell the students to imagine that they live in San Francisco and their friend lives in Philadelphia. Have the students find those places on the map. Ask the students to figure out how the times in those two places differ. They will likely look at the times at the top of the page and say that if it is 10:00 A.M. in San Francisco, it is 1:00 P.M. in Philadelphia.

8. Next have the students think about different scenarios: What time would it be in Philadelphia if it were 11:00 A.M. in San Francisco? What if it were 2:00 P.M. in San Francisco? What if it were 11:00 P.M. in San Francisco? Do several of these problems, making sure that the students understand the difference in time, when A.M. changes to P.M., and the fact that after midnight the day of the week and the date change.

9. Introduce the following problem to the students. Explain that they are going to imagine that they have a friend who lives on the other side of the world. Tell the students that they are going to look at a world map and choose a city in the northern hemisphere where their friend lives. Explain to the students that the northern hemisphere is the part of the world that is north of the equator. Explain that next they need to identify the country that city is in. Do an example with the students, such as London, England. Find London on the world map. Have the students explain how they know it is in the northern hemisphere. Then on the board write: *My friend lives in London, England.*

10. Now tell the students that their friend wants to call them on their birthday during their birthday party at 5:00 P.M. on a Tuesday. On the board write, *It is 5:00 P.M. on Tuesday.* Continue with your example. Find where your city would be on the map, and find the time at the top of the time zone. Then find London on the map, and find the time at the top of that time zone. With the students, figure out what time it is in London when it is 5:00 P.M. in your city. For example, if you live in San Francisco, you could touch the time zone at the top of San Francisco and say,

Somewhere
In the World
Right now

Turkey-Adana 8:00pm
My friend lives in Adana,Turkey.
My party starts at 5:00 pm
My friend calls 9 hrs after
5:00 pm. My friend calls at 2:00am
5 p.m 6 p.m 7pm 8pm 9p.m 10 p.m 11pm
12pm 1am 2am And My friend will call on
Wednesday

Figure 6–9 *Barbara imagined that her friend lived in Adana, Turkey, and decided she would call her at 2 A.M.*

"Five o'clock," and count on for each next time zone, "six o'clock, seven o'clock, eight o'clock, nine o'clock, ten o'clock, eleven o'clock, twelve o'clock, one o'clock, two o'clock." Note that the time has changed from P.M. to A.M. and it is now the middle of the night. Also note that since it is past midnight, it is no longer Tuesday but instead is Wednesday. On the board, write: *My friend will call me at 2:00 A.M. London time on Wednesday. I know this because* _____. Tell the students that they will fill the blank with an explanation of their thinking.

11. Do an additional example, if necessary. Then have students work in pairs to do the problem. After they do one example, invite them to find a new place for a different friend to live.

12. When the students have investigated several different places, begin a group discussion. Ask a pair of students to go to the wall map and point out the place that their friend lives. Have the other students look at their time zone chart to find that same place. Ask the class to figure out what time the friend in that country would be calling the students who are presenting. Then the students who are presenting should ask their classmates what they think and why. If the students don't agree on the answer, have them discuss their ideas until they come to an agreement.

13. Have several other pairs of students share in the same way. (See Figure 6–9.)

Temperature

CHAPTER 7

Introduction

Temperature impacts the decisions that children make on a daily basis: "Should I wear a coat or a sweater?" "Do I want to go swimming today or will the pool be too cold?" "Is my soup cool enough to eat or should I wait?" Although estimating temperature is a familiar activity for students, measuring it or attaching meaning to specific measurements frequently is not.

Students can easily see the effects of the presence or absence of heat but they cannot see heat itself or see degrees. Temperature is a measure of molecular movement, which is not visible to the eye. The numerical relationships that help students make sense of spatial measurement do not exist in temperature in the same way: Although an 80-inch piece of string is twice as long as a 40-inch piece of string, an 80-degree cup of water is not twice as hot as a 40-degree cup of water; it's molecules are not moving twice as intensely. Furthermore, the role of zero on a thermometer differs a great deal from the role of zero on a ruler and many other measurement tools: While the end of a ruler represents zero, or no distance, the 0 on a thermometer does not represent no heat. Zero on a Fahrenheit or Celsius thermometer is an arbitrary designation; molecules are still moving. True zero, or absolute zero, where molecules are nearly motionless, is -459.67 degrees Fahrenheit and -273.15 degrees Celsius, temperatures that are not particularly relevant to our daily lives.

The lessons in this chapter invite children to share what they already know about temperature and relate these understandings to measuring with thermometers. Students go on a temperature scavenger hunt, finding different temperatures inside and outside school. They explore patterns on thermometers and estimate and compare the temperatures inside a room and outdoors. Students learn to attach meaning to specific temperatures through understanding benchmark temperatures, such as room temperature, body temperature, and the temperature at which ice freezes. They have opportunities to use what they know about benchmark temperatures as they pack for an imaginary trip to another city, and practice reading thermometers and interpreting temperatures during experiments with ice and sunlight.

What Do You Know About Thermometers?

Overview

This lesson provides a window into students' prior information, conceptions, and misconceptions about thermometers and temperature. Students are invited to discuss what they think temperature is, what things have temperatures, and what things do not. They discuss how people estimate and measure temperatures. Then students examine thermometers and share what they notice.

Materials

❖ chart paper, 1–2 sheets

❖ thermometers, 1 per pair of students

❖ transparency of the thermometer students are using

Vocabulary: benchmark temperature, calibrate, Celsius, Centigrade, Fahrenheit, increments, Kelvin, multiple, negative, scale, temperature, thermometer, zero

Instructions

1. Share with the students that today they will begin a series of investigations about measuring temperature. Title a sheet of chart paper *Temperature Vocabulary*. Write the word *temperature* below it. On the board, write the following questions:

   • *What does temperature mean?*
   • *What things have temperatures and what things do not?*
   • *Why do we measure temperatures?*

   Ask the students to discuss those questions in their groups.

2. Begin a class discussion about how the groups answered the questions. On the board, list different statements that the students make and questions that arise. Encourage the students to discuss their own perspectives about statements that other students make. For example, some students might think that temperature means only that you get hot when you're sick, whereas other students may disagree and talk about oven temperatures and seeing the temperature on the news on television. Some students may say that everything has a temperature and others may say that things that are not alive do not have a temperature.

3. Provide the students with some information about temperature. Tell the students that all things in the world are made up of tiny particles that we can't see called *molecules*. Explain that these tiny particles move constantly, sometimes very

intensely and sometimes more slowly, and what we call *temperature* describes how intensely these molecules move. Tell the students that the hotter the temperature, the more intensely the molecules move, and the cooler the temperature, the more slowly the molecules move.

4. Next ask the students how people measure the temperatures of things. Encourage the students to think beyond just using thermometers to the ways people make estimates of temperatures. For example, ask if they have seen an adult feel a child's forehead with a hand to see if the child had a fever or if they have ever looked at a window's glass in the morning to see if they needed to wear a warm coat. Clarify the different ways we speak of temperature. Explain that while we commonly say, "You have a temperature," it is a short way of saying, "You have a high temperature," or "You have a fever."

5. Pass out a thermometer to each pair of students.

6. Ask partners to discuss what they notice about the thermometers and record on a sheet of paper the things they notice. Remind the students to look at all parts of the thermometer. Tell the students to record everything that they discover. (See Figure 7–1.)

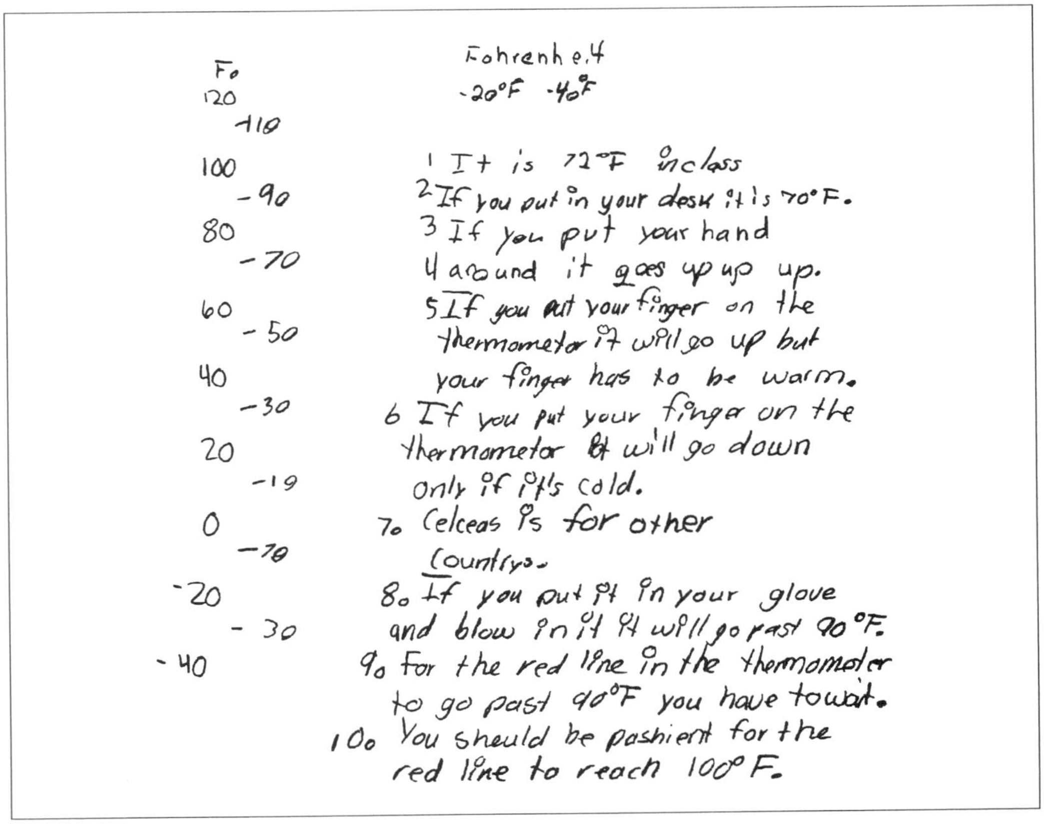
Fo
120
-110
100
-90
80
-70
60
-50
40
-30
20
-10
0
-10
-20
-30
-40

Fahrenheit
-20°F -40°F

1 It is 72°F in class
2 If you put in your desk it is 70°F.
3 If you put your hand
4 around it goes up up up.
5 If you put your finger on the thermometer it will go up but your finger has to be warm.
6 If you put your finger on the thermometer it will go down only if it's cold.
7. Celceas is for other countrys.
8. If you put it in your glove and blow in it it will go past 90°F.
9. For the red line in the thermometer to go past 90°F you have to wait.
10. You should be pashient for the red line to reach 100°F.

Figure 7–1 *Grace and Uyen discovered multiples of ten on their thermometer as well as ways to make their thermometer record higher temperatures.*

7. During a whole-group discussion, have students share what they discovered. As the students share, have the other students look for the same thing on their thermometers. Place the transparency of a thermometer on an overhead projector and refer to it as students share, so all the students understand what a volunteer has said. For example, if someone says the lines have multiples of ten: 10, 20, 30, 40, 50, and so on, point to those lines on the transparency and, as you do so, have the group count by tens. Write the word *multiple* on the "Temperature Vocabulary" chart. Explain that since the numbers increase by 10, we say the numbers grow in increments of 10. As you continue the lesson, continue adding important vocabulary to this chart.

8. If no one mentions the following points, bring them up yourself:
   • Point out the coldest and hottest temperatures that these thermometers can show.
   • Explain what the longer lines and the shorter lines on the scale mean.
   • Zero is a benchmark temperature, and temperatures are referred to as being above zero or below zero. For example, –10 degrees is read as "minus ten degrees" or "ten degrees below zero."
   • F stands for Fahrenheit and C stands for Celsius. It is customary to use the Fahrenheit scale in the United States, but most of the world uses the Celsius scale. In some parts of the world the same scale is called Centigrade, and scientists and engineers often use a different scale called Kelvin, where *zero* indicates absolute zero and there are no negative temperatures.
   • Zero degrees and 100 degrees in the Celsius scale match up to 32 degrees and 212 degrees, respectively, in the Fahrenheit scale. The lower temperatures in each scale refer to the temperature at which ice freezes, and the higher temperature on each scale refers to the temperature at which water boils.
   • Talk about the temperature that their thermometers currently indicate. The students' thermometers are likely to show slightly different numbers. Discuss why this might be the case. For example, the thermometers may be calibrated slightly differently, and some students may be touching the red tube.
   • Show them how to write that temperature and how to abbreviate it:
      68 degrees Fahrenheit
      68°F

9. Before erasing the board, copy down any students' questions or differences in opinion that were not addressed during this lesson. Plan how the students might research or figure out the answers. For example, you may find that some students think that only live things have temperatures, while other students may think that everything has a temperature. Invite students who have similar disagreements to find out which statement is correct by measuring things with their thermometers or by gathering data for things they cannot measure themselves.

Temperature Scavenger Hunt

Overview

In this lesson, the students become better acquainted with thermometers, not only with their scales but also with how to use them. During a temperature scavenger hunt, the students find as many different temperatures as they can and record what they discover. During the discussion the class creates a temperature reference chart listing benchmark temperatures.

Materials

◈ student thermometers, 1 per pair of students

◈ *Temperature Scavenger Hunt* recording sheets, 1 per student (see Blackline Masters)

◈ 2-by-3-foot chart paper, 1 sheet

◈ transparency of *Temperature Scavenger Hunt* recording sheet

Vocabulary: accurate, benchmark, cooler, degrees, estimate, Fahrenheit (or Celsius), hotter, increment, lines, multiples, scale, spaces, thermometer

Instructions

1. Prior to the lesson, decide whether you will do the investigation using the Fahrenheit scale or the Celsius scale. On the chart paper, draw a large thermometer to serve as a reference for benchmark temperatures. Pick a place for the scavenger hunt: in the classroom, inside the school building, and/or outside the school building.

2. Begin the lesson by telling the students that they are going to use thermometers to go on a temperature scavenger hunt. Review any safety ideas that they need to remember. For example, if you have thermometers with a flexible backing, make sure the students know that they should not bend it, as the tube will break.

3. Next place the transparency of the recording sheet on the overhead and have the students practice reading temperatures in the following way: Draw a line on the scale at 58°F. Have partners discuss the temperature they think is indicated. Then have them share their answers and explain their reasoning. Discuss the meaning of the space between the shorter lines on the scale and the space between the longer lines. Do this with several other benchmark temperatures that may be part of the students' background experience: 32°F for the temperature at which water freezes, 98.6°F for body temperature, and so on. Discuss how temperatures might differ on a cold day or a warm day.

4. Give one thermometer to each pair of students. Ask them to find the temperature of the room by reading the thermometer. There will likely be some variations in

what the thermometers say, so have the students discuss their ideas about why different temperatures resulted. Note that some differences occur because measurement is never exact, and the thermometers read a bit differently.

5. If any students find significantly higher temperatures, and the students have no idea why this might be, ask them to show the class how they are holding the thermometer. Have a student who found a typical reading show the class how he or she is holding the thermometer. When the students see the differences in how they are holding the thermometer, they will likely see that holding their fingers on the tube increases the thermometer reading, since it is measuring the body temperature rather than the air temperature. Remind the students that as they do the scavenger hunt, they should make sure that they hold the thermometer by the plastic backing.

6. Next have the students consider how long it takes for the thermometer to adjust to a new temperature. Have them check the clock, hold the bulb of the thermometer between their fingers, and find out how much time it takes for the red line to stop rising. Tell the students that during the temperature scavenger hunt, they will need to wait that long to take a reading to allow the thermometer to adjust to a new temperature. Remind the students that if they don't wait long enough, the temperature they record won't be accurate.

7. Now explain what they will do during the scavenger hunt. Tell the students that their task is to find as many different temperatures as they can within the area that you have chosen. Have students think of different places within that area that might yield different temperatures. Write them on the board. For example, they might suggest that the corner is cooler and under the heating vent is hotter. Next have the students estimate the temperatures that they will find in those places. Encourage the students to use what they know about the current room temperature, and their past experiences with temperatures, to make their estimates.

8. Distribute the *Thermometer Scavenger Hunt* recording sheets. Tell the students that each time they find a new temperature, they will draw a line to that place on the thermometer. At the end of the line, they will write that temperature in degrees and the place that they measured. On the transparency, show an example of how they are to record. Explain that both partners need to agree on the temperature before they write it down, and that they need to check each other's work to see that they both drew a line to the same place on their recording sheets.

9. As the students work, ask them to explain how they are identifying the temperatures. Encourage the students to use relevant mathematical terminology such as *degrees, Fahrenheit, scale, increment,* and *multiples.* Also ask the students whether their readings surprised them or not.

10. When the students finish, lead a whole-group discussion. Invite students to share what they discovered and what surprised them. For example, if students measured

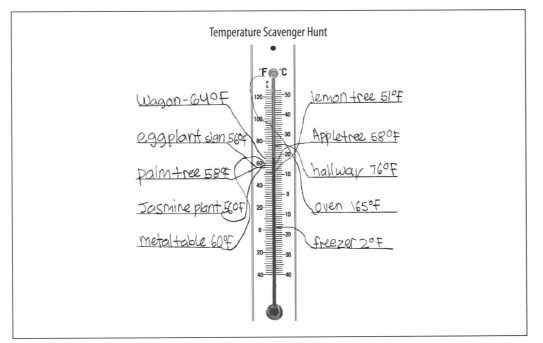

Temperature Scavenger Hunt

Wagon - 64°F
eggplant sign 56°F
palm-tree 58°F
Jasmine plant 50°F
metal table 60°F

lemon tree 51°F
Apple tree 58°F
hallway 76°F
oven 165°F
freezer 2°F

Figure 7–2 *Amanda measured the temperature of things in the school garden and the temperature in the office. The cafeteria worker told her the current temperature of the oven. The office temperature surprised Amanda.*

the temperature of an item in the sun, they may have discovered that the thermometer continually changed its reading as clouds passed by. On the board, record students' data (the temperature and the place). Discuss how the data compare with their predictions and why various temperatures resulted. Students may disagree about other students' data. If so, students may decide to verify their data by measuring a second time. (See Figure 7–2.)

11. Based on the data on the board, ask the students to predict what temperature might be found in places that they did not investigate, for example, in another classroom, in the cafeteria, or outside under a porch. Discuss how temperatures might differ on a colder day or a warmer day. For example, you might ask whether they would expect to find a temperature of 42°F in a house or of 112°F outside in December. Look for the coldest temperature they found and the warmest temperature they found.

12. Tape the drawing of the large thermometer on the board. Next to the thermometer list benchmark temperatures that will serve as a reference to help the students understand the magnitude of temperatures that they encounter in their lives. Make an arrow pointing to each referent temperature on the thermometer. For example, a referent list might include "Body temperature: 98.6°F," "Room temperature: 70°F," "Water freezes: 32°F," "Hot summer day: 110°F," and "Cold winter day: 40°F." Tell the students that this poster will serve as a reference during the remainder of the investigations (see page 256).

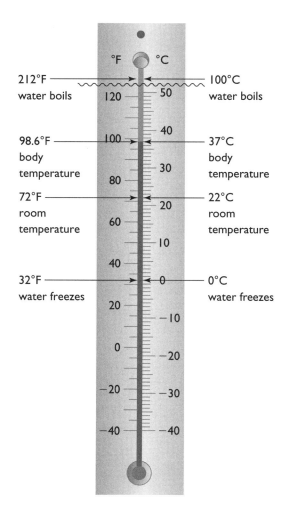

Inside and Outside Temperatures

. . . .

Overview

This lesson provides students with opportunities to create benchmarks for temperatures. Students estimate, then record, the temperature inside and outside the classroom and then use thermometers to determine the actual temperatures. They do this for five consecutive days and find out if their estimates get closer to the actual temperatures. Through daily class discussions, students discover strategies for taking accurate temperature readings and learn what room temperature is.

Materials

◈ thermometers, 1 per pair of students
◈ *Inside and Outside Temperatures* recording sheets, 1 per student (see Blackline Masters)
◈ chart paper, 1–2 sheets

Vocabulary: accurate, below zero, Celsius, degrees, Fahrenheit, increments, landmark temperature, minus, prediction, proximity, temperature, variation

Instructions

1. Prior to the lesson, decide whether to do this investigation using the Fahrenheit or Celsius scale.

2. Begin the lesson by discussing with the students how the temperature feels outside, what they are wearing as a result of the temperature, as well as some things they are able or not able to do as a result of the temperature. Suggest that the students keep this information in mind as they investigate the temperature during the coming week.

3. Hand out the recording sheets and ask the students to work in pairs to discuss their predictions of how many degrees a thermometer will show both inside the room and outside the school building today. After several minutes of discussion, ask each student to write his or her estimate on the recording sheet for Day 1.

4. Before providing the students with the thermometers, review any safety factors that they need to know. If the students are not comfortable using thermometers, draw a large section of the thermometer on the board and review what the increments mean. Discuss the benchmark temperature 0 degrees and how temperatures colder than 0 are referred to as "minus" the number of degrees below 0. It may be helpful to have the students practice identifying how the thermometer would look at different temperatures.

5. Now provide pairs of students with thermometers. Have them find out what the inside temperature is, record it on their sheets, and find out how far off their estimates were.

6. Discuss with the students the temperatures they recorded. If some students found very different temperatures, invite them to figure out why this happened. If students touched their thermometers with their hands as they measured, they may realize that they measured their hand temperature rather than the room temperature. Have these students measure the temperature a second time. Ask the students why smaller temperature variations occurred. Discuss how the variation between thermometers and proximity to windows, heaters, and doors could impact their readings. Remind the students that measurement is never exact.

7. Take the students outside to find out the temperature there. Again have them record the actual measurement, and figure out how far off their estimates were.

8. Continue this process throughout the week, recording the inside and outside temperatures at the same time each day.

9. After each session have students share how they made their predictions. Most students will pay attention to how the temperature feels that day and use that information along with the reading from the previous day. Ask these students to clarify

exactly how they knew it was colder or warmer than the previous day. For example, they may say that they had to choose a different kind of clothing to wear, or that they were shivering when they walked to the school building. Other students may have watched the news or read the newspaper.

10. Discuss strategies students used for taking temperatures. For example, many students realize the importance of taking their measurement in the identical place each day, and that changing location within the room or outside will make the temperature readings less reliable for comparison. Many students will also realize that they must keep their hands away from the tube of the thermometer in order to record the room temperature and not their hand temperature. If any students take outside measurements in the sun, they are likely to realize that as clouds cover the sun, the temperature changes, and that readings are more consistent in the shade.

11. At the end of the week ask the students whether their predictions became closer to their actual measurements as the week progressed. The students usually note that the temperature inside remained relatively stable, and that it was easier to predict than the outside temperature. On the board write *Room Temperature* and a temperature or range of temperatures that the students feel reflects their data. Emphasize that this benchmark temperature is important because it allows them to predict the temperature of many other places. Ask the students what other places might have that same temperature. They will likely name other classrooms or buildings such as their home or their friend's house. Encourage discussion about indoor spaces that are often uncomfortably cool or warm, and have the students use what they learned in this lesson to predict those temperatures. You may wish to invite a student to borrow a thermometer and take a reading in one of those places to allow the students to verify their predictions.

12. Last, ask the students what advice they would give to someone who wanted to measure the temperature accurately, inside or outside. As the students share, list their advice on chart paper. The list should include measuring in the same location every time, holding the thermometer so your hand is not touching the tube, and selecting a shady spot when finding the outside temperature.

Heat Experiments

Overview

Often we assume that students understand how heat functions, when in fact, many have beliefs that can surprise us. It is not uncommon for students to believe that hats, sweaters, coats, and closed-in places have heat of their own. In this lesson students discuss their beliefs about things that have heat. Then they conduct experiments to find out if items themselves can actually have their own warmth.

Materials

❖ thermometers, 1 per pair of students

❖ objects that students commonly think have heat of their own or are warm, such as a jacket, coat, winter hat, sweatpants, sweater, furry material, flashlight, reading lamp, and an item made of metal, at least 1 item per pair of students.

Vocabulary: calibration, degrees, estimate, heat, temperature, thermometer

Instructions

1. On the board, write the questions: *What is heat? What has heat?*

2. Have pairs of students discuss what heat is and their ideas about things—not people or animals—that have heat. When everyone is ready, list on the board the items that the students believe have heat. For example, students might suggest things such as fire, an oven, and a volcano. Encourage them to name things inside a house that have heat.

3. Move the discussion to situations that are often confusing to students, and add these to the list on the board. If students don't bring up these situations on their own, do so yourself. Ask them whether a sweater has heat, even when a person is not wearing it, or whether a sleeping bag is warm even when a person is not inside. Then discuss enclosed spaces. Some students may think that closed-in places, such as a desk or closet, will have warmer temperatures. Some students may think that a light is hot and may believe this to be true even when the light is turned off. Some students will erroneously predict that a piece of clothing not on a person will be colder than room temperature, since the item does not have a warm body against it. And other students may have the idea that metal is always hot or cold. Encourage discussion among the students, and have them explain the thinking behind their ideas.

4. Have students share their estimates of the temperatures of things on the list and explain why they chose them. Encourage the students to make temperature estimates by thinking about their prior experiences.

5. Next show the students the set of items that you collected. Have each pair select one of these items or a situation that was discussed, such as a closed-in space, a desk, or a closet, to investigate.

6. On lined paper have students title their experiment, for example, *Hat Experiment, Jacket Experiment,* or *Desk Experiment.* Ask each student to write *Prediction* at the top of their paper, and then record what they predict will be the temperature of their group's chosen item. Ask them to explain in writing why they selected that temperature.

7. Next have the pairs of students discuss their plan for their experiment, carefully deciding what they will do first, second, and so on. Make sure the pairs consider details such as how long to hold the thermometer against the item.

8. When the group has finished planning, remind the students of safety issues as well as strategies for accurate measurement, such as holding the thermometer by its plastic frame so that it registers the item's temperature rather than their hand's temperature. On the board write:

   a. *Do your experiment.*
   b. *Check the reading to make sure that it is correct.*
   c. *Compare the actual temperature with your prediction, and discuss the difference and whether the real temperature surprised you.*
   d. *On your paper write* Results, *and then record what you discovered and why you think that happened.*

9. Now have pairs of students get a thermometer and perform their experiment. Circulate as the pairs work. Have students explain how they know that they have read the thermometer correctly. Also ask them whether the reading surprised them, and why that temperature might have resulted. (See Figures 7–3 and 7–4.)

10. When the students finish, gather them together for a class discussion. Have students report the results of their experiments, and on the board list the temperatures that the students found. Compare the data from each pair. If any pairs found a significantly different temperature, discuss the discrepancy and, if necessary, have students perform their experiment again. Have the students discuss why the temperatures are so similar, and if the items actually are warm, that is, have heat of their own. Compare the temperatures with the air temperature in the classroom. The temperatures should all read very much the same. Differences will be due to small differences in the calibration of individual thermometers.

Pants Experiment

Prediction:

I think the pants will be 54° F because there's no body inside the pants and it would make it colder.

Results

The pants were 74° F. I was surprised. I think it was 74° F because of the air in the room was touching the pants and it made it 74° F.

Figure 7–3 *Nura predicted that the pants would be cold without a person wearing them, and then she discovered that the air temperature determined the temperature of the pants.*

Pants Experiment

Prediction:

I think the pants will be 54°F because there's no body inside the pants. If someone was in the pants, it might be hotter in them because that person might be hot from playing outside.

Results:

The pants were 74°F. I was surprised. I think they were 74°F because of the air in the room or it is just because of the way the pants are made. It doesn't matter what kind of pants because it would maybe be the same degrees.

Figure 7–4 *Even after the investigation, Andy was unsure about how air temperature affected the temperature of the pants.*

11. Now have the pairs discuss what they think as a result of the experiment and the discussion. Know that all of the children who think that "warm" clothes generate heat may not be convinced. One experience will not necessarily change well-entrenched student beliefs. Be open to suggestions from children, and continue doing other experiments, especially if they suggest it. For example, one student might suggest that keeping the thermometer in the jacket for three hours, or even overnight, might make the thermometer register a higher temperature.

Too Hot, Too Cold, Just Right

Overview

In this lesson, students play a game in which they try to guess a mystery temperature that is chosen by the teacher or another student. As students play, they gain facility with reading and recording temperatures on a thermometer and they develop strategies for guessing the temperature in as few guesses as possible.

Materials

- red overhead marker
- small sticky note
- paper thermometers, 1 per student for each game (see Blackline Masters)
- transparency of paper thermometer
- transparency with numbers 1 through 20 written vertically down the left side

Vocabulary: Celsius, degrees, Fahrenheit, minus, mode, negative numbers, scale, temperature, thermometer

Instructions

1. Provide each student with a recording sheet. Place a transparency of the same sheet on the overhead. Review with the students how to read the scale on the thermometer, and that the higher temperatures are toward the top of the thermometer while the lower temperatures are toward the bottom. Remind the students that the numbers below 0 are negative numbers and are read, for example, "minus ten degrees," or "ten degrees below zero."

2. Explain to the students that they will play a game with a thermometer in which they will try to guess your mystery temperature in as few guesses as possible. Decide as a group whether you will play this guessing game using the Fahrenheit scale or the Celsius scale.

3. To begin the game, choose a mystery temperature, such as 75 degrees Fahrenheit, but don't tell it to your students. With the overhead off, write it lightly in an upper corner of the transparency, and cover it with the sticky note so the students cannot see it.

4. Next ask a volunteer to guess a temperature. Remind the students to include the words *degrees Fahrenheit* in their guess. For example, a student might guess, "I think it's fifty-three degrees Fahrenheit. I picked a number in the middle to get rid of as many guesses as possible."

5. Now respond to the guess by providing a clue about the mystery temperature. Say, "Your guess is too hot," "Your guess is too cold," or "Your guess is just right."

6. Direct the students to find the location of the guess on their thermometers, and draw a line across that place on the scale. Mark the same place on your overhead transparency so students can verify that they interpreted the scale correctly. Ask the students to make a notation on their recording sheet to keep track of your clue. For example, some students might write *too hot*; other students might just write the letter *H*.

7. Write *Guesses* at the top of your transparency, and below it make a tally mark. Tell the students that this is how you'll keep track of the number of guesses. Remind them that their goal is to guess the mystery temperature in as few guesses as possible.

8. Assuming the volunteer did not correctly guess the temperature, have another student guess a different temperature. Provide a clue, have students record the guess on their sheets, and add the guess and a tally mark to the transparency.

9. At this point, ask the students to talk to a partner about what they think a good next guess would be and why. Ask several students to share their reasoning. Some students may share a strategy for eliminating as many numbers as possible, causing some discussion. For example, not all students will immediately realize that if 73 degrees is too hot, 93 degrees is also too hot.

10. Continue the game, stopping from time to time to have students share strategies for choosing a good next guess. If any guesses include negative temperatures, you may find that some students misinterpret the larger numbers as hotter. Encourage a discussion that helps students develop new understandings about how to correctly interpret temperatures below 0 degrees.

11. When the game is over, count the tallies. Then write *Game 1* on the board along with the number of guesses.

12. Play the game again as a group, this time inviting a student to select the mystery temperature, record it on the overhead, and cover it with the sticky note. At the end of the game, record on the board the number of guesses the game required.

13. Hand out paper thermometers to the students. Place the numbered transparency on the overhead. Tell the students to play the game with a partner twice, and then use a tally mark to record the number of guesses (from one to twenty) for each game on the transparency.

14. When the students finish, have a class discussion about the tallies. Note the largest number of guesses, the smallest number of guesses, the mode (the number of guesses that occurred the most), and any clusters or gaps. Have students share their strategies for choosing guesses.

Packing for a Trip

Overview
After selecting a large city that they would like to visit, students examine that city's weather data and review the data from three consecutive days. On a recording sheet, they note that city's high and low temperatures and temperature ranges. The students then consider this information as they decide what clothing they would need to pack for their visit and what outside activities they might do there.

Materials
◈ three days of current national weather data from newspapers or the Internet, 1 copy per pair of students and 1 for the teacher
◈ crayons, blue and red, 1 of each color per student and 1 of each for the teacher

◈ red overhead marker

◈ wall map of the United States or world

◈ *Packing for a Trip* recording sheets, 1 per student and 1 for the teacher (see Blackline Masters)

◈ transparency of *Packing for a Trip* recording sheet

◈ optional: rulers, 1 per pair of students

Vocabulary: degrees, Fahrenheit (or Celsius), high, low, precipitation, range, scale, thermometer

Instructions

1. Prior to the lesson, identify the source of weather data that the students will use. In this description, newspaper data are used.

2. Examine the newspaper weather page and the section that displays weather data for U.S. cities. Many urban newspapers list data for cities in the United States for three consecutive days: high and low temperatures for the previous day, predictions for that day, and predictions for the following day. This lesson is structured for this kind of data. If you want to have your students choose from cities outside the United States or if your newspaper does not present three days of data, provide the students with that weather information or data from more days of newspapers.

3. Provide the students with copies of the newspaper. Ask the students to find the weather section. When several pairs have found it, invite them to share their strategies for finding the section and discuss how the newspaper is organized. Then show the students the weather page for that day.

4. Ask the students how the weather section is organized and what they can learn about the weather. This free exploration provides the students with a chance to make sense of how lists of data are organized and to make connections with what they know about temperature, cities, and countries.

5. Explain to the students that they are going to select a city from the list that they would like to visit. Ask the students what they would need to know if they were going to pack a suitcase for that trip. They may say things such as "What I'm going to do there," or "If it's going to rain," or "How hot or cold it would be." Tell the students they are going to use the temperature information to help them plan for this imaginary trip. Have the students select a city and see if they can interpret the data that are listed for their city.

6. After a few minutes, ask students to share what they discovered. As each student shares, have the others look for that information on their own page. For example,

if a student found that the high temperature in Mexico City was 85°F, instruct the other students to find the section with international temperatures, the row with data about Mexico City, the column labeled "Hi," and the matching data. Make sure the students understand that *high* is abbreviated *hi*, and *low* is abbreviated *lo*. At this point you may wish to provide students with a ruler so they can more easily keep track of the rows in the table. Continue having students share, having the rest of the class find that data, and providing the students with any information that will help them interpret the data.

7. Now model what the students will do. Ask them to find the section with national data. Tell the students, for example, that you were born in Chicago. Provide each student with a recording sheet and crayons, and on the board write a sample of that sheet:

City: Chicago		
Thursday	Friday	Saturday

8. Have the students find Chicago's data in their newspaper. On the board list the data for each day. The following is an example of what you would write:

City: Chicago		
Thursday Hi Lo	Friday Hi Lo	Saturday Hi Lo
57°F 42°F	47°F 33°F	44°F 32°F

9. Examine the temperatures and react to them, so the students can understand what these numbers mean. For example, in this instance, you might note that on Saturday the low temperature would be freezing, and the highest temperature of 57°F, which occurred on Thursday, would be cool. Compare this temperature with the temperature outside your classroom on the day you are doing this lesson. Discuss with the students how this information would impact the clothing that you would need to take. Also discuss the things that people would be doing outside, or not doing outside, in the temperatures listed on the board. In this example, people might be walking briskly, they may be making sure that delicate plants are protected from the cold at night, and they would probably not be swimming or having picnics outside. Talk about how any listed precipitation, such as rain or snow, might impact what people do.

10. Next examine each day's temperature and discuss what the trend is: Will it get a little colder or a lot colder as the days progress? Or, will it get a little warmer or a lot warmer? Is it likely to rain during your trip?

11. Last, discuss what the temperature range is each day. Explain that the range is important, because it helps you know how different the temperatures you'll experience will be. Give an example such as this: "When there is only a small difference in temperature each day, people can be comfortable wearing the same clothing in the daytime and nighttime. If the range is large, you might have to pack different kinds of clothing." With the students, find the temperature range for each day, and write it on the board:

City: Chicago		
Thursday **Hi Lo**	**Friday** **Hi Lo**	**Saturday** **Hi Lo**
57°F 42°F	47°F 33°F	44°F 32°F
Range: 15°	Range: 14°	Range: 12°

12. Place the transparency on the overhead projector. At the top of your paper write *Chicago*. Beneath each thermometer on your recording sheet, write the days of the week. Also beneath each thermometer, write and label the high temperature, the low temperature, and the temperature range.

13. Now tell the students that they will record the high temperature with a red crayon. Show them how by drawing a red line with an overhead marker on Thursday's thermometer from the bulb upward to the line that indicates the high, in this case, 57 degrees. As you do this, remind the students what the lines on the scale represent. Next to the red line, make another line with the blue crayon, representing the low temperature of 42 degrees.

14. Last, list some of the clothing that the students said you would bring for those temperatures, as well as some of the things you would find people doing outside.

15. Review what the students' task is by writing the directions on the board:
    a. *Select the city to where you will travel.*
    b. *Label each thermometer with the day of the week.*
    c. *Beneath each thermometer, list the high temperature, the low temperature, and the temperature range.*
    d. *On each thermometer, record the high temperature with a red crayon and the low temperature with a blue crayon.*
    e. *At the bottom of the paper, list clothing you would pack for your trip.*

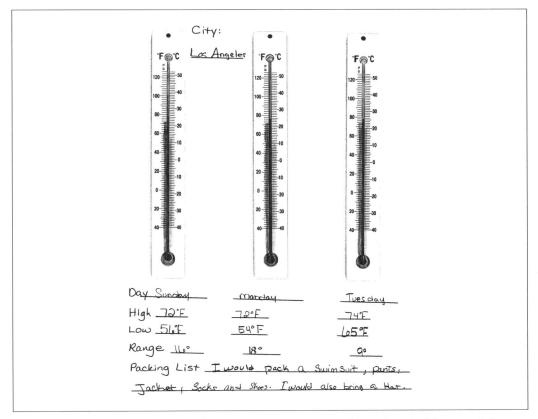

City: Los Angeles

Day	Sunday	Monday	Tuesday
High	72°F	72°F	74°F
Low	56°F	54°F	65°F
Range	16°	18°	9°

Packing List I would pack a swimsuit, pants, jacket, socks and shoes. I would also bring a hat.

Figure 7–5 *Jonathan investigated temperatures in Los Angeles and packed for a cool day at the beach.*

16. As the students work, have them check each other to see that they correctly interpreted the lines on the thermometer. Discuss with students what those temperatures would feel like, what they might need to wear, and what people would be doing—or not doing—outside. (See Figure 7–5.)

17. When the students finish, gather them close together for a group discussion. Have a student share the city he or she explored. Have the class find that place on a wall map. Have the student show the thermometers on his or her recording sheet, with the data covered. Ask the class to interpret the thermometer readings. Then predict the kinds of clothing that the student would bring on the trip, and discuss the kinds of things the student might do—or not do—outside in that temperature. Have the volunteer respond to the interpretations. Invite other students to share in a similar manner.

Patterns on a Thermometer

Overview

In this lesson, partners explore patterns on a thermometer. They choose a set of multiples to explore and then, on a paper copy of a thermometer, highlight on either the Celsius or the Fahrenheit scale where the multiples are. They write the multiples down the side of the paper. Then the students discuss and describe in writing the patterns they see in the numbers and in the highlighted lines. Last, in a class discussion, partners share the patterns they discovered.

Materials

- ◈ paper thermometers, 1 per pair of students (see Blackline Masters)
- ◈ overhead transparencies of paper thermometer, 4
- ◈ blank overhead transparency
- ◈ colored pencils, 1 per pair of students

Vocabulary: multiples, negative, pattern, positive, scale, thermometer, zero

Instructions

1. Before class, decide whether you will have students examine patterns on the thermometer's Fahrenheit scale or its Celsius scale.

2. Place one transparency of a thermometer on the overhead projector. Begin the lesson by explaining to the students that today they will focus on the number patterns that can be found on a thermometer. Point out the scale with which the students will work.

3. Review the meaning of *multiple*. Then tell the students that they will work in pairs to identify a number whose multiples they would like to explore. Do an example with multiples of five. On a blank transparency write the title *Multiples of Five on the Thermometer*. Explain to the students that they will write the title of their investigation on a sheet of lined paper.

4. With an overhead marker, highlight the lines on the scale that are multiples of five. Begin with 0 and go up: 5, 10, 15, and so on. Point out that zero is a multiple of every number. Ask the class to explain why.

5. Next, ask the students how they might extend that pattern to negative numbers. Highlight those numbers: −5, −10, −15, and so on.

6. Now have the students help you read those numbers on the thermometer, from the highest temperature to the lowest temperature. As they read the numbers, list what they say along the side of the overhead: *120, 115, 110, 105, 100,* and so on. Tell the students that they will also list a number pattern on the side of their thermometer handout.

7. Have the students examine your list of numbers and describe the patterns they see. Each time a student describes a pattern, list this information on the blank transparency. For example, a student may say that the numbers in the ones place alternate: 0, 5, 0, 5, 0, 5, and so on. Students may also note the patterns in the

tens place, starting with 10: 1, 1, 2, 2, 3, 3, 4, 4, and so on. The students will probably also notice the mirror symmetry in these numbers: −5, 5, −10, 10, −15, 15, and so on.

8. Next draw the students' attention to the patterns that they see in the lines that you drew on the thermometer transparency.

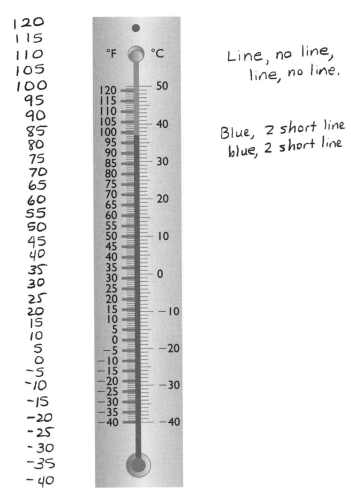

For example, your highlighted lines are on line, no line, line, no line, and so on. Write that observation on your pattern list as well. Another way they might interpret that pattern is two short lines, highlighted line, two short lines, highlighted line, and so on.

9. Tell the students that it is now their turn. Explain that they will select a number and explore its multiples in the same way as you just did with multiples of five. On the board, write the instructions:

   With a partner:

   a. *Select a number to explore: 2, 3, 4, 5, 10, 15, or 20*
   b. *Using a colored pencil highlight that number and its multiples on your thermometer picture. Continue coloring the pattern in the negative numbers. List those numbers on the side of your paper.*

c. *Examine the patterns in your highlights and in the numbers.*

d. *On your lined paper write what you notice about the patterns.*

e. *Explore a different set of multiples on another paper thermometer.*

10. Hand out the paper thermometer, colored pencils, and lined paper. As the students work, help them to correctly interpret the thermometer scales and engage them in discussions about what they notice about the patterns of highlighted lines. Provide a thermometer transparency to three pairs of students who investigated different sets of multiples. Ask them to use an overhead pen to highlight the multiples they found.

11. When the students finish, begin a discussion about the patterns they discovered in their multiples. Have the students to whom you gave a transparency share their patterns. As students describe the patterns they noticed, have the other students determine whether they agree. Then ask the other students whether the same patterns emerged in their multiples.

◈ Ice Water Investigations

Overview

During this activity, students investigate how adding ice changes the temperature of water. Students read thermometers at 30-second intervals, record the temperatures, and then graph their results. While doing this lesson, students practice using a thermometer scale, see how the temperature changes over time, and gain a sense of a reasonable temperature for water with and without ice.

Materials

◈ student thermometers, 1 per pair of students

◈ paper or plastic cups, 2 per pair of students

◈ water, enough to fill each paper cup

◈ pitcher to hold the water

◈ ice cubes, 3 per pair of students

◈ container and tongs for the ice cubes

◈ clock or watch with a second hand

◈ 1- by-8-inch red paper rectangle

◈ half-inch grid paper, 1 sheet per student (see Blackline Masters)

Vocabulary: elapsed seconds, estimate, Fahrenheit (or Celsius), graph, horizontal, maximum, minimum, scale, shape, temperature, vertical, *x*-axis, *y*-axis

Instructions

1. Begin by telling the students that they are going to investigate the temperature of water and how the temperature changes when ice cubes are put in it. Tell the students that they will be measuring using the Fahrenheit scale (or the Celsius scale if you prefer). Explain that they will keep a log of their information. Have them write *Ice Cube Investigations* at the top of a sheet of blank paper.

2. Next ask the students to think about what would be a reasonable estimate for the temperature of water without ice cubes and an estimate for the temperature when three ice cubes are put in it. Have the students talk in pairs about their estimates and then write their estimates on their log:

   • Temperature with no ice cubes: Estimate _____
   • Temperature with ice cubes: Estimate _____

3. Now help the students remember how to read the scale on a thermometer. Draw a portion of the scale on the board, from 60 to 80 degrees. Ask the students to recall the temperature that each of the lines stands for.

4. Hold the red paper rectangle vertically against the side of the scale, and explain to the students that this represents the red line on the thermometer. Have the students read the temperature by matching the top of the rectangle to the scale line, 72 degrees Fahrenheit in the following example.

   Move the rectangle to show a different temperature, such as 64 degrees. Do this several times to give the students practice reading the scale.

5. Next erase 60 and 80 and practice in a similar manner for temperatures between 30 and 50 and then between 40 and 60.

6. Explain to the students that they will practice reading the temperature quickly because, during this investigation, they will need to read a temperature at a specific moment of time, even though it is changing. Draw a new scale on the board, ranging from 60 to 80 degrees. Choose a target temperature within this range but don't

tell the students what it is. Hold the red rectangle at 80 degrees and slowly move it downward. When it's at your target temperature, say, "Time!" and see if the students agree on the temperature at that moment in time. Repeat this several times.

7. Help the students understand that although the temperature will keep changing during the experiment, they will identify the temperature at specific moments.

8. Give each pair a cup of water and a thermometer. Ask the students to read their thermometer and record that temperature in their log. Make sure that the students label the temperature *Beginning temperature*.

9. Tell the students that they will record the temperature of the water. Then they will place three ice cubes in their cup of water and record the temperature every 30 seconds for 6 minutes. Ask the students to make a vertical list in their log of the elapsed seconds that they will record:

Water temperature _____

30 sec. _____	210 sec. _____
60 sec. _____	240 sec. _____
90 sec. _____	270 sec. _____
120 sec. _____	300 sec. _____
150 sec. _____	330 sec. _____
180 sec. _____	360 sec. _____

10. Have the partners decide which person will read the thermometer first. Tell them to read and record the temperature of the water. Then explain that when you say, "Go," they will quickly place the ice cubes in their cups. Also explain that partners will alternate reading the thermometer out loud when they hear "Time!" and both will record the temperature in their logs. Remind the students that the temperature will continue changing, so when they hear "Time" they should look at the line on the scale that matches the red line at that moment.

11. Give each pair a cup with three ice cubes in it and then say, "Go!"

12. Watch the clock and, as every 30 seconds pass, say, "Time!" so the students can record the temperature at that moment. If students get behind, simply encourage them to record as soon as they can. The timing does not need to be exact.

13. Toward the end of the 6 minutes the temperatures will remain the same. You may end the investigation after the temperature remains the same three times, or you may wish to continue recording the temperature as the water warms up again.

14. After the investigation is over, have the students examine their data and share what they notice. Compare notes about the maximum temperatures and the

minimum temperatures. Find the difference between the two. Have the students consider the following questions: How did the temperatures change? Did the temperature change dramatically at the beginning and more gradually at the end, or was the change constant?

15. Tell the students that they will construct a graph to show more clearly how the temperatures changed. Give each student a sheet of half-inch grid paper. Show them how to list the seconds along the horizontal *x*-axis and label the axis *Time in Seconds*.

16. Next have the students list temperatures along the vertical *y*-axis. Show the students how to indicate the missing part of the *y*-axis that they don't need to draw. Then, beginning at 40 degrees, they should label the lines in 2-degree increments and end at the maximum temperature the students measured. Ask them to label that axis *Temperature in Degrees Fahrenheit*.

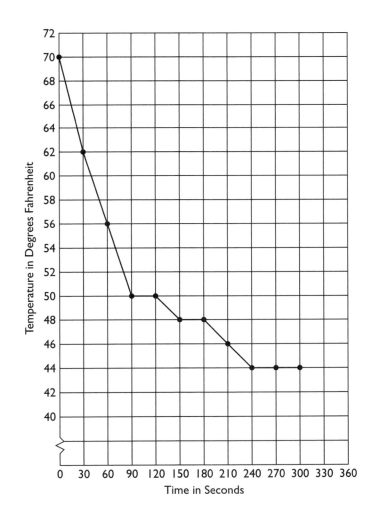

17. Have the students record each temperature by finding the seconds and placing a dot even with the temperature at that moment in time. Ask them to connect the dots to more clearly see how the temperature changed.

18. Remind the students that a graph, like a book, needs a title. Discuss what title would reflect what the graph represents.

19. Now remind the students that a graph, like a book, tells a story. Have the students examine their graph for the information it shows. Discuss the following questions: How did the temperature change? Did the temperature change dramatically at the beginning and more gradually at the end? Or was the change constant? Ask the students to compare their graphs and see if they all have a similar shape. Have a discussion about why that shape tended to occur.

◈ Color Experiments

Overview

In this lesson, the students use thermometers to test conjectures about the temperatures of orange, white, and black paper when placed in the sun. The students make predictions and then plan and carry out an experiment. They examine their temperature data, draw conclusions about which color was hottest, and then consider the implications this information might have.

Materials

◈ student thermometers, 1 per pair of students

◈ sets of 3 6-by-9-inch pieces of paper, 1 black, 1 orange, and 1 white, 1 set per pair of students

◈ chart paper, 1 large sheet

◈ optional: clipboards, 1 per pair of students

Vocabulary: degrees, Fahrenheit, landmark temperature, minus, prediction, scale, temperature, thermometer, zero

Instructions

1. Begin the lesson by reviewing any ideas about temperature that you think would be helpful to your students. For example, you might ask the students what temperature is and how we measure it.

2. To review how to read a thermometer, hold one up. Ask the students how they would explain to their little sister or brother how to identify the temperature. If necessary, draw a sample section of the thermometer scale on the board and discuss how to interpret the scale.

3. Now distribute a thermometer to each pair of students. Ask students where on the thermometer they will find hotter temperatures and where they will find colder temperatures. Have them find 0 degrees. Remind them that this is an important landmark on a thermometer. Tell the students to use 0 to help them find various temperatures: 100°F, 50°F, −20°F, 35°F, and so on.

4. Next introduce the experiment. Ask the students to imagine that it's a really, really hot day, and they are deciding which T-shirt would keep them coolest: Would they rather wear a black T-shirt, a white T-shirt, or an orange T-shirt? On the board, list the colors *black*, *white*, and *orange*. Discuss with the students the experiences they have had with different-colored cars or different-colored clothing, and how they think color impacts temperature. As students share, encourage them to explain their reasoning. Many students have a sense that black is hotter. They may even think that the color is what causes the heat, perhaps because things are black after they burn. Some students may think that orange is hotter because fire is orange. Simply accept the students' reasoning for now.

5. Tell the students that they will conduct an experiment to see how color affects temperature. Explain that they will go outside and measure the temperature first with just the thermometer; then they will place the thermometer under a piece of black paper and measure the temperature, and then they will do the same with a piece of white paper and a piece of orange paper. Ask the students to discuss with a partner how they think the temperature will differ each time.

6. Tell the students that they will create a science log to keep track of their experiment. Pass out a sheet of paper to each student. On the board list what the students will write in their logs:

   • *the title of the experiment: Color and Temperature*
   • *your question: How does color affect temperature?*
   • *your prediction*

7. Next make a plan with the students about how the experiment should be conducted. Explain that everyone needs to do the experiment the same way so the class can compare the data. Write the plan on the board. It may look like this:

   • *Step 1: Put the thermometer on the sidewalk, count to 180, read the temperature, and record what you find.* (**Note:** Choose a number that reflects the number of seconds that it takes to be sure that the new temperature has registered on your kind of thermometer. You may wish to have the students figure out what this number of seconds should be.)
   • *Step 2: Cover the thermometer completely with black paper. Count to 180, read the temperature, and record what you find.*
   • *Step 3: Do the same with white paper.*
   • *Step 4: Do the same with orange paper.*

8. Now have students prepare a section in their log where they will record their data. On the board, list the four sections it should have: *Thermometer Alone, Black Paper, White Paper,* and *Orange Paper.* Tell the students that they will work in pairs, and that both must agree on what the thermometer reads. Remind the students that they must record the temperature using the symbols for degrees and Fahrenheit.

9. Hand out the sets of colored paper and if you have them, clipboards. To perform the experiment, take the students outside. As the students work, provide them with any necessary support.

10. When the students complete their experiments, bring them back to the classroom. Tape the chart paper on the board, draw four columns, and label them like this:

Thermometer Alone	Black Paper	White Paper	Orange Paper

On the chart have the partners list their temperture data for each condition.

11. Allow time for students to examine the data and for partners to discuss what they notice. Next, have a class discussion about their observations. Have the students discuss trends—what seems to be true overall. Most students will find that the black paper is hottest, the white is coolest, and the orange is in the middle.

12. If a piece of data is very different from the others, invite the students try to make sense of it. For example, one pair of students might have found the orange paper had the highest temperature, but with some probing, they might remember that the paper had blown off, leaving the thermometer exposed to the sun.

    Have the students discuss reasons for the class results.

    Share with the students the following facts about when light energy hits the paper:

    • The color black absorbs a lot of the energy, so it keeps the heat and the paper becomes hot.
    • The color white reflects much of the light, so the heat does not get absorbed and the paper stays cooler.
    • The color orange absorbs some light but also reflects some, so the paper becomes medium hot.

    You may wish to draw a simple diagram of this:

COLOR EXPERIMENT

Before, I thought that papers would have the same temperature. I thought that because they're the same thing just different colors.
Now, I think that the papers wouldn't be the same degrees because some absorbs the heat, one bounces off and one absorbs and bounces off. If it was a hot day I would wear a white shirt to keep me cool. If it was a cold day I would wear black.

Figure 7–6 *Miguel's data surprised him. He was able to explain why different colors of paper were different temperatures and how that information would affect what he would wear on hot or cool days.*

13. Have the students discuss the implication their data might have for the choices they make. For example, have them consider which color T-shirt they would wear on a hot day or which color car they would buy.

14. Last, have the students write about how the experiment affected their thinking: what they thought before the experiment and how that compares with what they think now. Ask the students to reread their predictions and review their data. It may be helpful to provide the students with a sentence frame:

    • At first I thought . . .
    • But now I think . . .

15. Have a few students share their writing with the class. (See Figure 7–6.)

◆ A Temperature Story
....

Overview
In this lesson, students read a short story that has missing temperatures. Students use what they know about temperatures, do research, or use clues in the passage to fill in the missing temperatures for situations such as baking, a sunny day at the beach, and cold ocean water. In a class discussion students compare their answers and come to an agreement about which temperatures are reasonable.

Materials
◈ *A Day at the Beach* Story, 1 per pair of students (see Blackline Masters)

Vocabulary: degrees, Fahrenheit, reasonable, temperature

Instructions

1. Explain to the students that they will work in pairs to complete a story that is missing temperature information. Tell the students they are to select temperatures that might reasonably fill the blanks.

2. Instruct the pairs to discuss how they will justify their reasoning in a whole-class discussion. In some cases, students have background information that will help them solve the problem. For example, students who help family members bake may know that 350 degrees Fahrenheit is a common baking temperature. Allow students who do not have this information to search on the Internet or find a cookbook in the library. For the last paragraph in the story, students may find that working backward from the final temperature helps them figure out the previous missing temperatures.

3. When the students finish, begin a class discussion about the temperatures they chose. Have them justify their reasoning and discuss with each other different answers that may also be reasonable. As students hear other students' reasoning that they find more convincing, allow them to change the temperatures that they selected if they want to.

Blackline Masters

Paper Ruler

Finger Weaving Instructions

Finger Weaving

Centimeter Grid Paper

Brownie Shapes 1

Brownie Shapes 2

Inch Grid Paper

Sample House Plan

Put in Order—Volume

How Do They Relate?

Folding Boxes A

Folding Boxes B

Folding Boxes C

Folding Boxes D

Three-Fourths-Inch Grid Paper

Isometric Dot Paper

Measuring Angles

Measuring Polygon Angles

Waxed Paper Protractor

Angle Estimator

Target Angle

Put in Order—Mass

Weights

Time Line Paper

TV Time!

Let's Go to the Movies!

Patterns on the Clock Face

World Time Zones

Temperature Scavenger Hunt

Inside and Outside Temperatures

Paper Thermometer

Packing for a Trip

Half-Inch Grid Paper

A Day at the Beach

Paper Ruler

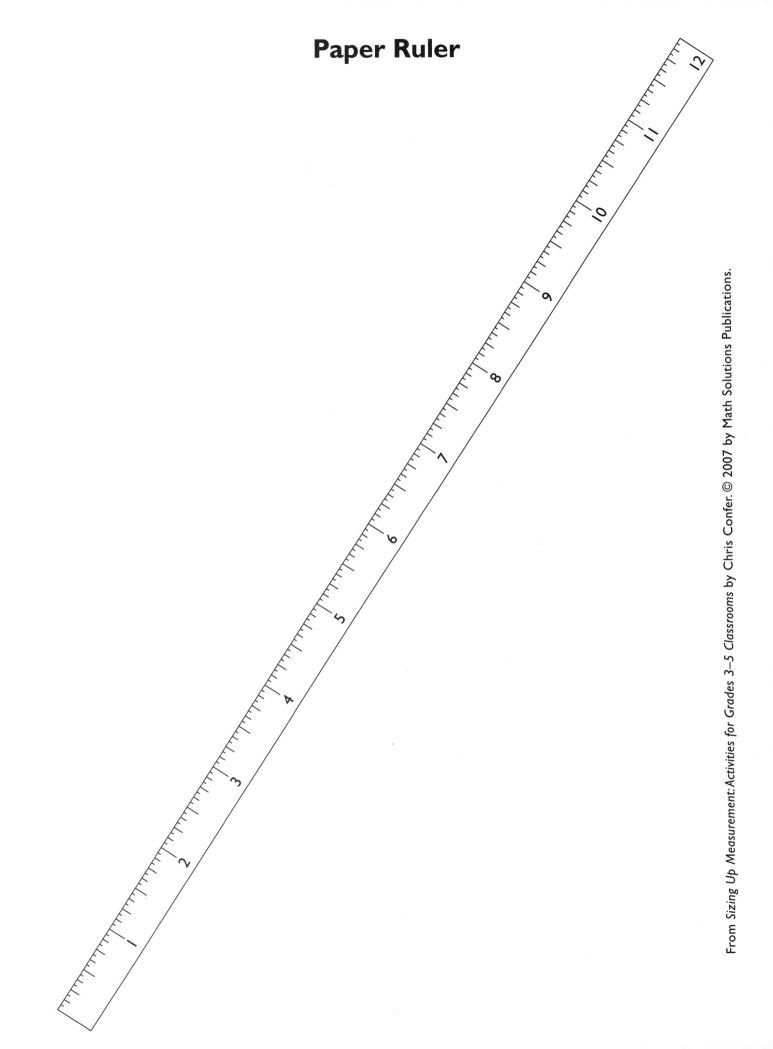

From *Sizing Up Measurement: Activities for Grades 3–5 Classrooms* by Chris Confer. © 2007 by Math Solutions Publications.

Finger Weaving Instructions

Step 1: Place loop over index finger. Grasp tail with other fingers.

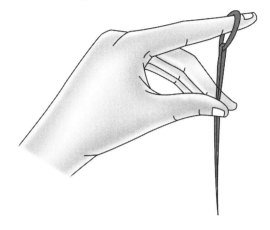

Step 2: Loop tail over index finger and grasp rest of tail with other fingers.

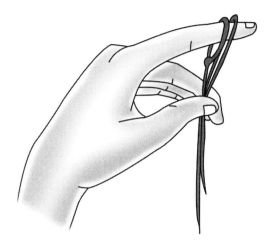

Step 3: Pull first loop over and off finger.

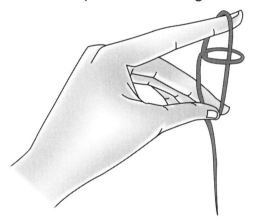

Step 4: Release tail and grab first loop. Loosen the loop over your index finger. You're ready to weave!

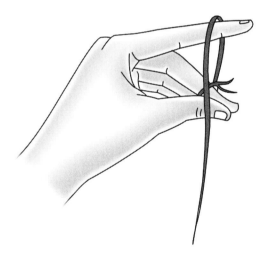

Step 5: Loop tail over in front of index finger as you did in Step 2. Grasp the rest of the tail with other fingers.

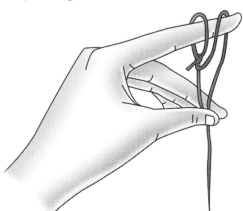

Step 6: Pull back loop over and off finger, as you did in Step 3. Pull loop down to form the chain. Continue repeating Steps 5 and 6.

From *Sizing Up Measurement: Activities for Grades 3–5 Classrooms* by Chris Confer. © 2007 by Math Solutions Publications.

Finger Weaving

Chain Letter	Meters	Decimeters	Centimeters	Total Length in Meters

From *Sizing Up Measurement: Activities for Grades 3–5 Classrooms* by Chris Confer. © 2007 by Math Solutions Publications.

Centimeter Grid Paper

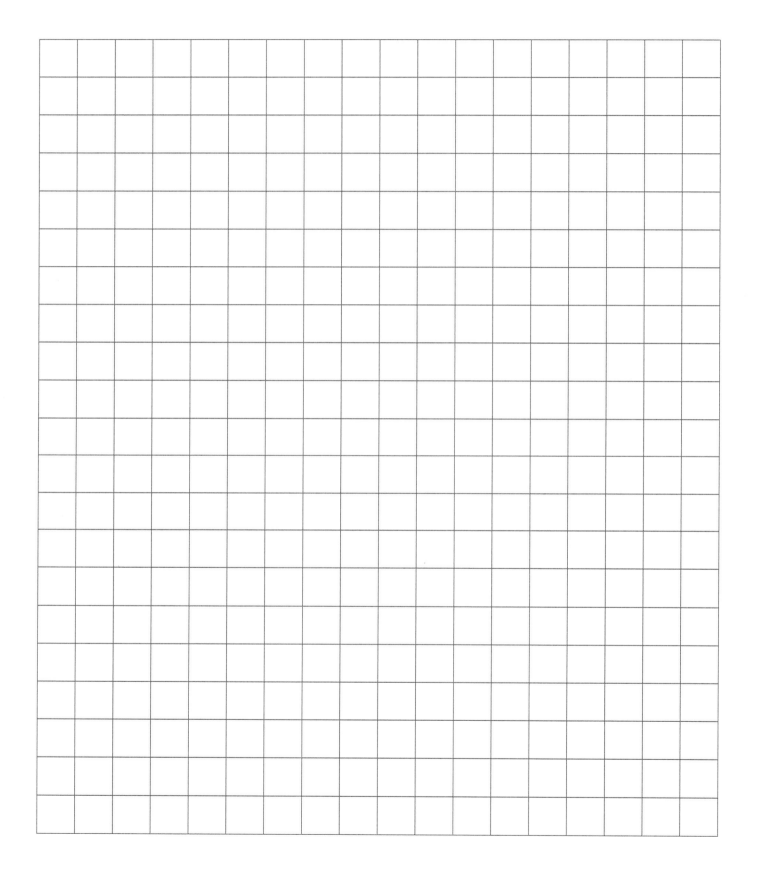

Brownie Shapes 1

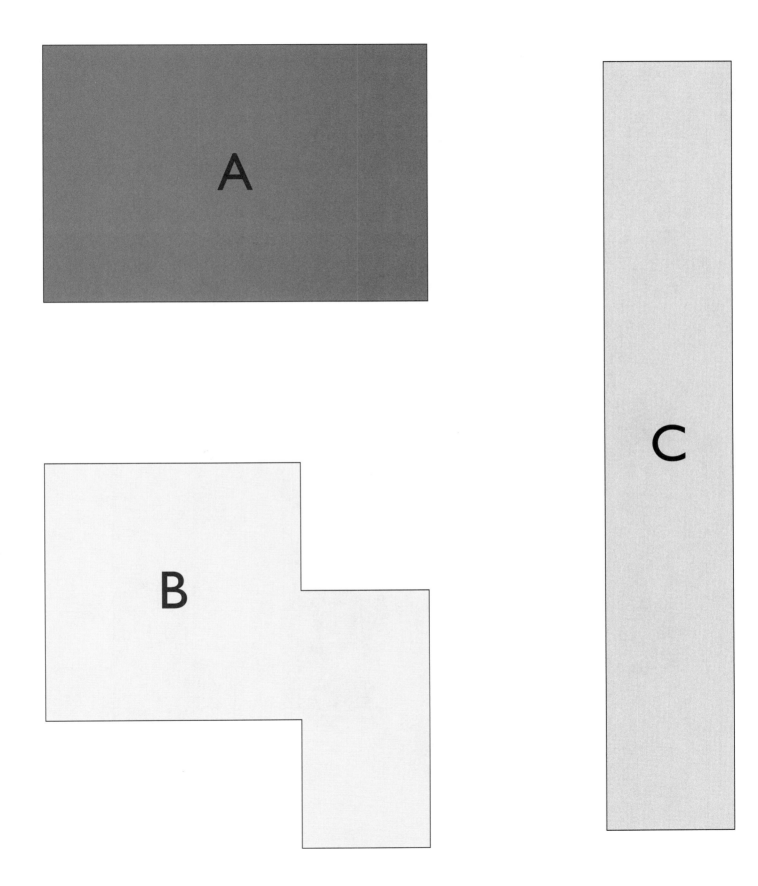

Brownie Shapes 2

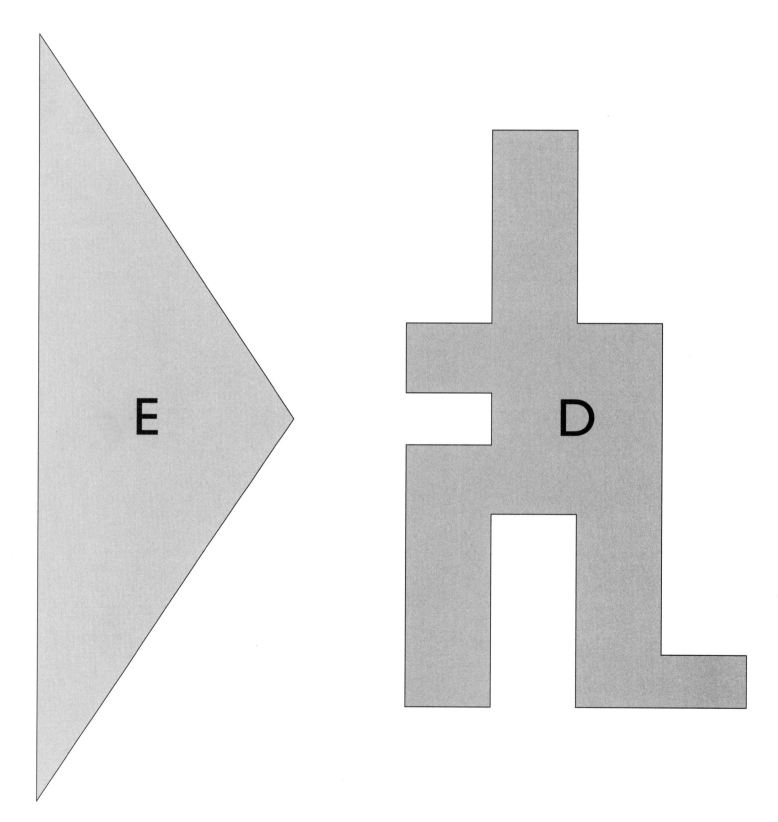

Inch Grid Paper

Sample House Plan

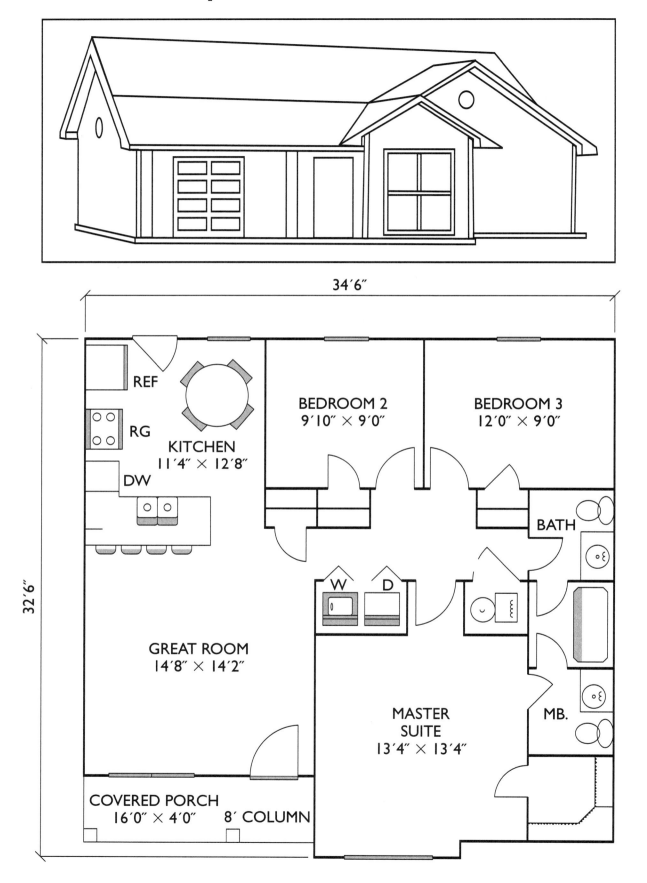

34'6"

32'6"

REF

RG

KITCHEN
11'4" × 12'8"

DW

BEDROOM 2
9'10" × 9'0"

BEDROOM 3
12'0" × 9'0"

BATH

W   D

MB.

GREAT ROOM
14'8" × 14'2"

MASTER
SUITE
13'4" × 13'4"

COVERED PORCH
16'0" × 4'0"   8' COLUMN

Put in Order—Volume

Prediction

Least   1.

2.

3.

4.

5.

6.

Greatest 7.

Comparing with Rice

Least   1.

2.

3.

4.

5.

6.

Greatest 7.

Measuring with Scoops

		Object Name	Number of Scoops
Least	1.		
	2.		
	3.		
	4.		
	5.		
	6.		
Greatest	7.		

How Do They Relate?

Comparing Volume Units, Small to Large

1 cup = _____ half-pint

_____ half-pints = 1 pint

_____ pints = 1 quart

_____ quarts = 1 half-gallon

_____ half-gallons = 1 gallon

Comparing Volume Units to a Gallon

_____ half-gallons = 1 gallon

_____ quarts = 1 gallon

_____ pints = 1 gallon

_____ cups = 1 gallon

Investigation

Use the above information to predict how these units relate:

❑ How many cups equal 1 quart?

❑ How many pints equal 1 gallon?

❑ How many cups equal 1 half-gallon?

❑ How many pints equal 1 half-gallon?

❑ How many half-pints equal 1 gallon?

From *Sizing Up Measurement: Activities for Grades 3–5 Classrooms* by Chris Confer. © 2007 by Math Solutions Publications.

Folding Boxes A

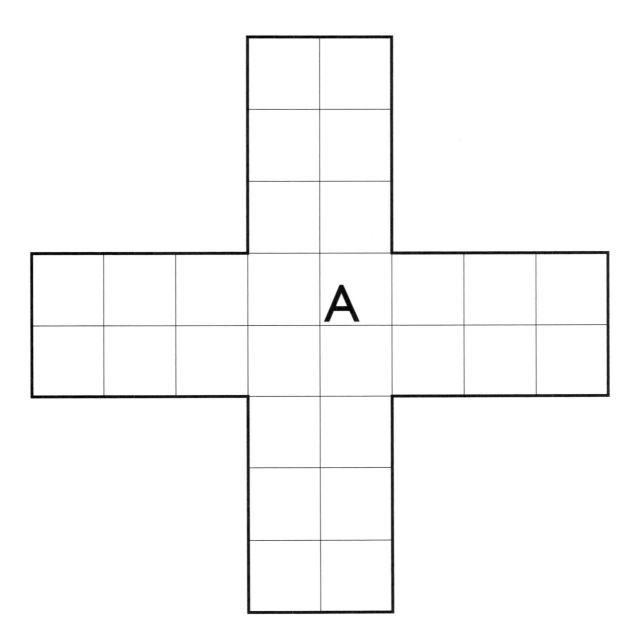

Folding Boxes B

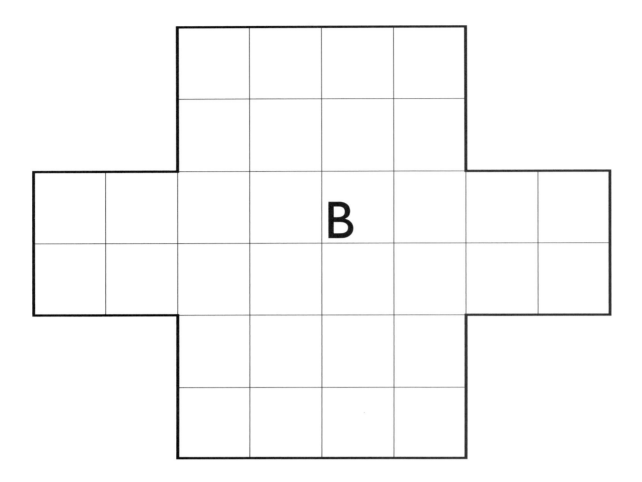

Folding Boxes C

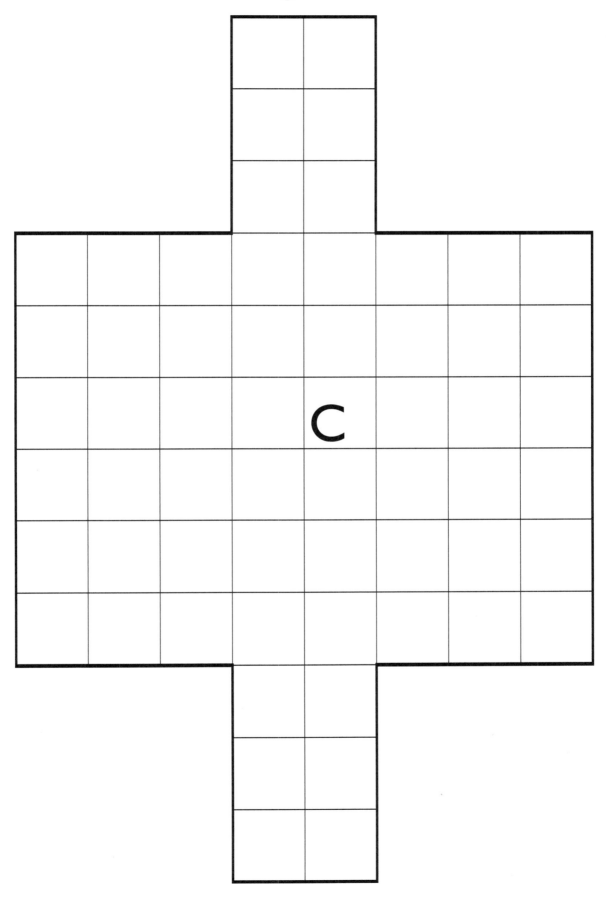

Folding Boxes D

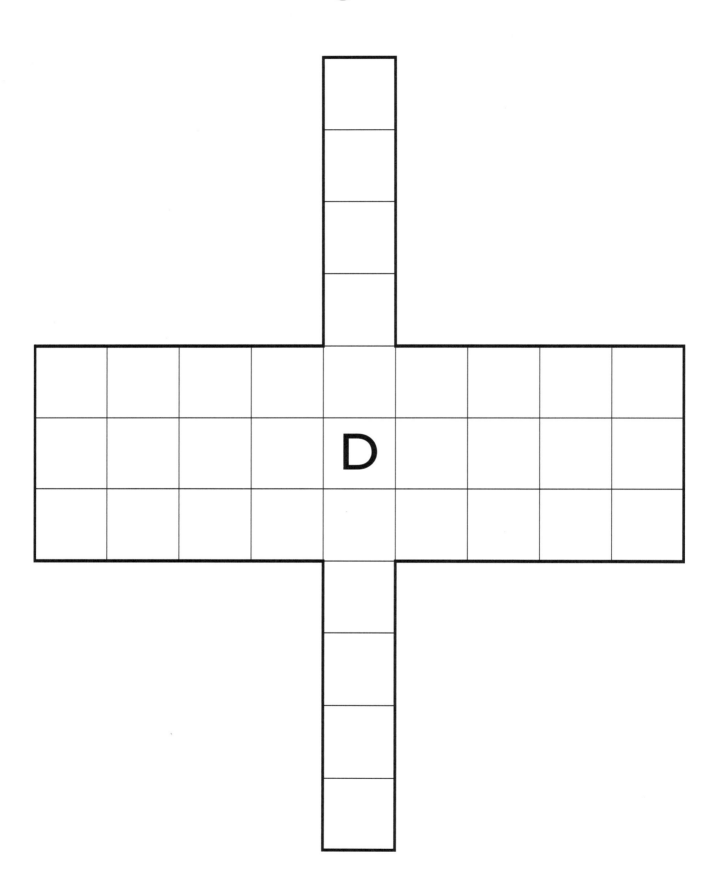

Three-Fourths-Inch Grid Paper

Isometric Dot Paper

Measuring Angles

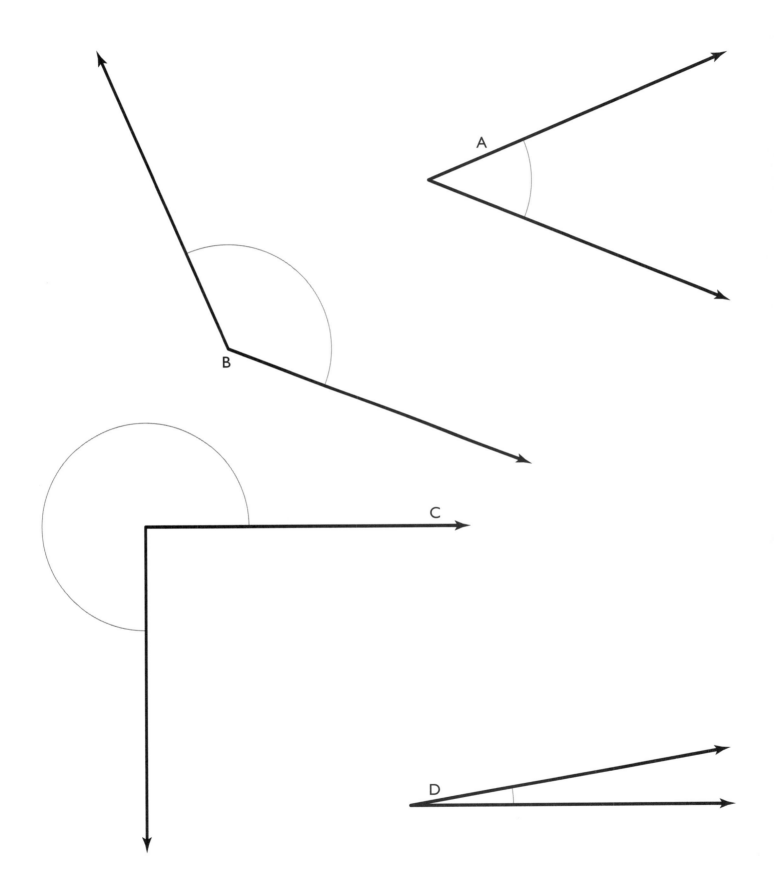

Measuring Polygon Angles

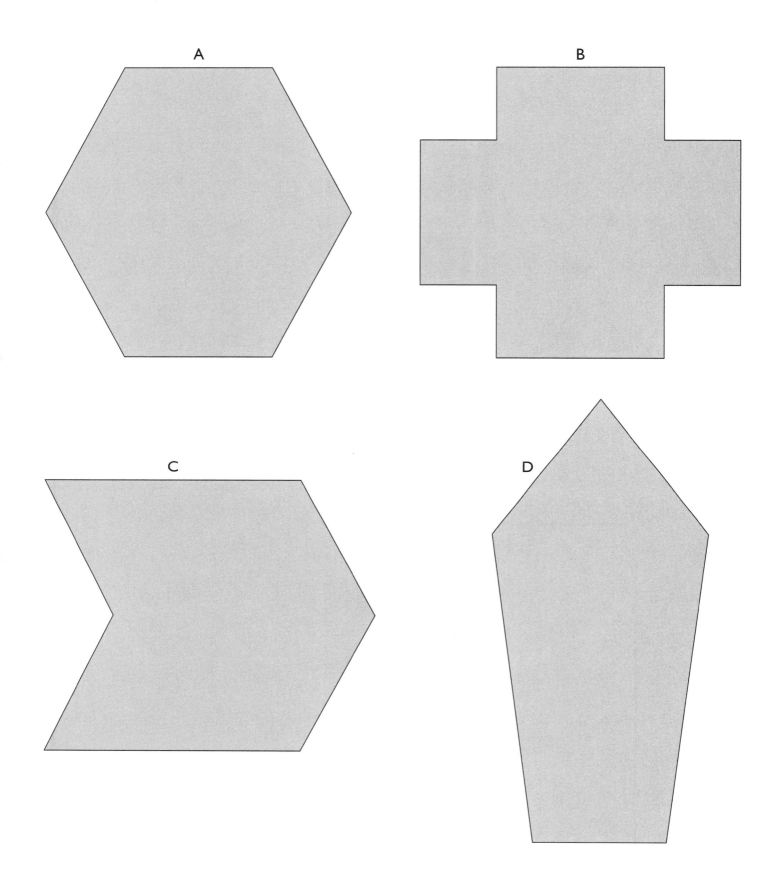

Waxed Paper Protractor

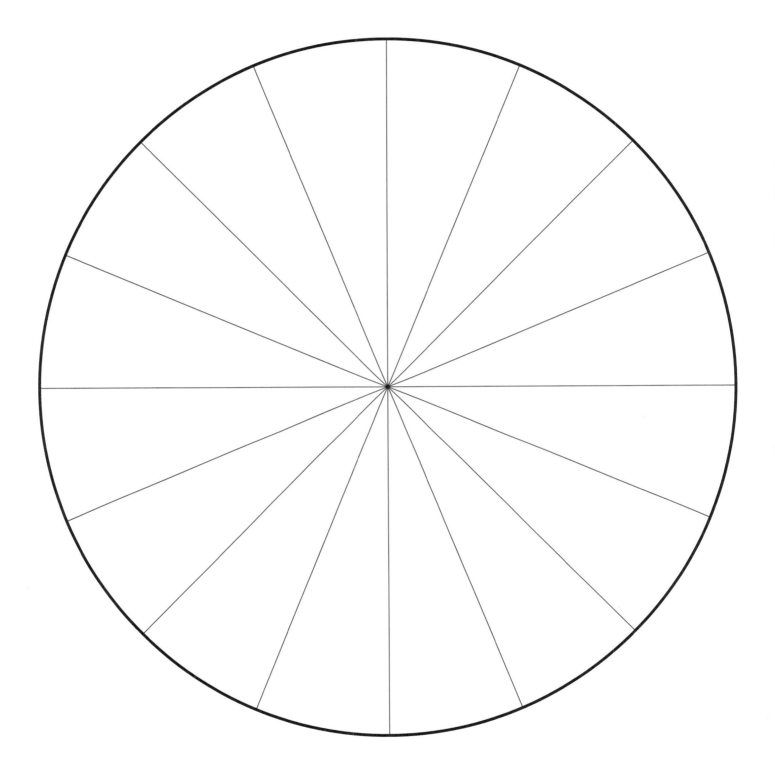

Angle Estimator

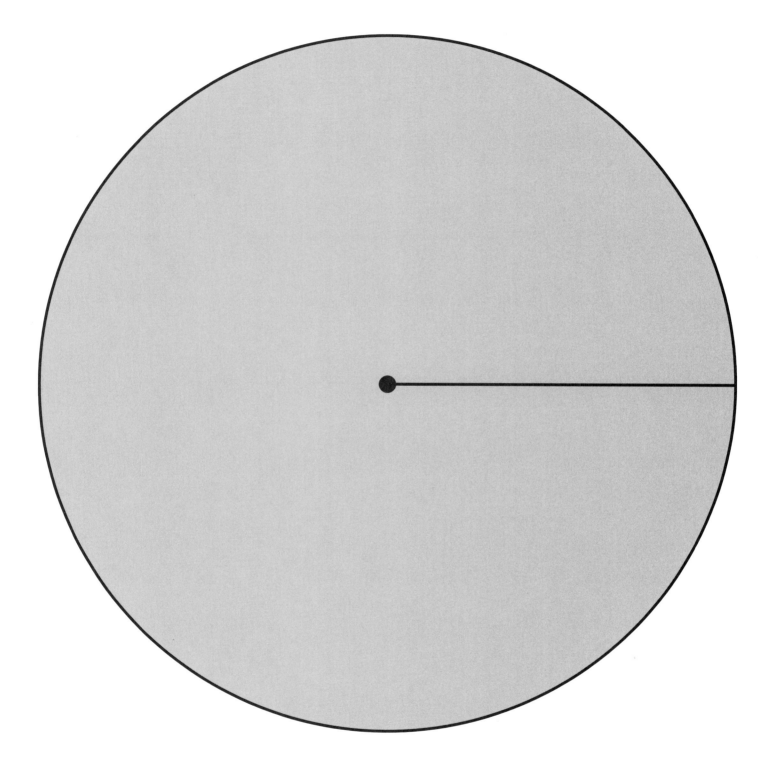

Target Angle

Target Angle	Estimate	Difference (Points)
__ __ 0°	_____	_____
__ __ 0°	_____	_____
__ __ 0°	_____	_____
__ __ 0°	_____	_____
		Total Score _____

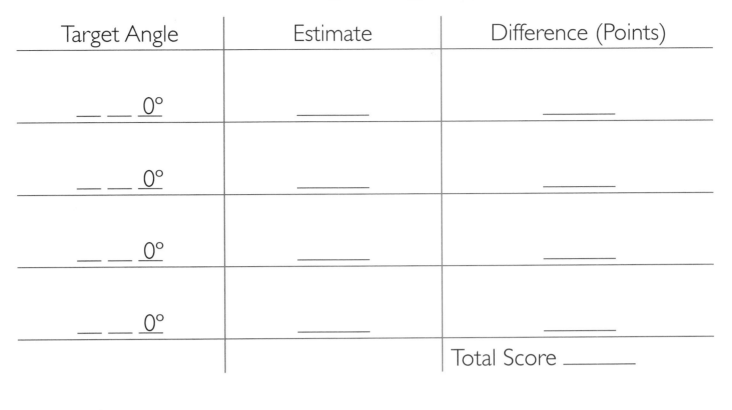

Target Angle

Target Angle	Estimate	Difference (Points)
__ __ 0°	_____	_____
__ __ 0°	_____	_____
__ __ 0°	_____	_____
__ __ 0°	_____	_____
		Total Score _____

Put in Order—Mass

Prediction

Lightest   1.

2.

3.

4.

5.

6.

Heaviest   7.

Comparing with a Balance

Lightest   1.

2.

3.

4.

5.

6.

Heaviest   7.

Measuring in Grams

		Object Name	Grams
Lightest	1.		
	2.		
	3.		
	4.		
	5.		
	6.		
Heaviest	7.		

Weights

Time Line Paper

TV Time!

Date	Start Time	End Time	Amount of Time

Let's Go to the Movies!

Peter Pan Returns   113 minutes
12:20   2:50   5:05   7:20

Lost on Mars   105 minutes
11:20   1:10   3:00   5:15   7:10

Bugs Ate My Computer   113 minutes
2:50   5:00   7:10

Ultimate Soccer Stars   84 minutes
11:45   2:20   4:35   7:05

Jim of the Jungle Swings into Action   115 minutes
11:35   2:15   5:20

Cartoon Capers   85 minutes
11:15   12:45   2:20   4:45

Robot Invasion 2   94 minutes
12:20   2:00   3:45   5:30

The Secret Ring of Galahad   111 minutes
11:40   1:35   3:50   6:10

Millions of Millionaires   124 minutes
11:15   2:00   4:15   6:50

The Flibberdiggibit   118 minutes
12:45   2:50   5:00   7:10

Patterns on the Clock Face

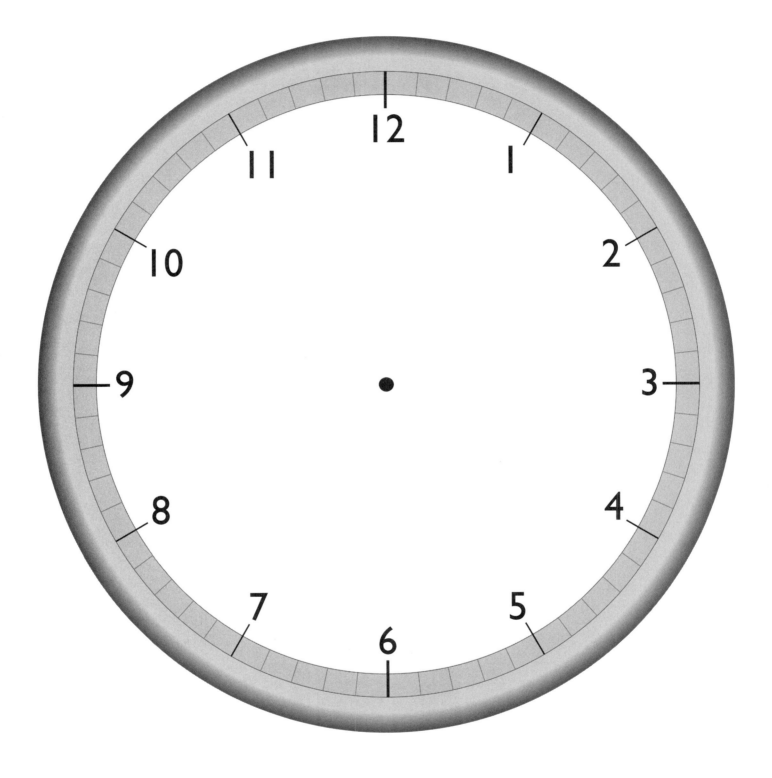

World Time Zones

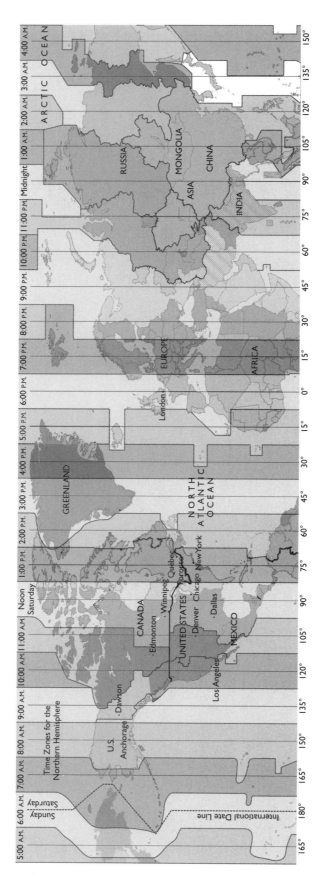

Temperature Scavenger Hunt

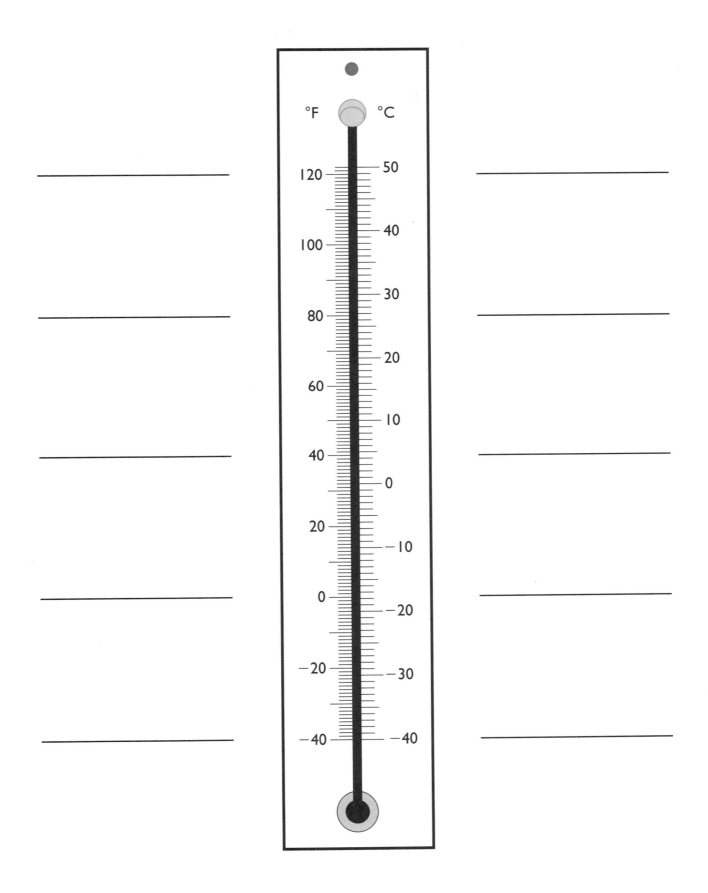

Inside and Outside Temperatures

	Day 1	Day 2	Day 3	Day 4	Day 5
Inside					
Estimate					
Measure					
How Far Off?					
Outside					
Estimate					
Measure					
How Far Off?					

Paper Thermometer

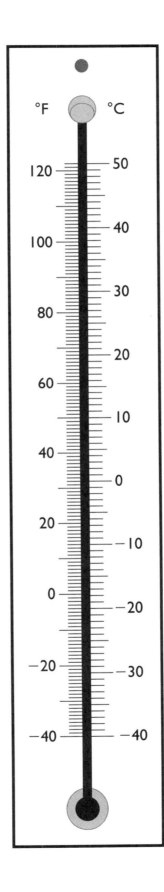

Packing for a Trip

City: _____

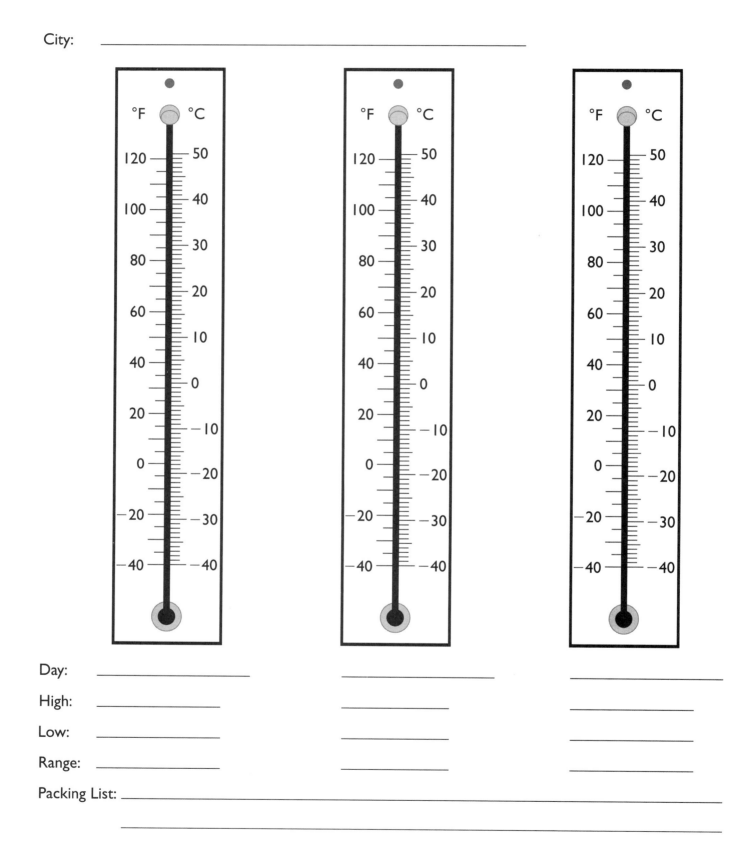

Day: _____   _____   _____

High: _____   _____   _____

Low: _____   _____   _____

Range: _____   _____   _____

Packing List: _____

_____

Half-Inch Grid Paper

A Day at the Beach

One summer day, my uncle read the weather section of the newspaper. "It's going to get up to _____ degrees Fahrenheit today!" he announced. "It's a perfect day to go to the beach!" As I called my friends, he mixed up some brownies for a snack, and when the oven read _____ degrees Fahrenheit, he popped them in. Of course I had to sample the brownies when they came out of the oven, but I waited until they were about _____ degrees Fahrenheit before I tasted them.

When we arrived at the beach, my friends and I dashed into the water. Was it ever cold! My lips turned blue as we played in the water. And no wonder! The water was only _____ degrees Fahrenheit. But we didn't care. It was such fun! We splashed each other, dug holes in the sand for the waves to fill, and buried each other up to our necks in the sand.

At 2:00 P.M. the temperature was the hottest it got that day. It was _____ degrees Fahrenheit, five degrees lower than what the newspaper had predicted. And then the clouds rolled in. The wind whipped the waves into foam. Ten minutes later the temperature had dropped fifteen degrees to _____. Another ten minutes later the temperature had dropped five more degrees, to 60°F.

Enough was enough! We knew our day at the beach was over. We gratefully pulled on our sweatshirts and drove over to Pizza Palace, still shivering. As we walked in the door, we were enveloped by the luscious smell of pizza and air warmed to _____ degrees Fahrenheit. Tired, happy, and warm, we dove into the pizza. It was a perfect ending to a perfect day at the beach!

Glossary

We've included in the glossary mathematical terms, phrases, and expressions that relate to measurement and are used in the K–2 book or the 3–5 book. Whenever possible, we use the correct terminology in the context of activities, often pairing the mathematical terminology with words students commonly understand. For example, when introducing the word *polygon*, we might use the word *shape* as well. During a lesson, we highlight key vocabulary for students, sometimes by recording these words on a vocabulary word chart. When appropriate, we encourage students to use this language as they discuss their thinking with each other and as they record their ideas in writing. In this way, over time, students acquire the language of mathematics.

A.M.: ante meridiem; between midnight and noon

acute angle: an angle that measures between 0 degrees and 90 degrees; an angle having a measure that is less than a right angle

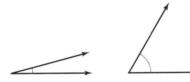

analog clock: a clock that shows the numerals 1–12, with a longer pointer to indicate the hour and a shorter pointer to indicate the minute

angle: a figure consisting of two rays with the same end point; its size is measured by the amount one ray has rotated in relation to the other

area: the measure of the amount of surface inside a closed boundary

array: a rectangular arrangement in rows and columns

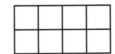

average: a typical or middle value for a set of numbers

balance scale: an instrument used to measure mass or weight; an object is placed in a weighing pan and a combination of standard weights are placed in a scale pan; standard weights are added to the scale pan until the pans are balanced

benchmark: a familiar length or object that is used as a point of reference to compare in estimation; a referent

Celsius: a scale for temperature measurement: water freezes at 0°C and boils at 100°C

centimeter: in the metric system, a unit of length equivalent to 10 millimeters or $\frac{1}{100}$ meter

circle: the set of all points in a plane that are the same distance (radius) from a point (the center of the circle)

circumference: the distance around a circle or sphere

column: a vertical arrangement of objects or numbers in an array or table

concave polygon: a polygon with at least one interior angle greater than 180 degrees

cone: a three-dimensional shape having a circular base, curved surface, and one vertex

conjecture: a reasonable guess

convex polygon: a polygon with all interior angles less than 180 degrees

cube: a three-dimensional shape with six square faces

customary units: units used in the United States for measuring length, volume, weight, and temperature; for example, inches, teaspoons, and pounds

cylinder: a three-dimensional shape with a curved surface and parallel, circular bases that are the same size

decimal: a number written in standard notation, often containing a decimal point, as in 3.45

decimeter: in the metric system, a unit of length equivalent to 10 centimeters or $\frac{1}{10}$ meter

degree: a unit of measure for temperature or angles; for angles, $\frac{1}{360}$ of a circle

diagonal: an arrangement of objects or numbers in an array or table from upper right to lower left or upper left to lower right

digital clock: clock that uses numbers to show the time in hours and minutes with a colon used to separate them, such as 3:20 A.M.

dimensions: a measure in one direction; for example, length, width, or height

distance: how far away something is; distance is measured in units of length

elapsed time: the amount of time between a beginning time and an ending time

end point: one of the points at each end of a line segment; the point at the end of a ray

equivalent: having the same value

estimate: a reasonable guess; a calculation of a close, instead of an exact, answer

Fahrenheit: a temperature scale; water freezes at 32°F and boils at 212°F

fluid ounce: in the customary system, a unit of capacity or volume; $\frac{1}{8}$ cup

foot: in the customary system, a unit of length equivalent to 12 inches or $\frac{1}{3}$ yard

gallon: in the customary system, a unit of capacity or volume containing 128 ounces

gram: a unit of mass equal to $\frac{1}{1,000}$ kilogram

heft: a hand movement used to estimate or compare weights

height: distance upward from a given point

hemisphere: half of a sphere

hexagon: a polygon with six sides

improper fraction: a fraction that names a number greater than or equal to 1; for example, $\frac{5}{4}$ or $\frac{8}{6}$

inch: in the customary system, a unit of length equal to $\frac{1}{12}$ foot

iteration: repeating the same steps or process over and over; unit iteration is the repetition of a single unit. If you are measuring the length of a desk with straws, it is easy to lay out straws across the desk and then count them. But if only one straw is available, then you must iterate (repeat) the unit (straw).

kilogram: in the metric system, a unit of mass equal to 1,000 grams

length: a measure of how long something is; length is measured in inches, centimeters, and so on

line segment: part of a line with two end points

liter: in the metric system, a unit of capacity or volume; a little less than a quart

mass: the amount of matter in an object; mass is usually measured against an object of known mass, often in grams or kilograms

mean: a typical value of a set of numbers

median: the middle data point in a set of data arranged in order of value

meter: in the metric system, a unit of length equal to 100 centimeters

metric system: a system of measurement built on the base ten numeration system; the units of measure in this system include millimeters, centimeters, meters, and kilometers for length, liters and milliliters for volume, grams and kilograms for weight, and degrees Celsius for temperature

millimeter: in the metric system, a unit of length equal to $\frac{1}{10}$ centimeter or $\frac{1}{1,000}$ meter

mode: the most frequently occurring data value in a graph

obtuse angle: an angle that measures between 90 degrees and 180 degrees

open number line: a number line with only the numbers relevant to a specific computational strategy. For example, for 36 + _____ = 60:

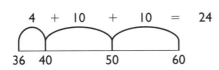

ounce: in the customary system, a unit of weight or volume; $\frac{1}{16}$ pound or $\frac{1}{8}$ cup, respectively

P.M.: post meridiem; between noon and midnight

parallelogram: a quadrilateral that has two pairs of parallel sides; opposite sides are the same length

perimeter: the distance around a two-dimensional shape

pint: in the customary system, a unit of capacity or volume equivalent to 2 cups or 16 fluid ounces

polygon: a closed two-dimensional figure made of line segments (sides) connected at their end points

pound: in the customary system, a unit of weight equivalent to 16 ounces

protractor: a device for measuring or drawing angles

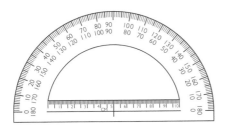

quadrilateral: a polygon with four sides

quart: in the customary system, a unit of capacity or volume

equivalent to 4 cups or 32 fluid ounces

range: the difference between the least and greatest values in a distribution

ray: part of a line with one end point

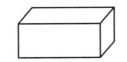

rectangle: a quadrilateral with four right angles and two pairs of opposite sides that are the same length

rectangular prism: a prism that has rectangles for all the faces

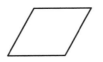

referent: a benchmark; a familiar length or object that is used as a point of reference to compare in estimation

rhombus: a parallelogram with all sides the same length

right angle: an angle that measures exactly 90 degrees

rotate: to turn around a center point

sample: a representative part of an entire set used to gather information about the whole group

scale: a way to measure length or distance with a graduated sequence of marks; an instrument for measuring weight

side: any of the line segments forming a polygon

spring scale: a type of scale used for measuring mass or weight; a spring scale determines an item's weight by identifying how far a spring stretches against a written scale

square: a rectangle with four sides that are the same length

square centimeter: in the metric system, a unit of area that is a square that has the measure of each side equal to 1 centimeter

straight angle: an angle measuring exactly 180 degrees

tablespoon: in the customary system, a unit of capacity or volume; 3 teaspoons or $\frac{1}{16}$ cup

teaspoon: in the customary system, a unit of capacity or volume; $\frac{1}{6}$ fluid ounce

temperature: a measure of molecular movement that underlies the ideas of heat and coldness

thermometer: an instrument used to display temperature

three-dimensional object: an object that has length, width, and depth; objects that fill space as prisms, pyramids, and spheres

time line: a scaled line used to display a certain length of time; a time line often has events displayed in positions according to when they occurred

ton: a unit of weight; in the U.S. system, 2,000 pounds

transitivity: a mathematical property that states, "If A = B and B = C, then A = C; if A < B and B < C, then A < C; if A > B and B > C, then A > C"; in measurement, when you can't compare two objects directly, you must

continued

continued from page 317

compare them by means of a
third object, for example, a ruler

trapezoid: a quadrilateral with
exactly one pair of parallel sides

triangle: a polygon with three sides

unit: a label, word, or unit of measure used with a number to show
its size or context; for example,
inches, quarts, centimeters,
degrees

U.S. customary system: system that
measures length in inches, feet,
yards, and miles, for example;
capacity in cups, pints, quarts,
and gallons, for example; weight
in ounces, pounds, and tons, for
example; and temperature in
degrees Fahrenheit

vertex: a point where rays of an
angle or sides of a polygon meet

vertical: straight up and down

volume: the measure of how much
space a three-dimensional shape
fills

weight: a measure of how heavy
something is; measured in units
including ounces, pounds, grams,
and kilograms

width: the horizontal measurement
made at a right angle to the height

yard: in the customary system, a unit
of length equal to 3 feet or 36
inches

References

Benton, Michael. 1984. *The Dinosaur Encyclopedia*. New York: Aladdin.

Briggs, Raymond. 1970. *Jim and the Beanstalk*. London: Hamilton.

Bunting, Eve. 1996. *Going Home*. New York: HarperCollins.

Burnie, David. 2001. *The Kingfisher Illustrated Dinosaur Encyclopedia*. London: Houghton Mifflin.

Burns, Marilyn. 1978. *This Book Is About Time*. Boston: Little, Brown.

———. 1982. *Math for Smarty Pants*. Boston: Little, Brown.

Carrick, Carol. 1985. *Patrick's Dinosaurs*. New York: Clarion.

Centers for Disease Control (CDC) National Center for Health Statistics. 2004. "Americans Slightly Taller, Much Heavier than 40 Years Ago." Accessed July 3, 2007: www.cdc.gov/od/oc/media/pressrel/r041027.htm.

Clement, Rod. 1991. *Counting on Frank*. Milwaukee: G. Stevens Children's.

dePaola, Tomie. 1984. *The Popcorn Book*. New York: Holiday House.

Frasier, Debra. 1991. *On the Day You Were Born*. San Diego: Harcourt Brace Jovanovich.

Jenkins, Steve. 1996. *Big and Little*. Boston: Houghton Mifflin.

Khan, Sarah. 1988. *Amazing Animal Facts & Lists*. London: Usborne.

Martin, J. A, B. E. Hamilton, P. D. Sutton, et al. 2006. "Births: Final Data for 2004." *National Vital Statistics Reports* 55 (1). Hyattsville, MD: National Center for Health Statistics. Accessed July 3, 2007: www.cdc.gov/nchs/fastats/birthwt.htm.

Most, Bernard. 1989. *The Littlest Dinosaurs*. San Diego: Harcourt Brace Jovanovich.

Myller, Rolf. 1990. *How Big Is a Foot?* New York: Dell Yearling.

Sachar, Louis. 1998. *Sideways Stories from Wayside School*. New York: Morrow Junior.

Schuett, Stacey. 1995. *Somewhere in the World Right Now*. New York: Alfred A. Knopf.

Schuster, Lainie, and Nancy Canavan Anderson. 2005. *Good Questions for Math Teaching: Why Ask Them and What to Ask, Grades 5–8*. Sausalito, CA: Math Solutions.

Schwartz, David M. 1985. *How Much Is a Million?* New York: Lothrop, Lee, and Shepard.

Stevens, Janet, and Susan Stevens Crummel. 1999. *Cook-a-Doodle-Doo!* San Diego: Harcourt Brace.

Taylor, David. 1995. *The Big and Little Animal Book*. Chicago: Heinemann Library.

———. 1996. *The Heavy and Light Animal Book*. Austin, TX: Raintree-Steck-Vaughn.

Index

A

absolute zero, 249
acute angles, 154
addition and subtraction, lesson on
    adding units of time, 222–24
Amazing Animal Facts & Lists (Khan), 24
anacondas, average weight, 219
Anderson, Nancy (*Good Questions for
    Math Teaching*), 202
angles, 149–82
    angle estimator, lessons on
        constructing and using an, 174–76,
        177–79, 300
    bodies, lesson on making angles with,
        152–55
    classifying, lesson on, 156–59
    combining, lesson on, 167–70
    constructing and measuring angles
        game, 177–79
    defining, lesson on, 150–52
    introduction, chapter, 149–50
    measuring, lessons on, 159–67,
        171–82, 297, 298
    objects made of angles, lesson on
        finding, 155–56
    in pattern blocks, measuring, 171–74
    of polygons, measuring, 164, 166–67
    problems understanding,
        student, 149
    quilts, lesson on estimating
        and measuring angles in, 180–82
    use of angles in outside world,
        lesson on, 164–67
animals
    life-size drawings of animals,
        lesson on making, 23–27
    weight lesson on heavy/light, 217–21
Apple Juice Container Debate,
    lesson, 210–13
area, 53–94
    bedroom floor plans, lesson on
        designing, 92–95
    of body parts, lessons on, 53–62
    decomposing areas, lesson on, 68–72
    defined, 53
    designing dog yards, lesson on,
        73–77
    different shape brownies, comparing
        areas of, 62–64, 285, 286
    equation writing for different shapes,
        lesson on, 65–68
    house floor plans, lesson on designing,
        87–92, 288
    introduction, chapter, 53
    polygons with equal perimeters, lesson
        on drawing, 78–81
    rectangles with equal perimeters,
        lesson on finding, 81–84
    use of Cuisenaire Rods to form
        polygons, lesson on, 84–87

B

balls, tennis, average weight,
    218, 219
bats, Kitti's hog-nosed, average
    weight, 221
beetles, Goliath, average weight, 221
benchmarks
    angles, 153–54, 171, 172
    height, 28–31
    length, 1, 14–16
    temperatures, 249, 252–58, 263–67
    time, 222, 224–26
    weights, 183, 190–91, 196–98,
        205–7
Benton, Michael (*The Dinosaur
    Encyclopedia*), 27
Big and Little Animal Book, The
    (Taylor), 23, 24
Big and Little (Jenkins), 24
Blackline Masters, 279–314
    Angle Estimator, 300
    Brownie Shapes 1, 285
    Brownie Shapes 2, 286
    Centimeter Grid Paper, 284
    A Day at the Beach, 314
    Finger Weaving Instructions, 282
    Finger Weaving Recording
        Sheet, 283
    Folding Boxes A, 291
    Folding Boxes B, 292
    Folding Boxes C, 293
    Folding Boxes D, 294
    Half-Inch Grid Paper, 313
    How Do They Relate?, 290
    Inch Grid Paper, 287
    Inside and Outside
        Temperatures, 310
    Isometric Dot Paper, 296
    Let's Go to the Movies!, 306
    Measuring Angles, 297
    Measuring Polygon Angles, 298
    Packing for a Trip, 312
    Paper Ruler, 281
    Paper Thermometer, 311
    Patterns on the Clock Face, 307
    Put in Order—Mass, 302
    Put in Order—Volume, 289
    Sample House Plan, 288
    Target Angle, 301
    Temperature Scavenger
        Hunt, 309
    Three-Fourths-Inch Grid
        Paper, 295
    Time Line Paper, 304
    TV Time!, 305
    Waxed Paper Protractor, 299
    Weights, 303
    World Time Zones, 308
Body Angles and Simon Says,
    lesson, 152–55
Briggs, Raymond (*Jim and the
    Beanstalk*), 43, 44
Broken Ruler 1, lesson, 16–19, 281
Broken Ruler 2, lesson, 20–23
Brownie Shapes 1 (Blackline
    Master), 285
Brownie Shapes 2 (Blackline
    Master), 286
Bunting, Eve (*Going Home*), 31
Burnie, David (*The Kingfisher
    Illustrated Dinosaur
    Encyclopedia*), 27
Burns, Marilyn
    Math for Smarty Pants, 13
    This Book Is About Time, 232
bustard, kori, 218–19

C

Calendar Patterns, lesson, 242–43
calendars
    ages of students, lesson on, 240–41
    characteristics, lesson on, 242–43
    understanding duration through,
        lesson on, 238–39
capacity, 96
Carrick, Carol (*Patrick's Dinosaurs*), 27
cars, average weight, 218, 219
Centimeter Grid Paper (Blackline
    Master), 284
centimeters, 43
Chihuahuas, average weight, 221
clams, giant, average weight, 219
classifying angles, lesson on, 156–59
Classroom Decisions, lesson, 222–24
Clement, Rod (*Counting on Frank*),
    9, 104, 112
clock faces, lesson exploring patterns on,
    244–46
Color Experiments, lesson, 274–77
Combining Angles, lesson, 167–70
Comparing Brownies, lesson, 62–64,
    285, 286
conservation of area, 62, 63, 64
conservation of length, xiv
Cook-a-Doodle-Doo! Great-Granny's
    Magnificent Strawberry Shortcake
    Recipe, lesson, 145–48
Cook-a-Doodle-Doo! Iguana's
    Mistakes, lesson, 120–22
Cook-a-Doodle-Doo! (Stevens and
    Crummel), 120, 121, 145
Counting on Frank (Clement), 9–10,
    104, 112
Crazy Quilts, lesson, 180–82
Creating Benchmarks for Height,
    lesson, 28–31
Crummel, Susan Stevens (*Cook-a-
    Doodle-Doo!*), 120, 145

D

"Day at the Beach, A," 277, 314
decimeters, 43
decomposing areas, lesson on, 68–72
deer, mouse, average weight, 221
dePaola, Tomie (*Popcorn Book*),
    100, 101
Design a House, lesson, 87–92, 288
Dinosaur Data, lesson, 27–28
Dinosaur Encyclopedia, The
    (Benton), 27
Dog Yards, lesson, 73–77
duration
    calendars, lesson on understanding
        duration through, 238–39

time lines, lesson on understanding
    duration through, 226–29

E

equivalence, in comparing different
    shape brownies lesson, 62, 63–64
estimation
    angle estimators, 174–76, 177–79
    of angles in polygons, 164, 166–67
    of inside and outside temperatures,
        256–58
    in lesson on creating benchmarks for
        height, 28–29
    of minutes, lesson on, 224–26
    ordering objects by mass, in lesson on,
        187–90
    of soda students drink in one year,
        lesson on, 116, 117
    volume, lesson on estimating, 104–6
    of volume of boxes without tops, lesson
        on, 122, 123
    of weight in food drive activity,
        213–17

F

Fewest Weights, The, lesson, 202–5
Filling Boxes, lesson, 122–24
Finger Weaving, lesson, 46–52,
    282, 283
floor plans
    for bedrooms, lesson on designing,
        87–92
    for houses, lesson on designing, 87–92
fluid ounces, 117
Folding Boxes, lesson, 124–27
    Folding Boxes A (Blackline
        Master), 291
    Folding Boxes B (Blackline
        Master), 292
    Folding Boxes C (Blackline
        Master), 293
    Folding Boxes D (Blackline
        Master), 294
Food Drive, A, lesson, 213–17
food drive activity, estimation and
    measurement in, 213–17
Foot-Length Rulers, lesson, 1–7
Frank's Dog Food, lesson, 112–15
Frasier, Debra (*On the Day You Were
    Born*), 240
Fruit Salad, lesson, 190–93

G

games
    I See Something, 193–96
    Simon Says, 152, 155

The Target Angle Game, 177–79
Too Hot, Too Cold, Just Right, 261–63
Going Home, lesson, 31–35
Going Home (Bunting), 31–32
Good Questions for Math Teaching
    (Schuster and Anderson), 202
gorillas, average weight, 219
grams, developing benchmarks
    for, 208–9
graphing, student hand size,
    55–56, 59–62
grid paper
    centimeter (Blackline Master), 284
    half-inch (Blackline Master), 313
    inch (Blackline Master), 287
    three-fourths-inch (Blackline
        Master), 295

H

Half-Inch Grid Paper (Blackline
    Master), 313
heat, lesson on functioning of, 258–61
Heat Experiments, lesson, 258–61
*Heavy and Light Animal Book,
    The* (Taylor), 217–18
Heavy and Light Animals, lesson,
    217–21
heavy/light
    animals, lesson on, 217–21
    introductory weight lesson on,
        183–87
hippopotamuses, average weight,
    219, 220
How Big Is a Foot?, lesson, 7–9
How Big Is a Foot? (Myller), 7
How Do They Relate?, lesson,
    108–11, 290
How Long a Line?, lesson, 9–14
How Many Rectangles?, lesson, 81–84
How Much Is a Kilogram?, lesson,
    205–7
How Much Is a Meter?, lesson,
    14–16
How Much Is a Million? (Schwartz),
    35–36
How Much Soda?, lesson, 116–19
How Old Are You?, lesson, 240–41
humans, average weight, 218–19
Hunt for Angles, lesson, 155–56

I

Ice Water Investigations, lesson, 270–74
Inch Grid Paper (Blackline Master), 287
Inside and Outside Temperatures,
    lesson, 256–58, 301
inverse relationships, xiv
I See Something, lesson, 193–96

isometric dot paper (Blackline
    Master), 296
iteration, 2–4

J

Jelly Bean Jar, lesson, 104–6
Jenkins, Steve (*Big and Little*), 24
Jim and the Beanstalk: Giant-Size
    Things, lesson, 43–46
Jim and the Beanstalk (Briggs), 43, 44

K

kangaroos, red, average weight, 219
Khan, Sarah (*Amazing Animal Facts &*
    Lists), 24
kilograms, lesson on developing
    benchmarks for, 205–7
Kingfisher Illustrated Dinosaur
    Encyclopedia, The (Burnie), 27

L

Last Day of School, The, lesson, 238–39
least to greatest, volume lesson
    ordering, 99–100
length, 1–52
    broken rulers, lessons for measuring
        activity cards with, 16–19,
        20–23, 281
    conservation of, xiv
    driving distances and map routes,
        lesson on, 31–35
    finger chains, lesson on measurement
        of, 46–52, 282, 283
    foot-length rulers, lesson on creation
        and use of, 1–7
    giant-size things, lesson on measuring,
        43–46
    height, lesson on creating
        benchmarks for, 28–31
    height of stacks of children, lesson on,
        35–40
    introduction, chapter, 1
    large measurements, lesson on,
        27–28
    life-size drawings of animals, lesson on
        making, 23–27
    of pencil lines, lesson on prediction
        and measurement of, 9–14
    relationships in metric system,
        lesson on, 41–43
    units, lesson on value of
        consistently sized, 7–9
    use of benchmarks with metric units,
        lesson on, 14–16

Let's Go to the Movies!, lesson,
    235–38, 306
Life-Size Zoo, A, lesson, 23–27
light/heavy, weight lesson on, 183–87
lines, lesson on predicting and
    measuring length of, 9–14
Little Red Hen, The, 121
Littlest Dinosaur, The (Most), 24

MN

Mailing a Birthday Package, lesson,
    198–202
maps, lesson on driving distances and
    routes, 31–35
Math for Smarty Pants (Burns), 13
Maximum Box, lesson, 127–32
measurement
    complexities of teaching, xiii
    historical overview, xiii
    lessons, focus of, xiii–xiv
    natural progressions in children's
        thinking, xiv–xv
    use of, by children in daily lives, xiii
Measuring Angles, lesson, 159–63, 297
Measuring Polygon Angles (Blackline
    Master), 298
Measuring with Plastic Protractors,
    174–76
median, in hand size lesson, 56, 62
Metric Hunt, lesson, 208–10
metric system
    connecting U.S. customary system
        with, lesson on, 46–52
    life-size drawings of animals, lesson on
        making, 24–27
    relationships in the, lesson on, 41–43
    units, use of benchmarks with metric,
        14–16
    weights, lesson on developing
        benchmarks for, 208–10
Minute Experiments, lesson, 224–26
minutes, lesson on exploring, 224–26
Mitten 1, The, lesson, 53–56
Mitten 2, The, lesson, 56–62
mode, in hand size lesson, 56, 62
molecules, 250–51
Most, Bernard (*The Littlest*
    Dinosaur), 24
mouse deer, average weight, 221
My Dream Bedroom, lesson, 92–95
Myller, Rolf (*How Big Is a Foot?*), 7

O

obtuse angles, 154
On the Day You Were Born
    (Frasier), 240
ostriches, average weight, 219
ounces, 116–17, 194–95

P

Packing for a Trip, lesson, 263–67, 312
Patrick's Dinosaurs (Carrick), 27
Pattern Block Angles, lesson, 171–74
patterns
    calendar characteristics, lesson on,
        242–43
    clock face, lesson on, 244–46, 307
    on thermometers, lesson on, 267–70
Patterns on a Thermometer, lesson,
    267–70
Patterns on the Clock Face, lesson,
    244–46, 307
perimeters
    bedroom floor plans, lesson on
        designing, 92–95
    drawing polygons with equal, lesson
        on, 78–81
    house floor plans, lesson on designing,
        87–92
    rectangles with equal perimeters,
        lesson on finding, 81–84
    use of Cuisenaire Rods to form
        polygons, lesson on, 84–87
Perimeters of 30, lesson, 78–81
Perimeters with Cuisenaire Rods, lesson,
    84–87
polar bears, average weight, 219
polygons
    angles in, lesson on measuring, 164,
        166–67, 298
    Cuisenaire Rods used to form,
        lesson on, 84–87
polygons with equal perimeters,
    lesson on drawing, 78–81
Popcorn Book (dePaola), 100, 101
Popcorn Containers, lesson, 100–103
pounds, 194–95
prediction
    in filling of jars lessons, 96, 98, 99–100
    of length of pencil lines, activity on,
        9–10
    in lesson on effect of color on
        temperature, 274, 275, 277
    number of cubes to fill a box
        pattern, lesson on, 124–27
    of volumes of liquids in containers,
        lesson on, 106, 111
    of width of cafeteria, 1–2
protractors
    angle estimator, lessons on
        constructing and using an, 174–76,
        177–79
    measuring angles with paper, 164,
        165–67
    quilts, measuring angles in, 180–82
Put in Order—Mass, lesson, 187–90, 302
Put in Order—Volume, lesson,
    99–100, 289

Q

quadrilaterals
  classification of angles, lesson on,
    156–59
  combining angles of, lesson on, 167,
    169–70

R

rectangles with equal perimeters,
  lesson on finding, 81–84
Relationships in the Metric System,
  lesson, 41–43
right angles, 153–54
rulers
  foot-length rulers, lesson on
    creation and use of, 1–7
  measuring activity cards with broken
    rulers, lesson on, 16–19, 20–23

S

Sachar, Louis (Sideways Stories from
  Wayside School), 132
Sample House Plan (Blackline
  Master), 288
scales (weight), introducing, 185–87
schedule-making lesson, 235–38
school buses, average weight, 221
Schuett, Stacey (Somewhere in the World
  Right Now), 246
Schuster, Lainie (Good Questions for Math
  Teaching), 202
Schwartz, David (How Much Is a
  Million?), 35–36
Scoops of Rice and Beans, lesson, 96–98
sea otters, average weight, 219
Sideways Stories from Wayside School
  (Sachar), 132–33
Simon Says (Game), 152, 155
Somewhere in the World, lesson, 246–48
Somewhere in the World Right Now
  (Schuett), 246
Sorting Angles, lesson, 156–59
square centimeters, use of term, 59–60
Stacks of Kids, lesson, 35–40
Stevens, Janet (Cook-a-Doodle-Doo!),
  120
straight angles, 154
Stuff a Bag, lesson, 196–98

T

Target Angle Game, The, lesson,
  177–79, 301
Taylor, David
  The Big and Little Animal Book,
    23, 24

The Heavy and Light Animal Book,
  217–18
T-charts
  combining angles with, 170
  in comparing areas of dog yards,
    lesson, 76–77
  in equivalent measure for recipes,
    lesson, 145, 147, 148
  for identifying patterns in angles,
    lesson, 166–67
  in I See Something game, 195
  relating feet and inches, 38
  in time elapsed lesson, 230–31
television, lesson on time spent
  watching, 232–35
temperature, 249–78
  characteristics, 249
  defined, 249, 252
  effect of color on temperature,
    lesson on, 274–77
  effect of ice on water, lesson on,
    270–74
  heat, lesson on functioning of,
    258–61
  inside and outside temperatures,
    lesson on, 256–58, 310
  introducing, lesson on, 250–52
  introduction, chapter, 249
  mystery temperatures, game for
    guessing, 261–63, 311
  patterns on thermometers, lesson on,
    267–70
  scavenger hunt, lesson, 253–56, 309
  in short story, lesson about placing,
    277–78, 314
  weather data, lesson on reviewing,
    263–67, 312
Temperature Scavenger Hunt, lesson,
  253–55, 309
Temperature Story, A, lesson, 277–78
ten, powers of, in metric system, 41–43
tennis balls, average weight, 219
thermometers
  effect of color on temperature, lesson
    on, 274–77
  effect of ice on water, lesson on,
    270–74
  game for guessing mystery
    temperatures, 261–63, 311
  heat, lesson on functioning of,
    258–61
  inside and outside temperatures, lesson
    on, 256–58, 310
  introductory lesson, 250–52
  patterns on thermometers, lesson on,
    267–70
  in temperature scavenger hunt lesson,
    253–56, 309
This Book Is About Time (Burns), 232
Three-Fourths-Inch Grid Paper
  (Blackline Master), 295

tigers, Siberian, average weight, 219
Tiling a Floor, lesson, 68–72
time, 222–48
  ages of students, lesson on, 240–41
  calendar characteristics, lesson on,
    242–43
  calendars, lesson on understanding
    duration through, 238–39
  clock face, lesson exploring
    patterns on, 244–46, 307
  elapsed, lesson on, 230–32
  importance of, 222
  introduction, chapter, 222
  minutes, lesson on exploring,
    224–26
  real-life decisions involving time,
    lesson on making, 222–24
  schedule-making lesson,
    235–38, 306
  spent watching television, lesson on,
    232–35, 305
  time lines, lesson on understanding
    duration through, 226–29, 304
  what students are doing in different
    parts of the world, lesson on,
    246–48, 308
time lines
  ages of students, lesson on, 240–41
  lesson on making, 226–29, 304
Time Lines of a Wonderful Day,
  lesson, 226–29
Time to Go Home, lesson, 230–32
Too Hot, Too Cold, Just Right, lesson,
  261–63
transitive reasoning, xiv–xv
triangles, lesson on combining
  angles of, 167–69
true zero, 249
TV Time!, lesson, 232–35, 305
typical, discussing use of term, 58

U

unit iteration, xiv
units of measure for liquids, lesson on,
  106–11
U.S. customary units
  connecting metric units of measuring
    length with, 46–52
  weight, 208–9

V

volume, 96–148
  amount of soda students drink in one
    year, lesson on, 116–19
  of boxes, lessons on, 122–24,
    127–32
  box pattern making lesson, 127–32

creating containers to hold popcorn, lesson on, 100–103

defined, 96

estimating volume, lesson on, 104–6

in filling of jars lessons, 96–98, 99–100, 289

introduction, chapter, 96

least to greatest volumes, lesson on, 99–100, 289

meaning of, lesson on, 96–98

number of cubes to fill a box pattern, lesson on predicting, 124–27

rectangular arrangements for schools, lesson on, 132–44

reliability of measuring, lesson on, 120–22

shopping bags, lesson on capacities of, 112–15

units to measure liquids, lesson on, 106–11

using equivalent measures in recipes, lesson on, 145–48

WXYZ

Waxed Paper Protractors, lesson, 164–67, 299

Wayside School, lesson, 132–44

Wayside School series, 132

weather data, lesson on reviewing, 263–67

weight, 183–221

benchmark weights, lesson on developing, 196–98

defined, 183

food drive activity, estimation and measurement in, 213–17

heavy and light animals, lesson on, 217–21

identifying classroom objects with a certain weight, lesson on, 193–96

introduction, chapter, 183

introductory lesson, 183–87

juice containers, lesson on selecting, 210–13

kilograms, lesson on developing benchmarks for, 205–7

metric system weights, lesson on developing benchmarks for, 208–10

ordering objects by mass, lesson on, 187–90

selecting objects whose weights get closest to given weight, lesson on, 198–202

selecting the fewest objects whose combined weight equals a given weight, lesson on, 202–5, 303

units of weight, lesson on developing sense of, 190–93

What Do You Know About Thermometers?, lesson, 250–52

What Do You Know? What Can You Discover?, lesson, 183–87

What Do You See?, lesson, 65–68

What Is an Angle?, lesson, 150–52

World Time Zones (Blackline Master), 308